4/05

PROMISES BETRAYED

PROMISES BETRAYED

WAKING UP FROM THE
AMERICAN DREAM

BOB HERBERT

TIMES BOOKS

Henry Holt and Company · New York

Times Books
Henry Holt and Company, LLC
Publishers since 1866
175 Fifth Avenue
New York, New York 10010
www.henryholt.com

Henry Holt® is a registered trademark of
Henry Holt and Company, LLC.

Library of Congress Cataloging-in-Publication Data

Herbert, Bob, 1945–
    Promises betrayed : waking up from the American dream / Bob Herbert.
        p. ; cm.
    Includes index.
    ISBN-13: 978-0-8050-7864-0
    ISBN-10: 0-8050-7864-9
    1. United States—Social conditions—1980– 2. Social justice—United States.
3. United States—Politics and government—2001– I. Title.
    HN59.2.H47 2005
    306'.0973'090511—dc22   2004616690

Henry Holt books are available for special promotions
and premiums. For details contact: Director, Special Markets.

First Edition 2005

Designed by Victoria Hartman

Printed in the United States of America

1 3 5 7 9 10 8 6 4 2

For Deborah,

my hero and my wife

CONTENTS

· PART ONE ·

WHY AMERICA STOPPED WORKING

Introduction: A Fire in the Basement   3

1. Power and the Powerless   13
   A FOOL'S ERRAND   13
   CASUALTIES AT HOME   16
   HOME ALONE   18
   CHANGE THE CHANNEL   21
   AN EMERGING CATASTROPHE   23
   WE'RE MORE PRODUCTIVE. WHO GETS THE MONEY?   26
   A JUSTICE'S SENSE OF PRIVILEGE   28
   OUR PLANET, AND OUR DUTY   31

· PART TWO ·

CRIMINAL INJUSTICE

2. A Disgrace in Tulia   37
   KAFKA IN TULIA   37
   "LAWMAN OF THE YEAR"   40
   TULIA'S SHATTERED LIVES   42
   RAILROADED IN TEXAS   45

JUSTICE GOES INTO HIDING   47

A CONFUSED INQUIRY   50

THE LATEST FROM TULIA   52

THE TULIA STORY ISN'T OVER   54

PARTWAY TO FREEDOM   57

A GOOD DAY   59

3. Innocence Is No Defense   63

A SENSELESS ASSAULT   63

TWO VICTIMS   65

HOW MANY INNOCENT PRISONERS?   68

A CHILD'S "CONFESSION"   71

HOW DID JAYLA DIE?   73

WITHOUT EVIDENCE   76

THE WRONG MAN   78

WHEN THE WEIGHT OF THE EVIDENCE SHIFTS   81

AN IMAGINARY HOMICIDE   83

WHEN JUSTICE IS MOCKED   86

4. The Ultimate Penalty   89

NEAR-DEATH EXPERIENCE   89

DEATH PENALTY VICTIMS   92

THE CONFESSION   94

TRAPPED IN THE SYSTEM   97

DEATH PENALTY DISSENTERS   99

COUNTDOWN TO EXECUTION NO. 300   102

PULL THE PLUG   104

· PART THREE ·

BARELY GETTING BY

5. Where Does the Money Go?   109

PICKING WORKERS' POCKETS   109

CAUGHT IN THE CREDIT CARD VISE   112

THE REVERSE ROBIN HOOD · 114
ADMIT WE HAVE A PROBLEM · 117

6. The Vanishing American Job · 120
OUT THE DOOR · 120
JOBLESS, AND STUNNED · 123
YOUNG, JOBLESS, HOPELESS · 125
TROUBLE IN BUSH'S AMERICA · 128
CAUGHT IN THE SQUEEZE · 130
NO WORK, NO HOMES · 132
THE WHITE-COLLAR BLUES · 135
EDUCATION IS NO PROTECTION · 137
DARK SIDE OF FREE TRADE · 139
WHO'S GETTING THE NEW JOBS? · 142

7. Corporate Values · 145
PURSUING THE CHILDREN · 145
NIKE BLINKS · 148
AMERICA'S LITTLEST SHOOTERS · 150
THE GIFT OF MAYHEM · 153
AN UGLY GAME · 155

· PART FOUR ·

BLACK AND WHITE

8. What Happened to the Dream? · 161
THE DREAM IGNORED · 161
STARING AT HATRED · 164
HAUNTED BY SEGREGATION · 166
WHERE FEAR RULES THE STREET · 169
CIVIL RIGHTS, THE SEQUEL · 171
BREAKING AWAY · 174

9. Double Standards   177
    EMPATHY FOR A KILLER   177
    BREATHING WHILE BLACK   180
    JUSTICE, NEW YORK STYLE   182
    A MOM'S VINDICATION   185
    POLICE RESTRAINT   187
    TRUTH, LIES, AND SUBTEXT   190

10. The Party of Lincoln   193
    A SLICK MIX   193
    RACISM AND THE GOP   196
    BUSH'S NOT-SO-BIG TENT   198
    SUPPRESS THE VOTE?   201
    VOTING WHILE BLACK   203
    A CHILL IN FLORIDA   206

· PART FIVE ·

THE AMERICA OF GEORGE W. BUSH

11. Compassionate Conservatism   211
    PUNISHING THE POOR   211
    OBLIVIOUS IN D.C.   214
    A STRANGE BUDGET CUT   216
    SICK STATE BUDGETS, SICK KIDS   219
    HEAVY LIFTING   221
    NOT SO FRIVOLOUS   224
    BLISS AND BIGOTRY   226
    STOLEN KISSES   229
    A WAR AGAINST THE CITIES   231

12. How Goes the War on Terror?   234
    "IT WASN'T A DREAM"   234
    HIGH-ALTITUDE RAMBOS   236
    STRATEGIC ADVICE FROM THE PUBLIC   239
    STAYING IN THE DARK   242

READY OR NOT 244

WAKING UP TO THE WAR 247

13. Misleadership in Iraq 250

WITH EARS AND EYES CLOSED 250

READY FOR THE PEACE? 253

WHAT IS IT GOOD FOR? 255

DANCING WITH THE DEVIL 258

THE HALLIBURTON SHUFFLE 260

AN INSULT TO OUR SOLDIERS 263

NO END IN SIGHT 265

THE WRONG WAR 268

"GOOKS" TO "HAJIS" 270

DID SOMEBODY SAY WAR? 273

14. Body Count 276

DEATH COMES KNOCKING 276

A PRICE TOO HIGH 279

OUR WOUNDED WARRIORS 281

A SOLDIER'S SACRIFICE 284

FROM DREAM TO NIGHTMARE 286

BUSH'S BLINKERS 289

PARALYZED, A SOLDIER ASKS WHY 291

LETTING DOWN THE TROOPS 294

HOW MANY DEATHS WILL IT TAKE? 296

THIS IS BUSH'S VIETNAM 299

· PART SIX ·

HERBERT'S HEROES

15. A Roll Call for Our Time 305

THE BEST OF AMERICA 305

REESE AND ROBINSON 308

THE GOOD TIMES 310

A DESIGNATED HERO 313

RIDING TO FREEDOM   315

A MUSCULAR IDEALISM   318

GET WELL, GEORGE   320

KEEPING THE BLUES ALIVE   323

LOVING RAY CHARLES   325

Conclusion: What Kind of America Do We Want to Live In?   328

Acknowledgments   335

Index   337

PART ONE

WHY AMERICA
STOPPED WORKING

INTRODUCTION

A FIRE IN THE BASEMENT

The eleven-year-old girl looked up at the police officers. "What's that word?" she asked. "Home-a-seed?"

She was told the word was homicide.

"What's that?" she asked.

The interrogation room grew quiet. No one answered.

Most of the stories I write are about people in trouble. Sometimes the wounds are self-inflicted, but most often they are the result of other people's bad behavior—sometimes the government's bad behavior. The frightened eleven-year-old who couldn't read the word *homicide* became the youngest person ever charged with capital murder in the United States. She was publicly humiliated and sent off to a juvenile prison in Texas by a coterie of ferociously self-righteous officials who could have stepped right out of the Middle Ages. It turned out that the girl was innocent, but she remained locked up for three years before lawyers and advocates could secure her release.

A reporter making the rounds will spend an inordinate amount of time trespassing in the precincts that were so well understood by the old blues masters, the places ravaged by hypocrisy and double-dealing, hatred and murder, acts of terror and endless war. These are the places where the suffering occurs and that tell us the most about the times in which we live.

I remember listening to a twenty-seven-year-old army sergeant in Dale City, Virginia, as he sat in a wheelchair in his parents' basement on a sunny summer afternoon and described the very weird experience of being blown up by a roadside bomb in Iraq. "Everything went in slow motion for about fifteen seconds," he said. He felt an excruciating sensation of flaming hot metal and a searing, all-encompassing pain. When his life resumed normal speed, everything he once knew about himself and the world had changed. His family life would be different. His days as a splendid athlete were over. His spinal cord had been severed in the blast.

I'm troubled as never before about what's happening in the United States right now. I grew up at a time when the great promise of America probably was at its peak. Optimism ruled in the 1950s and '60s. Jobs were plentiful and standards of living were improving. Access to a decent education was becoming easier. Despite tremendous problems—the war in Vietnam, bitter and sometimes deadly racial struggles, assassinations—there was a sense that the nation was trying to right its wrongs, that it was moving in the right direction, however difficult and dangerous the road might seem.

I don't feel that sense as I travel the country now, meeting and talking with ordinary men and women who are directly affected by the major events of our time. The winds have shifted and are blowing from a more ominous direction. There are too many stories now about anxious and bewildered men and women who are desperate for work but can't find jobs, about middle-class families drowning in debt, about public schools swarming with students but starved of books and supplies, about gays caught in the backlash of disputes over values, about sick people who can't afford lifesaving drugs, about hunger and homelessness and innocents sent off to prison, and about young men and women killed and maimed in George W. Bush's dark venture in Iraq.

It's not that life in America was better in the 1960s. It wasn't. But it seemed to be moving in a better direction. For me, a young person with energy, ambition, and prodigious dreams, that counted for a lot.

The United States today is more powerful and prosperous than ever, but it feels very much like a nation on edge. The electorate is sliced right down the middle, with the two sides glaring at each other, as if from armed camps. The joy and optimism that one would expect to be widespread in the most successful nation in the history of the world are oddly missing. Instead there is a sense of things out of whack, of the center caving, of obligations unmet and promises betrayed. A suburban school district in Oregon ran out of money during a budget meltdown a couple of years ago, so it chopped nearly a month off the school calendar. The schools were closed and the kids were sent home. A high school physics teacher that I interviewed seemed almost in despair. "During the Great Depression we didn't close schools," he said. "We didn't close schools during World War II." He wondered aloud if he wasn't part of the most civically irresponsible generation in a hundred years.

In Tulia, Texas, a dusty panhandle town not far from Amarillo, one of the worst criminal justice atrocities of the last half-century was carried out. Dozens of men and women, more than 10 percent of the town's entire black population, were arrested in a drug sting run amok. A few whites who had relationships with blacks were also arrested. A local newspaper hailed the sweeping of such trash from Tulia's streets. No drugs were found in the sting, and no money or weapons were recovered. There were no witnesses, save the lone rogue cop who fingered the suspects, a twisted individual who referred to black people as "niggers" and scribbled notes about his activities on his arms and legs. Nevertheless, prison terms of 20 years, 60 years, 90 years, 300 years were handed down. Innocent people began copping pleas to escape sentences that approached or exceeded life in prison. A woman named Tonya White avoided incarceration only after she managed to produce records of a bank transaction showing that she was in Oklahoma when she was supposed to have been selling drugs to the cop in Tulia.

I'll never forget the grief-stricken face of Freddie Brookins Sr., a man in his late forties whose son, Freddie Jr., was caught up in this episode. Brookins Sr. sat in the living room of his modest home and in a soft, cigarette-husky voice explained to me the dilemma his family had faced. Freddie Jr. had been offered a plea bargain and a relatively light prison sentence. But the family knew he was innocent. The father couldn't bear to advise his son to plead guilty to a crime he hadn't committed. So Freddie Jr. went to trial and was promptly convicted and sentenced to twenty years in state prison.

Eventually, because of the pressure of media coverage and lawsuits by the NAACP Legal Defense and Educational Fund, the truth emerged and nearly all of the Tulia defendants were freed. But that took a long time, and would never have happened if the case hadn't been picked up and relentlessly pursued by the press.

It would be one thing if stories like these were rare, if they were bizarre onetime occurrences that we learned a lesson from and prevented from happening again. But the stories I cover are not rare. They're distillations of problems that are widespread, deeply entrenched, and powerfully destructive. In many cases they are the stories of good people who get badly hurt, people whose lives are ruined, or even lost, because of conditions or decisions that should never have been allowed to prevail.

Problems left to fester are the seed corn of calamities. It's not pure coincidence that a nation that tolerates horrendous abuses in its criminal justice system would, in wartime, seek out ways to escape the constraints of the Geneva Conventions, and even to justify torture.

Some years ago I covered a story about an actor in New York who was stunned to find himself arrested, along with several other people, in the lobby of his apartment building. He'd done absolutely nothing wrong. When I asked a deputy police commissioner why the man had been arrested, she said the police were investigating a crime and had decided to grab everyone in the lobby and "sort it out later."

That's exactly the rationale that was used in the sweep of so-called terror suspects who ended up in U.S. custody at Guantánamo Bay in the aftermath of the September 11 attacks. It didn't matter whether the detainees had done anything wrong. The government would sort that out later.

I'm convinced that America itself, like so many of the people I write about, is in serious trouble. The essays in this book offer glimpses of a society that has stopped chasing the fundamental tenets of its mythic dream. The nation has grown largely indifferent to abuses of power and social injustice. Flag-waving politicians still give lip service to the great American ideals of freedom, justice, equality, and opportunity, but in an era of preventive war and so-called conservative values, we've all but stopped pursuing them. And that's dangerous. Throughout our history the pursuit of those ideals—however imperfect the effort, however strained, timid, slow, and haphazard—was the only thing that made the United States special.

The war in Iraq, immorally launched and incompetently waged, will not be characterized by history as the noble campaign of a powerful nation striding toward greatness. It will be seen as the tragically foolish act of a nation unwilling to learn the lessons of Vietnam. The abuse of prisoners abroad and the war on civil liberties at home are hardly evidence that the better angels of our nature are in the ascent. The United States was always at its best at those points in history when it chased its cherished ideals like a mariner following the stars.

At this moment, at the pinnacle of its power, the United States is a country that has lost its way. "When a nation goes down, or a society perishes," said Carl Sandburg, "one condition may always be found; they forgot where they came from. They lost sight of what had brought them along."

We are sliding backward in other ways. Franklin Roosevelt told us: "The test of our progress is not whether we add more to the abundance of those who have too much; it is whether we provide enough for those who have too little." Square that with the current appalling disparities in wealth and income in the United States and the emergence of a mind-bogglingly irresponsible ruling class whose core mission is indisputably to serve the interests of the very rich. The total wealth of the lucky 1 percent at the top of America's social pyramid is a colossal $2 trillion, more than the wealth of all the Americans in the bottom 90 percent combined.

I saw this in its starkest relief one rainy Tuesday morning during the Christmas shopping season. A group of shivering homeless men, one of them nibbling at the core of an apple, had gathered for shelter on the steps of a Presbyterian church on Fifth Avenue in Manhattan, near Rockefeller Center. Across the street, arrayed like glittering jewels, were some of the most exclusive shops the nation has to offer: Tiffany, Gucci, Fortunoff, Cartier, Versace. Among the items offered for sale were an emerald ring for $1.9 million and a diamond necklace for $10 million. A fountain pen could be had for a mere $102,000. Nearby was a candy emporium where the chocolate was $62 a pound.

Today's disparities rival, and maybe even exceed, the garish inequities of the Gilded Age at the end of the nineteenth century. The barons of twenty-first-century America, otherwise known as CEOs, have salaries 400 to 500 times the income of the workers, our present-day serfs, who labor for them full time.

In Chicago I spent time with a few of that city's 100,000 young people, ages sixteen to twenty-four, who are at the very bottom of the economic pyramid. They are out of school, out of work, and, in my view, all but out of hope. In New York there are 200,000 such youngsters, and across the United States a staggering 5.5 million. These kids haunt the streets and the malls and the bowling alleys all day and much of the night. They're part of the American family but there is virtually no effort to find employment for them, or get them into training programs, or back into school. They're not even counted when the official jobless statistics are tallied. They're ignored. So they hustle for money wherever they can, in some cases drifting into drug selling, gang membership, prostitution, or worse. A seventeen-year-old in Chicago named Audrey Roberts told me, "The stuff you hear about on the news, that's our everyday life. I've seen girls get raped, beaten up. I saw a boy get his head blown away. That happened right in front of me."

Connect the dots. Many of the young American men and women who ended up as the targets of snipers and bombers in Iraq had joined the military precisely because their economic opportunities and social options back home were grim. Again and again they will tell you that they joined the army to get a steady paycheck or an education, any opportunity to get ahead. Official statistics mask the reality of the nation's difficult economic landscape. Nearly 9 million Americans are out of work, and many millions more are underemployed and underpaid. Nearly a third of all American working families live in poverty. According to the Department of Agriculture, more than 12 million families are struggling just to feed themselves. Record levels of household debt and personal bankruptcies are being recorded as cash-strapped families increasingly borrow just to make ends meet.

In 1946, after a long depression and the worst of all wars, Harry Truman looked out at a world that was largely in ruins. He did not wring his hands or shrink faintheartedly from the task at hand. He embarked on the greatest renewal and reconstruction program the world has ever known. Recognizing the crucial importance of

American leadership, he led the way to the creation of the United Nations and NATO, and to the Marshall Plan to rebuild Western Europe.

Here at home he built the platform that was used to launch America's great postwar run. We built schools and housing and highways, and over the next few decades developed a standard of living that was the envy of the world. We made big advances in civil rights and women's rights and civil liberties. We committed ourselves to protecting the rights of workers and consumers, and even the criminally accused. We made the environment a priority.

All along the way there were astonishing strides in medicine and other disciplines, and technological advances that took us to the moon and beyond, and that brought us into a computer age that revolutionized the world.

It was a hell of a few decades.

Now where are we? At some point late in that postwar run, we took a wrong turn. That can-do era sputtered to an end, and we let the selfish, the vain, the greedy, and the incompetent take control of our nation and tell us what we can't do. We can't build first-class schools. We can't provide a reasonable wage for all working men and women. We can't follow through on the promise of Social Security. We can't deliver affordable drugs to the sick and infirm. We can't clean up the slums, or rescue the millions of children trapped in the clutches of poverty. We can't protect the environment.

The nation's leaders have looted the Treasury, mortgaged the future for generations to come, and driven us into a sinkhole in Iraq. And they've done it with impunity. Remember President Bush's "middle-class" tax cuts? "Over the coming decade," says Robert Reich, a former secretary of labor, "the Bush tax cuts will transfer more wealth to the richest one percent of the population than any fiscal policies in history."

If I had one wish for this country it would be for leadership that would arouse the consciousness of the masses to the deceit and injustice all around them. There are still plenty of valiant individuals who head out each day and put up a terrific fight on behalf of the poor and the oppressed and anyone else who might need a boost or a hand—or just a fair shake. But too often they're overmatched by the fat cats and the ideologues who have a stranglehold on the nation's financial resources and political power.

Time is not on our side. We've been attacked from without, but the greater danger to the essence of America is within. There's a fire in the basement of the United States and we're behaving as if we cannot even smell the smoke.

1

POWER AND THE POWERLESS

A FOOL'S ERRAND

Paul Conover and I met Michael Farmer during basic training at Fort Dix, New Jersey, in the mid-1960s. Conover and I were friends from Montclair. Farmer was a kid from Atlantic City, a seventeen-year-old who mumbled so badly you could never be sure what he was saying. He was big and good-looking, but the first impression was that he wasn't too swift.

One night Farmer came over to our barracks—uninvited—while Conover and I, who were a couple of years older and light-years cooler, were sitting on the floor, spit-shining our combat boots. Very tentatively and very politely, Farmer asked if he could join us.

I told him to get lost. Farmer must not have understood because he promptly sat down, took off his boots, and, over the next few minutes, proved to my satisfaction that he was as dumb as he sounded.

First he told us he had joined the army. Conover grinned and rolled his eyes. Then Farmer said he was in love with a girl in Atlantic City and planned to marry her. I shook my head. This was not a person worth spending time with. As a draftee, all I wanted was for my hair to grow back and to be reunited with that gleaming symbol of freedom and the good life, my Thunderbird.

But Conover liked Farmer and told him to come back the next night.

"He mumbles," I said.

But Conover said, "Ah, he's all right."

So Farmer came back, night after night, to smoke cigarettes, listen to Motown music, mumble about his girlfriend, and polish boots. To my chagrin, I started to like him, though I still needed a translator to understand him. For the longest time I thought his girlfriend's name was Merlin. It was Marilyn.

Farmer and Conover became very close. Eventually both of them were sent to Vietnam. I got lucky and was sent to Korea, which was no walk in the park. But it wasn't Vietnam.

The impact of the war on Conover and Farmer was strange. When Farmer came back, he seemed more sure of himself, more open and fun-loving, less insecure. He and Marilyn were married.

Conover, the most happy-go-lucky guy I had ever known, was a wreck. He was nervous. Jumpy. Some nights he would drink like a fiend. The cheerful optimism that had once defined his personality was gone.

He wouldn't really talk about Vietnam. All I ever heard him say was, "Didn't know I could get so scared."

Then the unthinkable happened. Farmer, who had enlisted for four years and was still in the service, got orders to go back to Vietnam. We told him not to go. Call your congressman, we said. Fight this thing. But Farmer didn't know how.

It's not hard to guess what happened. Farmer's second tour lasted only a few months. I was in the back of my father's upholstery shop one afternoon when Conover walked in.

"Farmer didn't make it," he said. And then he started crying.

A year passed. I got a job with a newspaper. Conover got married. Other buddies got killed in the war, which began to look like it might go on forever. My sister's boyfriend got shot.

I didn't realize it, but Conover's struggle was winding down. He wouldn't make it either. I never got the story straight. All I know is that he got his hands on a gun, and one night he waited in a car outside his house for his wife to come home. When she showed up he shot her dead. Then he killed himself.

Sunday was the twenty-fifth anniversary of the end of the war, which I cannot think about without thinking of Farmer and Conover. Neither had a clue about the politics or the history or the egos that sucked them up like dust from a carpet and consigned them to their pointless fates. Vietnam was a fool's errand, and the young and the ignorant went to their doom by the tens of thousands.

When David Brinkley, appalled by the carnage, asked Lyndon Johnson why he didn't just pull out of Vietnam, thus saving many lives, Johnson replied, "I'm not going to be the first American president to lose a war."

A couple of years ago I visited the Vietnam Memorial in Washington. I found Farmer's name, and then, not thinking, looked for Conover's. Of course, it wasn't there. But his short life and that of his wife, whose name I don't know, were wasted by Vietnam just as surely as the lives of those 58,000 other Americans listed on that bitter wall.

(May 4, 2000)

CASUALTIES AT HOME

Washington

On the day that President Bush asked Congress for the first install-
ment of the hundreds of billions of dollars needed to finance the war
in Iraq and its aftermath, the students and teachers at a high school
within walking distance of the White House were struggling through
their daily routine in a building that has no cafeteria, no gymnasium,
no student lockers, not even a fully reliable source of electricity.

A few weeks earlier bricks were falling from the façade of the
building, which is more than one hundred years old.

As we continue the relentless bombing of Baghdad, which the
military tells us is the necessary prelude to saving it, it's fair to ask
when the rebuilding of essential institutions like public schools will
begin here at home. (Don't hold your breath. The money for that
sort of thing has completely evaporated.)

"We actually have rooms where the water comes in when it rains,"
said Sheila Mills-Harris, the principal of the School Without Walls,
an academically rigorous high school that routinely finishes first or
second in the District of Columbia's rankings.

Laura Bush has visited the school, which has won a series of national honors. But academic honors and a visit by the First Lady are,
frankly, irrelevant in an era in which social concerns—such as support for public schools and health care, and the need to assist the
poor, the hungry, and the unemployed—have been forced to the
perimeter of public consciousness. Those issues, crucial to our conception of ourselves as a just and humane people, have been deval-
ued and shunted aside by an administration that is committed to an
ill-advised, budget-busting war and a devastating parade of tax cuts
for the very wealthy.

With our attention riveted on the death and destruction in Iraq, and the continued threat to Americans in the war zone, the other very serious problems facing the United States get short shrift. We knew last fall that the proportion of Americans living in poverty had risen, and that income for middle-class households had fallen. We know that unemployment, especially long-term unemployment, is a big problem. And we've known that the states are facing their worst budget crisis since the Great Depression, a development that has led, among other things, to drastic cuts in education aid that are crushing the budgets of local public school districts.

These issues aren't even being properly discussed. The Bush administration sounds the alarm for war and blows the trumpet for tax cuts, and Congress plunges ahead with the cuts in domestic programs that must inevitably follow. The voices of those who object are effectively silenced by the war propaganda and the fear of seeming unpatriotic.

With attention thus deflected, the administration and its allies in Congress have come up with one proposal after another to weaken programs that were designed to help struggling Americans.

In his most recent budget the president offered a plan to make it more difficult for low-income families to obtain government benefits, including tax credits and school lunch assistance. As the *New York Times*'s Robert Pear reported, the administration proposed changes in the Medicare program that would make it more difficult for elderly people, many of them frail, to appeal the denial of benefits like home health care and skilled nursing care.

The extent to which the most vulnerable Americans are being targeted is appalling. Billions of dollars in cuts have been proposed for food stamp and child nutrition programs, and for health care for the poor.

Collectively, these are the largest proposed cuts in history. Even cuts for veterans' programs are on the table—in the midst of a war!

The administration is actually fighting two wars—one against Iraq and another against the very idea of a humane and responsive government here at home.

At some point, hopefully sooner rather than later, the war against Iraq will end. Americans will then have the opportunity to look around and be stunned by the fix we'll be in. We'll look at the enormous costs of the postwar occupation in Iraq, and at the social and economic dislocation that's occurring here. And we'll look at the disaster that the federal budget has become. We'll be broke, and we'll ask ourselves, again and again, "What have we done?"

(March 27, 2003)

HOME ALONE

There was an interesting lead paragraph in an article on the front page of the *Wall Street Journal* in late August 2003:

"The blackout of 2003 offers a simple but powerful lesson: Markets are a great way to organize economic activity, but they need adult supervision."

Gee. They've finally figured that out. The nuns I had in grammar school were on to this adult supervision notion decades ago. It seems to be just dawning on the power brokers of the twenty-first century. Maybe soon the voters will catch on. You need adults in charge.

We barreled into Iraq with no real thought given to the consequences, and now we've got a tragic mess on our hands. California looks like something out of *Lord of the Flies,* and yet the person getting the most attention as a candidate to clean up that insane situation is an actor with a history of immature behavior whose cartoonish roles appeal most strongly to children. Maybe he'll shoot the budget deficit. *Hasta la vista,* baby.

Appalling behavior and appalling policies have become the norm among folks entrusted with the heaviest responsibilities in business and government. The federal budget deficit will approach half a trillion dollars next year. And that will be followed by huge additional deficits, year after irresponsible year, extending far off into the horizon. And, of course, the baby boomers, the least responsible generation in memory, will soon begin retiring and collecting their Social Security and federal health benefits, leaving the mountains of unpaid bills for the hapless generations behind them.

What this nation needs is a time-out.

Imagine if we had done some things differently. If, for example, instead of squandering such staggering amounts of federal money on tax cuts and an ill-advised war, we had invested wisely in some of the nation's pressing needs. What if we had begun to refurbish our antiquated electrical grid, or developed creative new ways to replenish the stock of affordable housing, or really tackled the job of rebuilding and rejuvenating the public schools?

What if we had called in the best minds from coast to coast to begin a crash program, in good faith and with solid federal backing, to substantially reduce our dependence on foreign oil by changing our laws and habits, and developing safer, cleaner, less expensive alternatives? This is exactly the kind of effort that the United States, with its can-do spirit and vast commercial, technological, and intellectual resources, would be great at.

Imagine if we had begun a program to rebuild our aging infrastructure—the highways, bridges, tunnels, and dams; the water and sewage facilities; the airports and transit systems. Imagine, on this Labor Day 2003, the number of good jobs that could be generated with that kind of long-term effort.

All of these issues, if approached properly, are job creators, including the effort to reduce our energy dependence. The big hang-up in the economic recovery we are supposed to be experiencing now is the continued joblessness and underemployment.

A fellow I ran into recently in San Jose, California, Andy Fortuna, said, "I've got a college degree and I'm washing cars. I'm working, but I'd like a good job. If the idea is for business to employ as few people as possible and keep their pay as low as possible—well, how's that good for me? Who speaks for me?"

Wise investments along these lines have dual payoffs—they help us take care of critical national needs and they help sustain the high levels of employment that are needed to keep the nation's high-powered consumer economy humming.

One other critical need that is not getting enough attention is homeland security. A series of recent reports has shown that two years after the September 11 attacks we remain dangerously unprepared for another terrorist strike inside the United States. And one of the major reasons we remain unprepared is that so many of the agencies responsible for our domestic defenses against terror are under-trained, understaffed, and underfinanced.

We are at a stage now where mature, responsible leadership is more essential than ever. All of the problems that we have ignored until now remain with us. But the money that might have started us on the road to solutions is gone. We are mired in Iraq, and not properly prepared at home.

We could use some adult supervision.

(September 1, 2003)

CHANGE THE CHANNEL

Saddam is now a staple of the Leno and Letterman shows.

And Paris Hilton outgunned President Bush in a prime-time shoot-out between Fox and ABC.

And we're already choosing up sides on Kobe's and Jacko's guilt or innocence.

We really are amusing ourselves to death, as Neil Postman pointed out a couple of decades ago. He might as well have been speaking into the void. It's only gotten worse.

Americans have more information available to them than any people in history. But we are experts at distancing ourselves from any real unpleasantness. Most of us behave as though we bear no personal responsibility for the deep human suffering all around us, and no obligation to try and alleviate it.

Paris, Jacko, Saddam. The world is like one big media show, a made-for-TV spectacular. We can change the channel if things get too ugly. Or just turn the television off. Genuine social consciousness is for squares.

Example: The nation's at war. Is there any reason to share in the sacrifices wars usually require? Nah. The grunts can do the fighting and the dying. And we can put the costs on a credit card. Future generations will pay for it.

And here at home? The headlines tell us things are pretty good. The economy's turned around and the president's poll numbers are up. Let's head for the mall.

The problem is, if you peel away the headlines and look more closely at reality, you'll see some things that aren't so amusing. In New York City, for example, there are more homeless people than at any time since accurate records started being kept in the late 1970s.

Each night more than 39,000 people—nearly 17,000 of them children—seek refuge in the city's shelters. "It's the greatest number of homeless since the Great Depression," said Patrick Markee, a policy analyst with the Coalition for the Homeless. The faces of the destitute are changing as more and more families with children—in New York and across the nation—find themselves without the money necessary for food or shelter.

The United States Conference of Mayors released a report showing that over the past year, hunger and homelessness have continued to rise in major American cities. A survey of twenty-five cities showed an increase of 17 percent in requests for emergency food assistance and an increase of 13 percent in requests for emergency shelter.

A surge in the Dow is big news. Surges in hunger and homelessness are not.

A broader look at the levels of serious distress being faced by increasing numbers of Americans comes from the latest Index of Social Health, which is published annually by the Institute for Innovation in Social Policy at the Fordham University Graduate Center, in Tarrytown, New York. The institute analyzes government statistics in a wide variety of areas, including infant mortality, children in poverty, teenage suicide, health insurance coverage, and homicide rates, as a way of monitoring the "social well-being of the nation."

The latest index, which covered the year 2001 (the latest year for which complete statistics were available), showed the social health of the nation taking a steep dive. It was the biggest decline in the index in two decades. And preliminary data for the years since 2001 show the decline continuing, according to Dr. Marc Miringoff, the institute's director.

The categories that worsened in the latest index were children in poverty, child abuse, average weekly earnings, affordable housing, health insurance coverage, food stamp coverage, the gap between rich and poor, and out-of-pocket health costs for those over sixty-five. Two indicators reached their worst levels on record, food stamp coverage (which correlates with increases in hunger) and income inequality.

"These numbers are usually invisible to us," said Dr. Miringoff. "They tell us an untold story, not just about the poor but the working poor and the middle class as well. It's shocking to see such a sharp decline in just one year. It tells us that something's going on with the basic fabric of our society."

We might actually pay attention to problems like hunger, homelessness, housing, and health costs, if only we could find a way to make them amusing.

(December 19, 2003)

AN EMERGING CATASTROPHE

Drive through some of the black neighborhoods in cities and towns across America and you will see the evidence of an emerging catastrophe—levels of male joblessness that mock the very idea of stable, viable communities. This slow death of the hopes, pride, and well-being of huge numbers of African Americans is going unnoticed by most other Americans and by political leaders of both parties.

A new study of black male employment trends has come up with the following extremely depressing finding: "By 2002, one of every four black men in the U.S. was idle all year long. This idleness rate was twice as high as that of white and Hispanic males."

It's possible the rate of idleness is even higher, said the lead author of the study, Andrew Sum, who is director of the Center for Labor Market Studies at Northeastern University, in Boston. "That was a conservative count," he said. The study did not consider homeless men or those in jail or prison. It is believed that up to 10 percent of the black male population under age forty is incarcerated.

While some of the men not working undoubtedly were ill or disabled, the 25 percent figure is still staggeringly high. And for some segments of the black male population, the situation is even worse.

Among black male dropouts, for example, 44 percent were idle year-round, as were nearly forty-two of every one hundred black men aged fifty-five to sixty-four.

"I was surprised by the magnitude of the population that was idle all year-round," said Professor Sum. "Typically, some groups will find work part of the year, but not the other part, and you end up with a high joblessness rate. But here we've got a growing number of men just not working at all."

Black men, already in an employment crisis, were hit particularly hard by the last recession and have not done well in the fitful recovery that followed. Jobless rates for some subgroups, black teenagers for example, have been all but off the charts.

Professor Sum and his colleagues got closer than official statistics usually get to the dismal employment reality of black men by using the so-called employment-population ratio, which represents the percentage of a given population that is employed at a given time. The government's official unemployment statistics are often misleading, particularly because people who have stopped looking for work are not counted.

Things fall apart when 25 percent of the male population is jobless. (This does not even begin to address the very serious problems of underemployment, such as part-time or temporary jobs, and extremely low wage work.) For the most part, jobless men are not viewed as marriageable material by women. And they are hardly role models for young people.

Those who remain jobless for a substantial period of time run the risk of becoming permanently unemployable.

This is a tragic situation for the men and their families and a serious problem for society at large. Such a huge all-but-permanently-unemployed population is an obstacle to efforts to achieve full employment and its accompanying benefits. These men are not contributing to tax revenues and they are consuming public and social services. And some, inevitably, are engaged in criminal and other antisocial behavior. Figuring out ways to get this population gainfully employed would turn a net societal deficit into a real benefit.

Finally, it's just wrong to allow so many Americans to remain in a state of social and economic degradation without attempting to alter the conditions responsible for their suffering.

Education is one of the keys here. As Professor Sum found, 44 percent of black men with no high school diploma were idle year-round versus 26 percent of those with a diploma, and 13 percent of those with a bachelor's (or higher) degree.

The distance from the idleness of the street corner to the warmth of a thriving family is not really that far, especially when a helping hand is offered. But we'll never offer the helping hand if we fail to recognize that there's a problem.

(July 19, 2004)

WE'RE MORE PRODUCTIVE.
WHO GETS THE MONEY?

It's like running on a treadmill that keeps increasing its speed. You have to go faster and faster just to stay in place. Or, as a factory worker said many years ago, "You can work 'til you drop dead, but you won't get ahead."

American workers have been remarkably productive in recent years, but they are getting fewer and fewer of the benefits of this increased productivity. While the economy, as measured by the gross domestic product, has been strong for some time now, ordinary workers have gotten little more than the back of the hand from employers who have pocketed an unprecedented share of the cash from this burst of economic growth.

What is happening is nothing short of historic. The American workers' share of the increase in national income since November 2001, the end of the last recession, is the lowest on record. Employers took the money and ran. This is extraordinary, but very few people are talking about it, which tells you something about the hold that corporate interests have on the national conversation.

The situation is summed up in the long, unwieldy, but very revealing title of a new study from the Center for Labor Market Studies at Northeastern University: "The Unprecedented Rising Tide of Corporate Profits and the Simultaneous Ebbing of Labor Compensation—Gainers and Losers from the National Economic Recovery in 2002 and 2003."

Andrew Sum, the center's director and lead author of the study, said: "This is the first time we've ever had a case where two years into a recovery, corporate profits got a larger share of the growth of national income than labor did. Normally labor gets about 65 percent and corporate profits about 15 to 18 percent. This time profits got

41 percent and labor [meaning all forms of employee compensation, including wages, benefits, salaries, and the percentage of payroll taxes paid by employers] got 38 percent."

The study said: "In no other recovery from a post–World War II recession did corporate profits ever account for as much as 20 percent of the growth in national income. And at no time did corporate profits ever increase by a greater amount than labor compensation."

In other words, an awful lot of American workers have been had. Fleeced. Taken to the cleaners.

The recent productivity gains have been widely acknowledged. But workers are not being compensated for this. During the past two years, increases in wages and benefits have been very weak, or nonexistent. And despite the growth of jobs in March that had the Bush crowd dancing in the White House halls, there has been no net increase in formal payroll employment since the end of the recession. We have lost jobs. There are fewer payroll jobs now than there were when the recession ended in November 2001.

So if employers were not hiring workers, and if they were miserly when it came to increases in wages and benefits for existing employees, what happened to all the money from the strong economic growth?

The study is very clear on this point. The bulk of the gains did not go to workers "but instead were used to boost profits, lower prices, or increase C.E.O. compensation."

This is a radical transformation of the way the bounty of this country has been distributed since World War II. Workers are being treated more and more like patrons in a rigged casino. They can't win.

Corporate profits go up. The stock market goes up. Executive compensation skyrockets. But workers, for the most part, remain on the treadmill.

When you look at corporate profits versus employee compensation in this recovery, and then compare that, as Sum and his colleagues did, with the eight previous recoveries since World War II, it's like turning a chart upside down.

The study found that the amount of income growth devoured by corporate profits in this recovery is "historically unprecedented," as is the "low share . . . accruing to the nation's workers in the form of labor compensation."

I have to laugh when I hear conservatives complaining about class warfare. They know this terrain better than anyone. They launched the war. They're waging it. And they're winning it.

(April 5, 2004)

A JUSTICE'S SENSE OF PRIVILEGE

Antoinette Konz is a young education reporter for the *Hattiesburg American,* a daily newspaper with a circulation of about 25,000 in Hattiesburg, Mississippi. Konz, twenty-five, has been in the business only for a couple of years, so her outlook hasn't been soiled by the cranks and the criminals, and the pretzel-shaped politicians that so many of us have been covering for too many years to count.

She considered it a big deal when one of the schools on her beat, the Presbyterian Christian High School, invited her to cover a speech that was delivered by Supreme Court Justice Antonin Scalia.

About 300 people, many of them students, filled the school's gymnasium for the speech. They greeted Justice Scalia with a standing ovation.

Konz and a reporter for the Associated Press, Denise Grones, were seated in the front row. They began to take notes. And when Justice Scalia began speaking, they clicked on their tape recorders.

What's important about this story is that Justice Scalia is a big shot. Not only is he a member in good standing of the nation's most august court, he's almost always among those mentioned as a possible future chief justice.

Compared with him, Konz and Grones are nobodies.

Justice Scalia, the big shot, does not like reporters to turn tape recorders on when he's talking, whether that action is protected by the Constitution of the United States or not. He doesn't like it. And he doesn't permit it.

"Thirty-five minutes into the speech we were approached by a woman who identified herself as a deputy U.S. marshal," Konz told me in a telephone conversation a couple of days after the speech. "She said that we should not be recording and that she needed to have our tapes."

In the United States, this is a no-no. Justice Scalia and his colleagues on the court are responsible for guaranteeing such safeguards against tyranny as freedom of the press. In fact, the speech Scalia was giving at the very moment the marshal moved against the two reporters was about the importance of the Constitution.

Konz said that neither she nor Grones wanted to comply with the marshal's demand. "It was very distracting, very embarrassing," she said. "We were still trying to listen to what he was saying."

The marshal, Melanie Rube, insisted.

The AP reporter tried to explain that she had a digital recording device, so there was no tape to give up. Konz said that the deputy seemed baffled by that.

Eventually both recordings were seized.

If this had been an old-time Hollywood movie, the Supreme Court justice would have turned a kindly face toward the marshal and said, in an avuncular tone, "No, no. We don't do that sort of thing in this country. Please return the recordings."

But this is the United States in the twenty-first century, where the power brokers have gone mad. They've deluded themselves into thinking they're royalty, not public servants charged with protecting the rights and interests of the people. Both recordings were erased. Only then was the reporters' property returned.

When agents acting on behalf of a Supreme Court justice can just snatch and destroy information collected by reporters, we haven't just thumbed our noses at the Constitution, we've taken a very dangerous step in a very ugly direction. The depot at the end of that dark road is totalitarianism.

I called Jane Kirtley, a professor of media, ethics, and law at the University of Minnesota, and asked her what was wrong with what the marshal did. She replied, "Everything."

Not only was it an affront to the Constitution to seize and erase the recordings, Kirtley believes it was also a violation of the Privacy Protection Act, a law passed by Congress in 1980. "It protects journalists not just from newsroom searches," she said, "but from the seizure of their work product material, things like notes and drafts, and also what's called documentary materials, which are things like these tapes, or digital recordings."

Konz told me: "All I was doing with that tape recorder was making sure that I was not going to misquote the justice. My only intention was to report his words accurately."

After the encounter with the marshal, she said, "I went back to the office and I just felt absolutely— I just felt horrible."

(April 12, 2004)

POSTSCRIPT

Justice Antonin Scalia sent a letter of apology to Antoinette Konz and changed his policy to allow print reporters to make audiotapes of his talks for reference purposes only, not for broadcast.

OUR PLANET, AND OUR DUTY

One moment the kids were laughing and skylarking on the beach, yelling and chasing one another, sweating in the warm bright sun. The next moment they were gone.

The world is used to horror stories, but not on the stupefying scale of the macabre tales coming at us from the vast and disorienting zone of death in tsunami-stricken southern Asia. Einstein insisted that God does not play dice with the world, but that might be a difficult notion to sell to some of the agonized individuals who have seen everything they've lived for washed away in a pointless instant.

The death toll now is more than twice the number of American GIs killed in all the years of the Vietnam War. Not just entire families, or extended families, but entire communities were consumed by waters that rose up without warning to destroy scores of thousands of people who were doing nothing but going about their ordinary lives.

The *New York Times* ran a big front-page picture taken in a makeshift morgue in southern India. It certainly captured the horror. It looked for all the world like a sandy playground covered with dead children.

Imagination pales beside the overwhelming reality of the tragedy. There were, for example, the grief-stricken throngs, clawing through mud and rubble, peering into the faces of the severely injured, wandering through piles of decaying corpses, in search of loved ones.

The *Boston Globe* quoted a young man whose college sweetheart was among the more than 800 people killed when a train carrying beachgoers in Sri Lanka was slammed by a thirty-foot wall of water that lifted it from the tracks and hurled it into a marsh. "Is this the fate that we had planned for?" cried the young man. "My darling, you were the only hope for me."

Perhaps a third of those killed were children. Many were swept away before the eyes of horrified, helpless parents. "My children! My children!" screamed a woman in Sri Lanka. "Why didn't the water take me?"

The killer waves that moved with ferocious speed across an unprecedented expanse of global landscape flung their victims about with a randomness that was all but impossible to comprehend. People in beachfront dwellings ended up in trees, or entangled in electrical power lines, or embedded in the mud of hillsides. People died in buses, cars, and trucks that were swept along by the waves like leaves in a strong wind. Sunbathers were swept out to sea.

In that environment, Einstein must stand aside for Shakespeare, whose Gloucester said: "As flies to wanton boys are we to the gods. They kill us for their sport."

Any tragedy is awful for the relatives of those who perished. But this is a catastrophe of a different magnitude. "This," as one observer noted, "is like confronting the apocalypse."

"What makes it especially frightening is that whole communities have been annihilated," said John Clizbe, a psychologist in Alexandria, Virginia, who, until his retirement a couple of years ago, had served as vice president for disaster services at the American Red Cross. "We've known for years now that the emotional devastation that survivors feel and experience is often greater than the physical devastation."

The recovery process is easier, he said, when there is a supportive community to bolster those in need. But in some of the most devastated regions of southern Asia, the regions most in need of support, those communities have vanished.

It's a peculiarity of modern technology that people anywhere in the world can sit back and watch in real time, like voyeurs, the life-and-death struggles of their fellow humans. The planet is growing smaller and its residents more interdependent by the day. We're fully aware that our planetary neighbors in southern Asia are desperately drawing upon the deepest reservoirs of fortitude and resilience that our troubled species has at its disposal.

What this means is that we're the supportive community. All of us. This catastrophe would at least have a silver lining if it moved the people of the United States and other nations toward a wiser, more genuinely cooperative international posture.

William Faulkner, in his Nobel Prize acceptance speech, said: "I believe that man will not merely endure: he will prevail. He is immortal, not because he alone among creatures has an inexhaustible voice, but because he has a soul, a spirit capable of compassion and sacrifice and endurance."

That's what Faulkner believed. We'll see.

(December 31, 2004)

PART TWO

CRIMINAL
INJUSTICE

2

A DISGRACE IN TULIA

KAFKA IN TULIA

Tulia is a hot, dusty town of 5,000 on the Texas Panhandle, about fifty miles south of Amarillo. For some, it's a frightening place—slow and bigoted and bizarre. Kafka could have had a field day with Tulia.

On the morning of July 23, 1999, law enforcement officers fanned out and arrested more than 10 percent of Tulia's tiny African American population. Also arrested were a handful of whites who had relationships with blacks.

The humiliating roundup was intensely covered by the local media, which had been tipped off in advance. Men and women, bewildered and unkempt, were paraded before TV cameras and featured prominently on the evening news. They were drug traffickers, one and all, said the sheriff, a not particularly bright Tulia bulb named Larry Stewart.

Among the forty-six so-called traffickers were a pig farmer, a fork-lift operator, and a number of ordinary young women with children.

If these were major cocaine dealers, as alleged, they were among the oddest in the United States. None of them had any money to speak of. And when they were arrested, they didn't have any cocaine. No drugs, money, or weapons were recovered during the surprise roundup.

Most of Tulia's white residents applauded the arrests, and the local newspapers were all but giddy with their editorial approval. The first convictions came quickly, and the sentences left the town's black residents aghast. One of the few white defendants, a man who happened to have a mixed-race child, was sentenced to more than 300 years in prison. The hog farmer, a black man in his late fifties named Joe Moore, was sentenced to 90 years. Kareem White, a twenty-four-year-old black man, was sentenced to 60 years. And so on.

When the defendants awaiting trial saw this extreme sentencing trend, they began scrambling to plead guilty in exchange for lighter sentences. These ranged from eighteen years in prison to, in some cases, just probation.

It is not an overstatement to describe the arrests in Tulia as an atrocity. The entire operation was the work of a single police officer who claimed to have conducted an eighteen-month undercover operation. The arrests were made solely on the word of this officer, Tom Coleman, a white man with a wretched work history, who routinely referred to black people as "niggers" and who frequently found himself in trouble with the law.

Coleman's alleged undercover operation was ridiculous. There were no other police officers to corroborate his activities. He did not wear a wire or conduct any video surveillance. And he did not keep detailed records of his alleged drug buys. He said he sometimes wrote such important information as the names of suspects and the dates of transactions on his leg. In trial after trial, prosecutors put Coleman on the witness stand, and his uncorroborated, unsubstantiated testimony was enough to send people to prison for decades.

In some instances, lawyers have been able to show that there was no basis in fact—none at all—for Coleman's allegations, that they came from some realm other than reality.

He said, for example, that he had purchased drugs from a woman named Tonya White, and she was duly charged. But last April the charges had to be dropped when White's lawyers proved that she had cashed a check in Oklahoma City at the time that she was supposed to have been selling drugs to Coleman in Tulia.

Another defendant, Billy Don Wafer, was able to prove—through employee time sheets and his boss's testimony—that he was working at the time he was alleged by Coleman to have been selling cocaine. And the local district attorney, Terry McEachern, had to dismiss the case against a man named Yul Bryant after it was learned that Coleman had described him as a tall black man with bushy hair. Bryant was five-foot-six and bald.

In a just world, this case would have been no more than a spoof on *Saturday Night Live*. Instead it's a tragedy with no remedy in sight.

The NAACP Legal Defense and Educational Fund, the William Moses Kunstler Fund for Racial Justice, the Tulia Legal Defense Project, and a number of private law firms are trying to mount an effort to free the men and women imprisoned in this fiasco.

The idea that people could be rounded up and sent away for what are effectively lifetime terms solely on the word of a police officer like Tom Coleman is insane.

(July 29, 2002)

"LAWMAN OF THE YEAR"

The state agency that monitors standards for law enforcement officers in Texas had already been warned about Tom Coleman when he was hired to conduct a bizarre one-man undercover drug operation that targeted the black population in Tulia, a small town on the Texas Panhandle.

Dozens of black people, and a handful of whites who had relationships with blacks, were arrested on July 23, 1999, after an eighteen-month "investigation" by Coleman that at times was as farcical as a Jim Carrey movie.

Coleman, who is white, was a clownish and inept officer who threw away important evidence, made terrible mistakes when identifying suspects, routinely used racist language, and on at least one occasion discharged his weapon accidentally. And yet, on his uncorroborated, unsubstantiated testimony, defendant after defendant was convicted of selling drugs, and some were sentenced to prison terms of twenty years, sixty years, ninety years, and more.

For his exploits in Tulia, Coleman was given a state "Lawman of the Year" award.

But even before the curtain rose on the Tulia farce, the sheriff in another jurisdiction, Cochran County, had complained to the Texas Commission on Law Enforcement about Coleman's conduct.

In a letter to the commission dated June 14, 1996, the sheriff, Ken Burke, said, "It is my opinion that an officer should uphold the law. Mr. Coleman should not be in law enforcement if he is going to do people the way he did in this town."

Officials in Tulia said they didn't know about that complaint when they hired Coleman. But in the middle of his Tulia operation, Coleman was hit with misdemeanor charges of theft and abuse of his official position in Cochran County, where he had run up thousands of dollars in debts before abruptly leaving. Coleman's boss in Tulia, Swisher County sheriff Larry Stewart, conveniently allowed his undercover cop to put his investigation on hold, giving him time to borrow money and resolve the Cochran County charges.

Coleman's investigation in Tulia was incredibly shabby, but it led to the arrest of more than 10 percent of the town's black population.

Erick Willard, a lawyer who defended two women accused by Coleman, said he had been stymied in his efforts to get Coleman's original, handwritten accounts of individual arrests. In some cases, said Willard, "The way he would record it was he'd lift up his pants leg and he'd write it on his leg."

Notes committed to paper were just as difficult to come by. Willard said that during the discovery process he learned that secretaries had supposedly typed some of Coleman's reports from notes that were then "thrown away in a trash Dumpster."

He said he was never able to find out who the secretaries were.

Coleman liked to brag that he was "deep undercover," and that no one knew where he was or what he was doing, "not even the police."

Willard's clients insisted they were innocent. Both took polygraph tests and, in Willard's words, "passed with flying colors." But lie detector tests are not admissible in court, and the district attorney's office would not dismiss the charges.

Both women pleaded no contest. They were sentenced to time already served, fined, and released.

Top officials in Tulia acknowledged that drugs were also sold and consumed by white and Hispanic residents, but Coleman focused almost exclusively on blacks. In a videotaped interview, parts of which were aired on a local television station, Coleman said he used the term *nigger* both on the job and in casual conversations with friends and family. He said he believed the word was no longer "as profane" as it once was.

Coleman eventually packed up and left Tulia, but he soon found himself in trouble again—this time in Ellis County. Joe Grubbs, the district attorney of Ellis County, whose office had hired Coleman, told me that, among other things, Coleman had engaged in contact with a woman that was "inappropriate." He would not give details. He said Coleman had also accidentally discharged his weapon during a drug raid, but no one had been injured.

There were other problems, a "multiplicity" of problems. Said Mr. Grubbs: "He, in effect, put me in a position where I had to discharge him, and I did."

(August 1, 2002)

TULIA'S SHATTERED LIVES

Tulia, Texas

"There," said Mattie White, squinting against the hot sun. "That's where the kingpin lived."

Her voice was thick with disgust and bitter irony as she uttered the word *kingpin.* She pointed to the absolute ruin of a house that had belonged to Joe Moore, a pig farmer in his late fifties who was said by law enforcement authorities to be the lead trafficker of the dozens of alleged cocaine dealers rounded up in an infamous series of raids on July 23, 1999.

The house—little more than a shack, really—seemed about to collapse from the weight of its crumbling concrete and rotting wood. Windows were broken, screens were shredded, and the corrugated tin roof was a study in rust and corrosion.

Moore was no major gangster. But he had been swept up in the raids that followed an eighteen-month "deep undercover" investigation by a narcotics agent named Tom Coleman. There was no evidence that anyone arrested was a substantial dealer of cocaine, as alleged. No drugs, money, or weapons were found in the raids. And the evidence against the suspects consisted almost solely of Coleman's uncorroborated, unsubstantiated word.

But in Tulia, a hot, dusty, and racist town on the Texas Panhandle, that was enough. Coleman, who is white, targeted poor black residents and a handful of whites who had relationships with them. Some of the targets had had previous run-ins with the law, and one of those was Joe Moore. Although he insisted he had sold no drugs, he was convicted on the word of Coleman, and the court was merciless. He was sentenced to ninety years in state prison.

"Joe Moore didn't sell no drugs," said White. "All he did was sell his hogs. Me and him was real good friends. He was a nice person, and he would help anyone."

Coleman's investigative shenanigans (he worked alone, kept no detailed records, and fingered obviously innocent people) have devastated the tiny black community here. And they have taken an extreme toll on White, a serious, hardworking, and very religious black woman of fifty-one. Her thirty-three-year-old daughter Tonya was accused of selling drugs to Coleman. Not only was Tonya not in Tulia when she was supposed to have been selling the drugs, she didn't even live in Texas.

The charges against Tonya White had to be dropped when lawyers produced bank records that proved she was in Oklahoma City at the time that Coleman said the drug transaction had occurred.

Mattie White's son Donald, thirty-two, was not as fortunate. He, too, was accused of selling to Coleman. And Donald was known to have struggled with a drug habit in the past. He was convicted and sentenced to fourteen years in prison. Because of good behavior, and perhaps because there was mitigating evidence offered at trial, Donald was paroled after serving two years.

White's daughter Kizzie, twenty-five, was also accused of selling drugs to Tom Coleman. She was convicted and sentenced to twenty-five years in prison.

White's son Kareem, twenty-six, was also accused of selling drugs to Tom Coleman. He was convicted and sentenced to sixty years in prison.

This goes on and on. Kizzie White has two children, an eight-year-old girl and a five-year-old boy. The father of the boy is a white man named Cash Love. He, too, was accused of selling drugs to Tom Coleman. Love was awarded a special measure of Tulia's venom. He was convicted and sentenced to more than 300 years in prison.

It may be that some people sold some small amounts of drugs to Coleman, a troubled man who has had his own difficulties with the law. But there is no evidence that anyone caught in his net was a major dealer. And there is plenty of evidence that innocent people were snared and sent off to prison.

Mattie White is now working two jobs as she tries to care for Kizzie's children, maintain her own home, and offer hope and support for Kizzie and Kareem, who are in prisons far from Tulia.

"It's very difficult," she said. "These children miss their mama, and I've fallen behind on my mortgage and taxes. It's terrible what that man has done with his lies. He has ruined so many lives. I just pray and ask God to help me, because I know he knows the difference between right and wrong."

(August 5, 2002)

RAILROADED IN TEXAS

The malicious intent of the law enforcement authorities in Tulia, Texas, was almost immediately evident as police officers fanned out early on the morning of July 23, 1999. They weren't just going to arrest dozens of the town's black residents for alleged drug trafficking, they were going to publicly humiliate them.

Some suspects rousted from their beds were refused permission to dress before being paraded in front of television crews, which had been alerted in advance. At least one man was clad only in his underpants.

Kizzie White, a young woman who was arrested that morning, said in a videotaped prison interview that the officers had come into her house with their guns drawn and that some wore masks. "They wouldn't let me put on my clothes," she said. "I had on boxers and a T-shirt, with no underclothes on. With no shoes on. Basically, they took me out half-naked."

White was among those convicted of drug trafficking in the subsequent assembly-line trials in which guilty verdicts were a foregone conclusion. She is serving a sentence of twenty-five years in state prison.

White was fingered, as was everyone else, by Tom Coleman, a narcotics agent with an atrocious employment history and a penchant for making criminal allegations against innocent people. (He claimed, among other things, that Kizzie White's sister Tonya had sold him drugs in Tulia when it turned out that Tonya had not even been living in Texas.)

If Coleman had any professional or ethical standards, he managed to keep them well hidden. His methods of identifying people who allegedly sold him drugs were notoriously unreliable and sometimes bizarre. But in Tulia they resulted in convictions nevertheless.

Consider, for example, the case of Freddie Brookins Jr., who was sent to prison for allegedly selling cocaine to Coleman. When asked how he had identified Brookins, Coleman said, according to a habeas corpus petition now pending before the Court of Criminal Appeals in Austin: "I believe I talked to the sheriff on this occasion. I gave him the description of the subject. And I believe the sheriff asked city police officers or somebody, and told me—says, 'Well, we got a Freddie Brookins.' And I said, 'Okay. I need a picture of him.' And then I called Linda, Deputy Sheriff Linda Swanson, and got a picture of him. When she showed it to me, I came back, I think—I don't remember—when I came back on Wednesday or so, she showed me the picture. 'That's him.' So, there you go."

There you go. People were sent to prison for decades on these kinds of flimsy and unsubstantiated identifications and recollections.

According to an appeal filed on Brookins's behalf by the NAACP Legal Defense and Educational Fund, Deputy Sheriff Swanson testified at Brookins's trial but "provided no photograph and could not answer a single question about when she was asked to make a copy of the alleged photograph which Coleman allegedly used to identify Mr. Brookins."

That didn't matter to the jury. Freddie Brookins was convicted and sentenced to twenty years in prison.

Swanson answers the phone for the Swisher County sheriff, Larry Stewart. When I called and asked to speak to the sheriff, she began asking me questions, including what my "religious preference" was.

I called another time to ask Swanson specifically about her role in the identification of Brookins. "I'm not going to answer any questions," she said. When I asked why, she said the sheriff had told her not to.

A few days ago I visited Brookins's father, Freddie Brookins Sr., at his home in Tulia. He's a slender, athletic-looking man of forty-eight, who is filled with grief over his son's fate.

He told me his son had been offered a plea bargain that would have required him to serve five years. "He had already told me he was innocent," said Freddie Sr., "but I asked him again. I said to him, 'Did you do it?' He said, 'No, I didn't.'"

Freddie Sr. said he couldn't bear to advise his son to take a plea to something he hadn't done. So Freddie Jr., twenty-five years old, went to trial.

The entire Brookins family knew what the outcome would be. When it came time for sentencing, Freddie Sr. told each relative who was in the courtroom not to cry.

"I said, 'Don't give them the benefit of seeing your tears. Don't give them the satisfaction of knowing how much they've hurt you.'"

(August 8, 2002)

JUSTICE GOES INTO HIDING

Top law enforcement officials in Texas and at the Justice Department in Washington were aware of the hateful treatment of black people caught in a drug sting gone haywire in the small panhandle town of Tulia, but no one bothered to do anything about it.

The fact that a monstrous, racially motivated miscarriage of justice was occurring, that innocent people had been wrongfully accused, and that entire families were being ruined did not prompt anyone to intervene.

"Certainly we're concerned in any case about fair justice," said Tom Kelly, a spokesman for the Texas state attorney general, John

Cornyn. But he said Cornyn had not become involved in the events in Tulia because it was his understanding that the Justice Department had been conducting a criminal investigation.

"Attorney General Cornyn does stand ready to assist federal authorities in any way that we can assist them in their ongoing investigation," said Kelly.

You can file that comment in the empty-gesture folder. There is no ongoing criminal investigation. A couple of years ago, the Justice Department, after receiving complaints from the NAACP and others, did open an investigation of Tom Coleman, an undercover narcotics agent who conducted a clownish one-man sting operation that resulted in the arrests in the summer of 1999 of more than 10 percent of Tulia's black population. Bill Clinton was president at the time, and the lead investigator was an FBI agent from Amarillo.

Coleman should have been an easy target. A white man who was fond of the word *nigger*, he focused his "investigation" entirely on black people and a handful of whites who had relationships with them. He fingered people who were obviously innocent, routinely discarded evidence, scrawled important investigative information on his legs and arms, changed some of his testimony from trial to trial, and stumbled frequently into legal trouble himself.

But George W. Bush was the governor of Texas during Coleman's Tulia shenanigans. And when Bush became president and appointed John Ashcroft attorney general, the Justice Department investigation was doomed. Lori Sharpe Day, an adviser to Ashcroft, informed the president of the American Bar Association last month that "an investigation of events in Tulia was conducted by the Criminal Section and recently closed."

Late one afternoon I got a call from a Justice Department spokesman who said that while the criminal investigation has been closed, the Tulia matter is still under "review" by their Civil Rights Division.

Cornyn, meanwhile, is running for a U.S. Senate seat in Texas against a black opponent. One of the items you are not likely to find in his campaign material is the photo of him presenting Tom Coleman with a Texas "Lawman of the Year Award" for 1999.

With state and federal officials unwilling to aid the victims of this fiasco, and with several people serving unconscionably long prison sentences, it has fallen to a small group of dedicated lawyers to try to right some of these grievous wrongs.

One of the members of this cadre, a white lawyer from Amarillo named Jeff Blackburn, who has offered his services pro bono, has managed to get the charges against two defendants dismissed. "This is an injustice that has to be corrected," he said.

The legal challenges, supported by a number of private law firms, are being coordinated by the formidable Elaine Jones, president of the NAACP Legal Defense and Educational Fund.

"It is rare that we've seen an entire community preyed upon in this way," said Jones. "But we're in it now and we're going to stay with it. I'm not going to rest until all the convictions are overturned. I just hope no one dies in prison. You know, the hog farmer Joe Moore, who is in his late fifties and serving a sentence of ninety years, is now in poor health."

The local authorities, including the prosecutor, Terry McEachern, are now keeping remarkably low profiles. The right thing to do would be to throw in the towel, to admit that there was not sufficient evidence to justify these cases.

Tom Coleman's investigation was a nightmarish blend of incompetence and malevolence, and no one should have to spend even an hour in jail because of it.

(August 12, 2002)

A CONFUSED INQUIRY

Under pressure, and after a great deal of confusion among its own officials, the U.S. Justice Department has said it will continue its criminal investigation into a drug sting gone haywire in the Texas Panhandle town of Tulia.

Just last month an adviser to Attorney General John Ashcroft, Lori Sharpe Day, wrote in a letter to the president of the American Bar Association: "An investigation of events in Tulia was conducted by the Criminal Section and recently closed."

Those "events" included the arrests on July 23, 1999, of dozens of Tulia residents on narcotics trafficking charges. Local authorities rounded up more than 10 percent of the town's black population.

The arrests were the culmination of an absurd one-man "investigation" by Tom Coleman, a narcotics agent who did not wear a wire or conduct any video surveillance, did not keep detailed records of his alleged drug buys, and wrote such important information as the names of suspects and the dates of transactions on his legs and other parts of his body.

After a series of columns in this space, an outcry arose and several public officials asked the Justice Department to take action.

Senator Charles Schumer of New York, in a letter to Ashcroft, said: "This is far worse than Keystone Kops police work. It looks more like deliberate racial profiling, arresting and prosecuting with trumped-up evidence. Officer Coleman's 'investigation' is more reminiscent of the Old South of 1962 than the New South of 2002."

Senator Hillary Rodham Clinton noted in a letter to Ashcroft that Coleman had made criminal allegations against people who were subsequently shown to be innocent. But most of the time his word was enough to send people to prison, sometimes for astonishingly long sentences.

The "evidence" in those cases, said Clinton, "was simply the testimony of Mr. Coleman. Yet any reasonable review of the public information made available clearly establishes that Mr. Coleman's testimony in many cases was at best inconclusive, and at worst constituted perjury."

In a direct plea to Ashcroft, Clinton said, "I implore you to reopen the criminal investigation of Mr. Coleman as soon as possible."

As requests for some sort of action continued to come in, Justice Department officials seemed baffled about the status of their alleged investigation into the events in Tulia.

A criminal investigation of Tom Coleman's activities was started two years ago, when Bill Clinton was president. I called the Justice Department to ask about the status of that investigation. A spokesman, Mark Corallo, said that it was continuing. I told him I had a copy of the letter from Day to Robert Hirshorn, president of the Bar Association, saying the investigation had been closed.

Corallo seemed surprised. He said Day had probably been mistaken, but that he would check. He called back and said, "Mystery solved!"

According to Corallo, the criminal investigation had, in fact, been closed, but the matter was still under "review" by the Civil Rights Division.

After that conversation the official account changed yet again. In a letter to the editor of the *New York Times,* the Justice Department's director of public affairs, Barbara Comstock, said the information given to the Bar Association was erroneous, and the criminal investigation "remains open."

"The department apologizes," said Comstock, "for any confusion resulting from the issuance of that letter."

She said, "The Criminal Section is working expeditiously to review all of the relevant evidence to determine whether to prosecute for federal criminal civil rights laws violations."

If the department is serious about this matter—and that remains to be seen—it will not limit its investigation to Coleman's activities. There was an entire criminal justice hierarchy that worked in concert to send the Tulia defendants to prison, including the district attorney who prosecuted the cases, the sheriff who hired Coleman, and the regional narcotics task force that trained and supervised him.

Federal investigators who are both honest and diligent will find plenty of evidence of official wrongdoing waiting for them in Tulia.

(August 22, 2002)

THE LATEST FROM TULIA

Some tentative, very preliminary steps are being taken to address one of the great miscarriages of justice in the country—the roundup and prosecution of dozens of black men and women on specious drug trafficking charges in the Texas Panhandle town of Tulia.

There is no reason to believe that any of the people arrested in the humiliating roundup on July 23, 1999, were guilty of trafficking. No drugs, money, or weapons were found. Several defendants have already been proved innocent. All were arrested solely on the word of a clownish undercover cop named Tom Coleman, who had a penchant for making up charges, throwing his "evidence" into the garbage, scrawling important investigative information on his arms and legs, changing his testimony from trial to trial, making false statements while under oath, referring to black people as "niggers," and stumbling into legal trouble himself.

On the uncorroborated, unsubstantiated testimony of this officer, defendants arrested in Tulia on that shameful summer day were convicted and given prison sentences of twenty years, sixty years, ninety years, and more. When the first astonishingly harsh sentences were handed down, the remaining defendants quickly began agreeing to plead guilty in return for more lenient punishment. Thirteen defendants remain in prison, serving sentences of up to ninety-nine years.

In the bleak and twisted world of criminal justice in Texas, this case was considered cause for celebration. Coleman was hailed as a hero and given the state's "Lawman of the Year" award.

Local officials had every reason to believe that no one would pay attention to the terrible doings in Tulia. But the media spotlight has remained on the fiasco, and the case has become a Texas-size embarrassment. The offices of the U.S. attorney general, John Ashcroft, and the Texas attorney general, John Cornyn, have said they are investigating. But the investigations have been extremely quiet, and so far no developments have been reported.

There has been a significant development in the courts, however. The Texas Court of Criminal Appeals, responding to petitions filed by a local attorney, Jeff Blackburn, and lawyers from the NAACP Legal Defense and Educational Fund, has sent a number of the cases back to the trial court for additional fact-finding.

Among other things, the appeals court wants to know if there was evidence available to impeach Coleman's testimony, and if there had been any knowledge by the prosecution of such evidence.

Ordinarily the original trial judge would handle the response to the request by the appeals court. But District Judge Ed Self, who presided over most of the Tulia trials, recused himself after defense lawyers called his impartiality into question. The judge, who had leaned heavily in favor of the prosecution during the trials, had defended his rulings in a letter to the editor of a local newspaper. He was also quoted as saying that local residents were "tired of all the talk about the drug bust."

A new judge from an entirely different judicial district—Judge

Ron Chapman of Dallas—has been assigned to the case. This is a very hopeful sign. The criminal justice crowd in and around Tulia worked as a team to perpetrate this outrage. And these good ol' officials have shown no inclination to blow the whistle on their own bad behavior. A pair of fresh and impartial eyes is in order.

Meanwhile, the district attorney who prosecuted most of the Tulia cases, Terry McEachern, has a problem of his own to deal with. He was arrested in New Mexico the day before Thanksgiving on a misdemeanor charge of driving while intoxicated. Police said he was pulled over after his Jeep Cherokee was spotted weaving from lane to lane. He reportedly said he had consumed some alcohol and also the prescription drug Valium. But he said he was not drunk. He refused to take a blood alcohol test.

John Cornyn, the state attorney general whose office is supposed to be investigating the Tulia arrests, had a much better November. Cornyn, who actually presented Tom Coleman with his Texas "Lawman of the Year" award, was elected to the United States Senate. He will take his seat as part of the Republican majority in January.

(December 26, 2002)

THE TULIA STORY ISN'T OVER

A grand jury in Texas has indicted the ex-cop who conducted a slimy undercover operation that devastated much of the black community in the small panhandle town of Tulia.

But we should hold off on the champagne toasts. The perjury indictment against Thomas Coleman, a self-styled "deep undercover" narcotics agent who concocted one of the worst criminal justice atrocities of recent years, is not really that big a deal.

Thirteen of the people improperly targeted by Coleman's racist, lunatic investigation are still locked in the hellish environment of the Texas prison system. And the lies that Coleman is accused of telling under oath were not directly related to his investigation in Tulia, which has now been officially discredited.

It would be outrageous if Coleman were nailed for perjury but the higher-ups who enthusiastically encouraged his activities—and prosecuted and imprisoned his victims—were allowed to escape all responsibility for their actions.

Coleman's undercover operation and his uncorroborated, unsubstantiated testimony led to the imprisonment of more than three dozen individuals, nearly all of them black. When the defendants were rounded up in a humiliating series of arrests on July 23, 1999, the police found no guns, no drugs, and no money.

The defendants were characterized as major drug dealers and vilified in Tulia's small-town, racially charged environment. Some of the sentences were extraordinarily, cruelly long—ninety years and more.

It has since been shown that Coleman was a bizarre individual who fingered people who were obviously innocent, scrawled important investigative information on various parts of his body, had been in trouble with the law himself, had once blown out the windshield of a patrol car with a shotgun, had routinely referred to blacks as "niggers," and had a widespread professional reputation as unreliable and untrustworthy.

In short, Tom Coleman was a clown, although a dangerous one. His activities should be thoroughly investigated by competent authorities, and his superiors should be investigated as well.

In Texas the Tulia fiasco was characterized as a criminal justice triumph. Coleman was hailed as a hero and presented with the state's "Lawman of the Year" award by John Cornyn, who was then the state attorney general and has since been elected a United States senator from Texas.

"Tulia is not just the story of a rogue cop," said Vanita Gupta, a lawyer with the NAACP Legal Defense and Educational Fund, which is handling the appeals of several Tulia defendants.

Among the larger issues here are why this happened at all, who allowed it to happen, and why the law enforcement establishment refused to intervene even after it was clear that a great injustice was occurring.

Tom Coleman's activities were financed by the federal government. He was hired and was supposed to have been supervised by the Panhandle Regional Narcotics Trafficking Task Force, one of the many federally financed task forces that are supposed to be waging an all-out war against the scourge of drugs in the United States.

The task forces in Texas are great examples of a drug war gone haywire. They squander millions of dollars on amateurish investigations that snare mostly low-level offenders, and they tend to focus like lasers on people who are black or Hispanic.

The way the money is distributed by the Department of Justice encourages the task forces to rack up as many arrests as possible, whether they are quality arrests or not. The more people they arrest, the more money the task forces get.

In Tulia, Tom Coleman's capers were so freakish they became impossible to defend. Last month the authorities threw in the towel. Prosecutors conceded that they had made an awful mistake in relying on Coleman's uncorroborated testimony and moved in court to overturn every conviction, including those in which defendants had pleaded guilty. (Some defendants, after seeing the excessively harsh sentences being handed down, rushed to plead guilty in exchange for more lenient punishment.)

The Texas Court of Criminal Appeals has the final say on whether the convictions will be vacated. The decent thing to do at this point would be to ease the suffering of the thirteen individuals still incarcerated by releasing them on bail pending the final ruling of the appeals court.

That would be the decent and honorable thing to do. But this is Texas we're talking about.

(April 28, 2003)

PARTWAY TO FREEDOM

Amarillo, Texas

At least twelve of the people who were sent to prison on the word of a lying, reckless, bigoted lawman in Tulia, Texas, will finally be allowed to step into the sweet light and fresh air of freedom. But they have not yet been exonerated.

District Judge Ron Chapman, who has thoroughly investigated the case and recommended that all convictions be thrown out, will authorize the release of the prisoners at a special bail hearing in Tulia today. Because of jurisdictional reasons, three others who are still in prison will not be part of the proceedings. A decision on whether to release one other prisoner has not been reached.

Every branch of the Texas state government has now acknowledged, in one form or another, that the Tulia defendants were railroaded. Two weeks ago, in an extraordinary ceremony for a state that likes to view itself as beyond tough on crime, Governor Rick Perry signed a bill that permitted Judge Chapman to grant bail to those who were still behind bars.

The sixteen people still imprisoned were among forty-six Tulia residents arrested on felony drug charges four years ago after an absurd "deep undercover" investigation by a clownish officer named Tom Coleman. The men and women targeted by Coleman were characterized as major drug traffickers. But no drugs, guns, or money were recovered when they were rounded up, publicly humiliated, and paraded before the news media, which had been alerted in advance.

The subsequent trials were outrageous pro forma proceedings in which convictions were a foregone conclusion. After the first few trials resulted in grotesque sentences—in some cases, ninety years or more—the remaining defendants began lining up to plead guilty in return for lesser punishment. A total of thirty-eight defendants either were convicted or pleaded guilty.

Coleman's activities in Tulia have since been completely discredited, and he's been indicted for perjury. Prosecutors threw in the towel in April. They said they had made a terrible mistake in relying on Coleman's uncorroborated testimony, and they agreed that all convictions, including those of individuals who had pleaded guilty, should be overturned.

But justice is always elusive in Texas, so that was not the end of the story. Judge Chapman's formal recommendation that the convictions be overturned has to be approved by the Texas Court of Criminal Appeals, which has not yet acted. And no one knows when it will act or what it will do. Meanwhile, the convictions stand.

The prospect of the Tulia defendants sitting in prison for months while awaiting a decision from the Court of Criminal Appeals led the State Legislature to pass the bill that made the granting of bail possible.

State Senator John Whitmire, chairman of the criminal justice committee, said, "It is clear to me that the only reasonable alternative at this point is to release these individuals."

An unfavorable ruling by the Court of Criminal Appeals could result in the defendants' being sent back to prison. But there is another potential route to exoneration. Governor Perry has asked the Texas Board of Pardons and Paroles to review the Tulia convictions to determine if some form of clemency is in order. In a letter to the board's chairman, Gerald Garrett, Governor Perry wrote:

"I urge you to begin an expeditious investigation into each of these cases and recommend whether a pardon, commutation of sentence or other clemency action is appropriate and just." He added: "A recent review by the trial court concluded that the key witness, an undercover agent, was not credible."

Among the prisoners to be released is Joe Moore, a pig farmer, now in his sixties, who was sentenced to ninety years. I remember standing outside his vacant and absolute ruin of a house, his shack, and thinking, "This has to be the most poverty-stricken drug kingpin ever."

Moore nearly died from illness while in prison.

Elaine Jones, president of the NAACP Legal Defense and Educational Fund, which represents several of the people still in prison, told me yesterday: "I can't get into a celebratory mood yet. This is progress, but the convictions have not been overturned and our clients will still be under the jurisdiction of the state, even after they're released. I don't want anybody to lose sight of that."

(June 16, 2003)

A GOOD DAY

Tulia, Texas

The first time I ever saw a smile flicker across the face of Freddie Brookins Sr. was on Monday.

Brookins is a compact, athletic-looking man in his late forties. He could serve as a model for that mythic American figure, the tough, soft-spoken, no-nonsense father who puts in decades of hard work to build a reasonably secure and comfortable life for his family.

Brookins is a beef processor. Four years ago his son, Freddie Jr., a young man with no history of trouble with the law, was arrested in the now-notorious Tulia drug sweep. After taking out a home equity loan to get his son released on bail, Brookins asked Freddie Jr. if he had, in fact, sold drugs to an undercover agent named Tom Coleman, as the authorities were alleging.

Freddie Jr. said no. Which created a situation. Tremendously long prison sentences were already being handed down, and everybody understood that there was more of a chance that the people of Tulia would begin to fly than that a jury would acquit any of the blacks caught in the sweep.

But prosecutors were willing to accept a guilty plea from Freddie Jr. in exchange for a five-year sentence.

When I met Brookins in the summer of 2002, Freddie Jr. was already in prison doing twenty years. Brookins told me he couldn't bear to advise his son to take a plea to something he hadn't done. So the young man went to trial in the spring of 2000 and was convicted, as he knew he would be.

I got a chance to talk to Brookins on Monday afternoon, soon after Freddie Jr. and eleven other Tulia defendants were released on a special personal-recognizance bond. The Tulia drug cases have completely fallen apart, and all convictions are likely to be overturned.

I spotted Brookins taking a quiet moment alone outside a building where a welcome-home celebration for the newly released defendants was being held.

"How you doing?" I asked.

That's when I saw the smile spread across his face. He took my hand in both of his and gave it a great squeeze.

"He's finally home," he said. His voice was a little husky from cigarette smoke, and still as quiet as ever. "It's a great day. A great day."

I asked if he was bitter about the authorities, or the system, or Tom Coleman, the chronic liar who set the Tulia madness in motion.

"That's a hard question," said Brookins. "In a way I'm bitter. And in a way I feel sorry for them."

Also released on Monday was Joe Moore, a kindly, overweight sixty-year-old pig farmer who "can't read or write too good" and is in such poor health he can barely walk without assistance. He was smiling, too.

"Well, I had kind of a hard time for a while there in prison," he said, "because I have sugar diabetes and I wasn't getting my medication there for a while. I began to lose some of my sight. But then I got my medication, so I'm all right now."

Except for the fact that he is destitute. "I lost all my hogs because of this trouble," he said. "I lost everything, really."

There seemed to be a special measure of cruelty in the treatment of Moore. He was sentenced to ninety years in prison as an alleged drug kingpin, and at one point was assigned to a maximum-security unit populated by hard-core predators. Even the inmates were astonished.

"They said to me, 'What are you doing here? You don't need to be in here, old man.'"

Rather than abusing Moore, the inmates looked out for him. "They were very protective," he said.

There were smiles and hugs everywhere on Monday as defendants were reunited with their children, their parents, other relatives, and close friends. But if you paid close attention it was easy to see signs of discomfiture, wariness, anger, and even rage behind many of the smiles.

The events over the past four years were not just bizarre, they were profoundly destructive. Some of the defendants seemed bewildered, not fully understanding all that had happened to them, or what might be in store.

None of those I spoke to had solid plans for the future. And no one had any money to speak of. Their liberty had been taken away from them capriciously and, in their view, almost as capriciously returned.

So Monday was a good day. But given everything that had happened, no one was placing heavy bets on Tuesday.

(June 19, 2003)

POSTSCRIPT

I wrote about a dozen columns on the travesty in Tulia. At first there was not a great deal of public interest and no interest at all among officials in Texas. But a number of lawyers and activists continued working tirelessly on behalf of the defendants, and over several months the interest in the story and support for the defendants began to grow. Eventually it became widely understood that this was a tremendous miscarriage of justice and that the story was not going away. The NAACP Legal Defense and Educational Fund, the American Civil Liberties Union, the William Moses Kunstler Fund for Racial Justice, and several private law firms all did extraordinary work on the case.

This sustained effort reached a successful conclusion on August 22, 2003, when the governor of Texas, Rick Perry, granted full pardons and restored full citizenship rights to all of the individuals who had been wrongfully convicted.

A number of lawsuits were filed on behalf of the defendants and eventually a settlement totaling $6 million was reached.

In January 2005 Tom Coleman was convicted of one count of perjury in a case unrelated to his activities in Tulia. He was sentenced to seven years' probation.

3

INNOCENCE IS NO DEFENSE

A SENSELESS ASSAULT

John Padilla was crossing Sheffield Avenue at the corner of Liberty Avenue in the East New York section of Brooklyn when he saw the car approaching. Its headlights were off and it was traveling fast, he said.

This was late on the night of October 7, 1994. Padilla crossed the street safely, but within seconds the car with its headlights off crashed into another car at the intersection.

Padilla, twenty-eight at the time, ran back into the street to see if he could help. It turned out that the car with no headlights was an unmarked police vehicle carrying three officers. Padilla, an immigrant from Honduras, recalled that no one was seriously injured, but within minutes several other police cars and an ambulance arrived at the scene. Padilla still thought he could be of help.

He spotted a police officer with a notebook and went up to him.

I interviewed Padilla on Tuesday in the lower Manhattan offices of his attorneys, Marvin Salenger and Robert Sack. He remembered telling the officer with the notebook: "Would you like to hear what I saw? I could tell you what happened because I saw what happened."

The officer with the notebook ignored him. But another officer walked up and said, according to Padilla, "Shut the [expletive] up and take a hike."

Padilla naïvely tried to explain that he wasn't a crank, that he had information he thought the police should have. He said the second officer told him if he didn't take a hike he'd be arrested. So, as even the police acknowledge, Padilla turned around to leave. For some reason, the second officer, later identified as John Coughlin, grabbed Padilla from behind, flipped him, and slammed him face first to the pavement.

Then several cops jumped him. Padilla said he was hit in the back of the head with a heavy object and his face was pounded into the ground. "I couldn't see how many cops there were," he said. "But I could see so many feet surrounding me and kicking me. It was horrible. I felt like I was going to be killed. I was totally scared. I was shaking."

Padilla was taken to the 75th Precinct stationhouse, where he was given a summons for disorderly conduct. The specific charge was making unreasonable noise. To Coughlin it was not a big deal. He would later describe his encounter with Padilla as a "minor incident."

But when Padilla left the stationhouse he was a mess. His face was swollen and he was bleeding from his forehead, his chin, his hands, and his knees. He went home, and on Monday morning he went to work as usual. But instead of gradually feeling better, he felt worse. He suffered excruciating headaches. And within a few days he began to lose the sight in his right eye. The optic nerve, which transmits visual impulses from the eye to the brain, had been damaged in the beating inflicted by the cops.

Padilla is now legally and permanently blind in that eye. "All he can see are shadows," said Salenger.

Salenger and Sack filed a lawsuit on Padilla's behalf, charging that he had been falsely arrested and that the police had used excessive force. The case recently came to trial. At one point Coughlin, now a sergeant, was asked to demonstrate for the jurors how he flipped Padilla. He seemed happy to do so. He stepped behind an attorney who volunteered for the demonstration, grabbed him, flipped him, and slammed him to the floor. There was a collective gasp in the courtroom. Jurors later commented on the grin of apparent satisfaction that Sergeant Coughlin displayed after the demonstration. Coughlin assured the lawyer that he had taken it easy on him.

There were at least ten cops on the scene when Padilla was arrested. But Coughlin testified that he could not recall the name of even one officer who witnessed the arrest.

The jurors did not find the attack on Padilla to be funny or trivial. Last week they returned an $8.2 million verdict against the city and the Police Department.

Padilla is a hardworking body-and-fender repairman who is married and has two young children. "He is just a terrific guy," said Salenger. "All he wanted to do was help."

Said Sack: "The police, by violating their oath, violated the rights of an innocent man, causing him to suffer a devastating injury."

(February 18, 1999)

TWO VICTIMS

On the evening of May 18, 1982, a woman who was visiting a nature preserve with her husband in Buffalo, New York, was attacked and raped. The woman had walked away from her husband and was on an isolated path when the attack occurred. She told police she had been heading back to their parked car, where she had planned to sit and read.

The woman was twenty-three years old and white. She said the man who had attacked her was black. She got only a glimpse of his face, she told police, because he was wearing a hooded jacket and had blindfolded her.

Four and a half months later, police picked up Vincent Jenkins, a forty-three-year-old black man who would never qualify for a good-citizenship award. He had been involved in the illegal numbers game and had served a prison sentence for a manslaughter conviction in the early seventies. (His lawyer had argued that the killing was in self-defense, and Jenkins had in fact been cut with a knife in the fatal encounter, but a jury convicted him anyway.)

Jenkins was taken by investigators to a police garage, where he was viewed by the victim through a one-way glass. She had been told that he was a suspect. She looked at him for more than fifteen minutes but was unable to identify him as the man who had raped her.

The police then showed the victim a four-year-old photo of Jenkins. They told her it was a current photo. They allowed her to look at Jenkins again. Finally she said yes, he was the man who had attacked her.

Jenkins was arrested and charged with rape.

The trial court ruled that the initial identification process had been unconstitutionally suggestive, so the "evidence" from that process—the viewing of Jenkins in the garage, the four-year-old photo—was excluded from the trial. But the victim was allowed to testify that Jenkins was the man who had raped her.

Jenkins's current lawyer, the Manhattan attorney Eleanor Jackson Piel, said, "The jury believed her, even though his physical appearance was dramatically different from the description the victim had originally given the police."

The jury also disregarded the analysis of hairs found on the victim that were determined to have come from a black person, but not from Jenkins.

Jenkins was convicted and sentenced to twenty years to life in prison.

In the early nineties Piel contacted the lawyer Barry Scheck, who has pioneered the use of DNA testing in criminal cases. At their request, the court ruled that evidence originally collected as part of the so-called rape kit be submitted for DNA testing. This was done over the objections of the Erie County district attorney's office.

The test was inconclusive. Nothing in the test results pointed to Jenkins as the rapist, but some of the results were confusing. That was in 1993.

By the late nineties the DNA testing procedures had become much more sophisticated. Another series of tests was done in the Jenkins case. No one, including the prosecutors, disputes the scientific accuracy of the tests. Based on material from vaginal and cervical swabs, the tests showed DNA from two males, which was consistent with the victim's testimony that she had had sex with her husband twenty-four hours before she was raped.

The tests unequivocally ruled out Jenkins as the source for any of the DNA. But they also ruled out the victim's husband. This has thrown prosecutors into a theoretical tailspin. All sorts of wild hypotheses are emerging as they search for any scenario that can be used to keep Jenkins in prison.

Piel and Scheck have asked John Elfvin, a federal judge in Buffalo, to order the release of their client, who has now spent nearly seventeen years in prison. But prosecutors continue to object. Now they are suggesting that maybe there were two rapists, or even three, and that Jenkins was one of them, but that he left no genetic evidence.

Those hypotheses, born of desperation, are contradicted by the victim, who said immediately after the attack, and at the trial, and for all these years, that she had been raped by one man and that he had ejaculated.

That one man, according to the DNA evidence, was not Vincent Jenkins.

(July 8, 1999)

HOW MANY INNOCENT PRISONERS?

One way or another Vincent Jenkins will be freed from the Green Haven Correctional Facility in upstate Dutchess County, where he has served nearly seventeen years of a twenty-to-life sentence for a rape he didn't commit.

The question now is when.

DNA tests have ruled out Jenkins as the man who attacked and raped a woman in a nature preserve in Buffalo in 1982. But it is easier to learn to fly by flapping one's arms than it is to get a district attorney to admit having sent an innocent person to prison.

So lawyers from the office of Erie County district attorney Frank Clark told me that they will not oppose Jenkins's release on his own recognizance. And they will not oppose any motion in state court to have his conviction vacated. But they will continue to oppose the effort by Jenkins's lawyers to have a federal judge rule that he should be freed because his innocence has been established.

Got that?

This is a case in which the victim has said for seventeen years that she was attacked by one man, and one man only, and that he ejaculated. And DNA tests, done in collaboration with the county's own experts, have ruled out Jenkins as that man. And still the D.A.'s office is unwilling to concede that a tragic error occurred, and that the wrong man was convicted.

Most Americans would be shocked to learn how many innocent people are behind bars in this country. Jenkins is represented by the New York City lawyers Eleanor Jackson Piel and Barry Scheck. Scheck noted that the FBI has been doing DNA testing in rape and rape-homicide cases since 1989. "They only get the cases when there has either been an arrest or an indictment," he said. "Then they do DNA to confirm or exclude the person. In 25 percent of the cases where they can get a result, they exclude the primary suspect."

Think about that. In one out of four of those cases, the wrong person gets arrested. These are cases that carry extraordinary prison sentences, and in some cases the death penalty.

Said Scheck: "How many of those people would have been convicted had there been no DNA testing?"

If even 1 percent were convicted, that would translate into thousands of innocent people in prison, he said.

"Then you ask the question, 'What about all the other cases that don't involve biological evidence?' It's not like people who are making identifications in rape cases are far less accurate than someone who makes an eyewitness identification in a purse-snatching, or a robbery, or any other crime."

This is not a subject that the criminal justice system has been willing to honestly engage.

Scheck is the co-director, with Peter Neufeld, of the Innocence Project at the Benjamin N. Cardozo School of Law in Manhattan. The two men have pioneered the use of DNA testing in criminal cases.

Scheck said sixty-four people—more than half of them with the assistance of the project—have had their convictions overturned as a result of DNA testing. In eight of those cases, the convicts were on death row.

Scheck said thousands of others "have been exonerated after an arrest, in the middle of a trial, things like that." Those thousands represent only a small percentage of the individuals wrongfully arrested and imprisoned for serious crimes. Scheck said that in 70 percent of the Innocence Project cases, the evidence he would like to test can't be located.

In the Jenkins case, Piel and Scheck have asked a federal judge to rule that their client is innocent, and that therefore his imprisonment is a violation of his constitutional guarantees of due process and protection against cruel and unusual punishment.

A ruling in their favor would be groundbreaking. It would be the first time a federal court cited innocence as the constitutional basis for ordering the release of a prisoner. It would establish that imprisoning an innocent person was in and of itself a constitutional violation.

The reluctance of prosecutors to admit that they have sent the wrong person to prison—even after incontrovertible evidence has been produced—is a huge problem. That, and the cumbersome procedures of state court systems, makes it perversely difficult to secure the release of the innocent.

Piel, Scheck, and Neufeld are trying to find a better way.

(July 18, 1999)

POSTSCRIPT

Vincent Jenkins was completely exonerated by the courts. A federal judge vacated his conviction on August 30, 1999, and he was released from prison two days later. The following November, a state judge dismissed his rape indictment. Jenkins sued the state and won the largest wrongful conviction settlement in New York history—$2 million.

A CHILD'S "CONFESSION"

LaCresha Murray is a fourteen-year-old prisoner at the Giddings State Home and School in Giddings, Texas, about sixty miles east of Austin, the state capital. She is serving a term of twenty-five years after being found guilty in 1996 of criminally negligent homicide and injury to a child in the death of a two-and-a-half-year-old girl named Jayla Belton.

The case was a local sensation. Excited prosecutors and other law enforcement officials stumbled over one another in their rush to portray LaCresha, just eleven years old, as a juvenile monster, a homicidal maniac who attacked Jayla and inflicted a savage beating, eventually breaking four of her ribs and rupturing her liver. The medical examiner said the injuries were like those that might result if a person went through the windshield in a high-speed car accident. Prosecutors referred to LaCresha in private as "La Creature."

LaCresha was convicted twice (the first verdict was overturned), but a close look at the case shows that she was the victim of a colossal miscarriage of justice. She remains trapped in a Texas-size nightmare, a naïve child with learning difficulties who was tricked into signing a confession she could barely read and surely didn't understand.

Prosecutors ignored evidence that Jayla had long been the victim of child abuse. There was no legitimate evidence against LaCresha. None. No witnesses, no forensic evidence—not so much as a drop of blood or a speck of body fluid of any kind. Twenty or more police officers scoured the premises where she supposedly killed the child. They found nothing.

Jayla had been dropped off on the morning of May 24, 1996, at a small, one-family house in Austin, where LaCresha lived with three siblings and their grandparents, R. L. and Shirley Murray. Shirley

Murray provided day care for Jayla and a number of other children. But Jayla's mother, Judy Belton, and her boyfriend, Derrick Shaw, had been told not to bring the child on May 24 because Shirley Murray would be away. Shaw dropped the baby off anyway.

According to the Murrays and a number of people who visited the house that day, Jayla was clearly ill. She was listless, refused to eat, perspired profusely, and was vomiting. In the early evening, the Murrays said, LaCresha noticed that the baby was "shaking real bad." In fact, the child had gone into convulsions.

R. L. Murray and LaCresha rushed the child to a hospital, but frantic efforts to save her failed.

Enter the Austin police. The medical examiner is reported to have told investigators that no one could survive more than fifteen minutes with a ruptured liver. The investigators, still without a suspect, took that to mean there was a good chance that the last person seen with the child was the killer. LaCresha had carried Jayla into the hospital. The cops zeroed in on her.

LaCresha was kept away from her family for four days and finally was subjected to a lengthy police interrogation, without the benefit of a lawyer. An officer ran through what was surely to her an incomprehensible reading of her rights, after which he said: "You've heard them before, on TV shows probably, huh?"

LaCresha insisted she had done nothing harmful to Jayla. "Why would I want to hurt a child?" she asked.

The cops told her that a doctor, "with over twenty years of experience," had said the baby died at precisely the time that LaCresha said she noticed the baby was shaking.

"I didn't do nothing," LaCresha replied. "I promise to God."

The interrogation was a travesty. Unable to shake her protestations of innocence, the police finally resorted to asking if it were at least "possible" that LaCresha had dropped the baby, or even kicked her.

She was told, "We're going to stay here until you tell us the truth."

Isolated and without a lawyer's help, LaCresha eventually said that the suggestions made by the interrogators were possible, even "probable." She developed a fantastic scenario that could in no way account for the injuries Jayla suffered. But it was enough for the police.

A confession was typed up. LaCresha was asked, "Can you read pretty good?"

"No," she said, "but I try hard."

As she read over her "confession," LaCresha asked the officers, "What's that word? Home-a-seed?"

When she was told that the word was *homicide,* she asked, "What's that?"

No one answered.

(November 15, 1998)

HOW DID JAYLA DIE?

Dr. Linda Norton offers us a voice of sanity in the nightmarish case of LaCresha Murray, a fourteen-year-old in Texas who is serving a twenty-five-year prison term after being found guilty of beating a two-and-a-half-year-old girl to death. The killing occurred in Austin in 1996, when LaCresha was eleven.

Dr. Norton is a former Dallas County medical examiner who is now in private practice. She is recognized as an expert in matters of child abuse and neglect and has testified frequently for the prosecution in child-abuse cases.

This time, for the first time, she testified for the defense.

"I have been doing forensic pathology since 1974," she said in an interview, "and I have never had a case affect me like this one. LaCresha Murray is an innocent child."

LaCresha, who has learning difficulties and is big for her age (which played into the prosecution's efforts to portray her as an eleven-year-old monster), was convicted of criminally negligent homicide and injury to a child in the death of Jayla Belton. LaCresha was said to have attacked Jayla with such force that she broke four ribs and ruptured her liver.

There was no legitimate evidence against her, just a "confession" that even prosecutors have acknowledged would not have accounted for the injuries that killed Jayla. There were no witnesses and no murder weapon, and police investigators who scoured the premises where the killing supposedly took place could find no forensic evidence of any kind.

That, said Dr. Norton, is because LaCresha did not kill Jayla.

Dr. Norton believes that Jayla Belton was a chronically battered and malnourished child. She noted that dozens of bruises had been found on her body. "A lot of those bruises and some of the healing abrasions were clearly quite old," she said.

Dr. Norton was openly and harshly critical of the Travis County medical examiner, Dr. Roberto Bayardo, for not conducting the kind of tests during his autopsy that she believes would have confirmed that Jayla had long been physically abused and had not been adequately fed.

"He didn't even weigh the body," she said.

Dr. Bayardo acknowledged that "the baby was small, that's for sure." But he said he hadn't weighed the body because "at that time we were in an old building. We didn't have a scale." So, he said, "We just estimated the weight, whatever it was."

He told me he had seen many bruises but had not conducted the microscopic examinations that would have indicated when they had been inflicted because there was no need for that.

"They only tell you when the injuries are old," he said. "When they are old I can see it by my naked eye."

His eye, he said, told him that the bruises had only recently been inflicted. He said he did not believe Jayla had been chronically abused.

When I asked if he thought an eleven-year-old girl could have exerted enough force to rupture the baby's liver, he replied, "This was not your usual eleven-year-old girl."

On the morning of May 24, 1996, Jayla's mother's boyfriend, Derrick Shaw, dropped Jayla off at the one-family home in Austin where LaCresha lived with three siblings and their grandparents, R. L. and Shirley Murray.

Dr. Norton believes Jayla had been seriously injured, perhaps by a kick or some other blow to the abdomen, before she was dropped off. The child's behavior that day, as described by members of the Murray family, was consistent with that, she said. Jayla, usually ravenous, refused to eat. She brought up whatever food was given to her. She wanted only to sleep.

Dr. Norton said she believed the child's liver had already been damaged, and that Jayla was bleeding and "going into shock all day long."

LaCresha and her grandfather rushed the child to the hospital early in the evening. Hospital personnel tried for more than twenty minutes to revive her.

Said Dr. Norton: "With CPR on a child, you're talking about one hundred compressions a minute." That's more than 2,000 powerful chest compressions on a very thin child. Dr. Norton believes the rupture of the already damaged liver occurred then.

LaCresha became a suspect because Dr. Bayardo told the police that Jayla could not have survived more than a few minutes with a ruptured liver, so the killer was probably the last person with the child. LaCresha had carried Jayla into the hospital.

(November 19, 1998)

WITHOUT EVIDENCE

The prosecutors who brought homicide charges against eleven-year-old LaCresha Murray for allegedly killing a two-and-a-half-year-old girl now concede that LaCresha's so-called confession, obtained during a lengthy grilling by the police in Austin, Texas, was worthless.

"She never confessed to anything," said Gary Cobb, an assistant district attorney in Travis County who was the lead prosecutor in the case. "She said she may have accidentally dropped and accidentally kicked the child, which is totally inconsistent with the injury. So that played no part in what we did with the case." (Cobb may have forgotten, but it certainly did play a part. Over the objections of the defense, Cobb's team fought successfully to have LaCresha's signed statement introduced at her trial.)

LaCresha, now fourteen, is serving a twenty-five-year sentence for the fatal beating of Jayla Belton in May 1996. There was no forensic evidence linking her to the crime, nor were there any witnesses alleging that she attacked the child.

In interviews I asked Cobb and his boss, the Travis County district attorney, Ronnie Earle, what evidence had convinced them that LaCresha was the killer.

"There's a great deal of evidence that taken all together is what points to her," said Cobb. He said LaCresha had the "opportunity" to kill the child because she had "access" to the room Jayla was in at approximately the time of death, "or at least the time that the child started dying."

When I asked what LaCresha had specifically done to Jayla, both Cobb and Earle said they believed she had stomped on her. And given the number of injuries, said Cobb, it was clear that "she did something else to her."

I asked what that might have been. Cobb said: "Well, she could have hit her with her fist. She could have hit her up against something. She could have kicked her more."

I said, "But you don't know whether she did or not?"

Cobb replied, presumably sarcastically, "We don't have a videotape of her doing anything."

I asked several more times about the apparent lack of evidence against LaCresha.

Earle said, "This is a child murder, a baby murder. Almost all murders of infants, of children, happen when just two people are present—the killer and the decedent. So there is almost never any evidence of any kind."

He then said there was evidence in this case and it "all points to LaCresha."

There were two trials, one in the summer of 1996 and another in February 1997, each resulting in a guilty verdict. The first verdict was thrown out. In that case, the prosecution theorized that LaCresha's grandfather, R. L. Murray, had been mistaken when he said he had heard LaCresha bouncing a ball in the house on the afternoon in question. The prosecutors said that what he heard was not a bouncing ball, but LaCresha slamming Jayla against the walls of a room less than a dozen feet from where Murray was sitting.

That theory was abandoned in the second trial. The new theory, never mentioned at the first trial, was that LaCresha had stomped on Jayla and that one of her tennis shoes had left an impression on the child's chest.

That theory, in the view of Earle and Cobb, is still viable.

Cobb told me, "We do have a footprint that matches a shoe belonging to LaCresha that we were able to match as leaving a skin impression on the child."

Earle described that as "fairly powerful evidence."

Neither of the men mentioned why such "powerful" evidence had not been introduced at the first trial. It turns out that the alleged match was bogus, even though it was presented to the second jury as "evidence."

As the second trial was approaching, the D.A.'s office put together photos of marks on Jayla's body with photos of a pair of sneakers found in the Murray home. They turned the photos over to the state crime lab, hoping, apparently in desperation, to have a match declared.

In a letter dated February 5, 1997, Juan Rojas, an official with the crime lab, informed the prosecution team that "we were unable to testify that the marks on Belton's body were made by these shoes due to insufficient general characteristics."

In other words, no match.

The jury was never told of that letter.

(November 22, 1998)

POSTSCRIPT

LaCresha Murray, the youngest Texan ever charged with capital murder, was released from juvenile prison in the spring of 1999 after a federal appeals court overturned her conviction. The court ruled that her confession had been improperly obtained. All charges against her were dropped in August 2001.

THE WRONG MAN

A little before 12:30 p.m. on December 30, 1997, a masked gunman walked into a bodega on Strauss Street in the Brownsville section of Brooklyn. There were four other people in the store: the owner, Jesus

Martinez, known affectionately in the neighborhood as "Poppy," a teenage employee named Frankie Rodriguez, and two young customers, Candace Daniel, thirteen, and Steven Green, fifteen.

The gunman raised his .38-caliber revolver and shot Mr. Martinez in the chest, killing him. Frankie Rodriguez turned and ran. The gunman chased him down an aisle, shooting at him. When Rodriguez stumbled and fell, the gunman stood over him and fired a fatal shot into his back.

Candace Daniel ran out of the store and was not hurt. Steven Green, who had been playing a video game near the rear of the store, hid in a back room until the gunman left. He was not injured either.

The police described the crime as a botched holdup.

A little over a week later, on January 8, 1998, cops arrested a twenty-seven-year-old rapper and songwriter named Antowine Butts. The office of the Brooklyn district attorney, Charles Hynes, then went to work putting together a first-degree murder case against Butts. This was not easy because Butts was innocent. But Hynes's office has shown on several occasions that innocence is no impediment to prosecution.

Jay Salpeter, a private investigator and former New York City detective who did investigative work for the defense, told me, "This was a really bad one. The guy was totally innocent. He was home with his three kids."

The police and the district attorney's office used smoke, mirrors, and two of the world's worst witnesses to try to convict Butts. Both witnesses picked him out of a lineup. One of the witnesses was a self-confessed crackhead who all but implicated himself in the crime. The other was a terminally confused young woman who said she had just happened to be passing by when the murders occurred, saw Butts, and decided, on the spot, to hang out with one or two other men who she said were involved.

To read the transcript of the trial of Butts (who once was caught jumping a turnstile, his only previous brush with the law) is to immerse oneself in the frightening reality of a criminal justice system gone mad—a system that simply closed its eyes to the most elementary aspects of truth and falsity, guilt and innocence.

The key witness against Butts was Martin Mitchell, a criminal with a long record. Mitchell told investigators that he had been at a meeting at which the murder of Martinez was planned. And Mitchell was outside the bodega the next day when Martinez and Rodriguez were killed. Did it occur to the police and the prosecutors that maybe Mitchell was involved in the crime?

Apparently not. He wasn't charged with anything.

A top aide to Hynes told me: "You can be at a meeting where an event is planned and not be a member of the conspiracy."

So the police and the D.A.'s office took Mitchell at his word when he said he was not involved in the crime, and they believed him when he said that Butts was. If you want a sense of how worthless Mitchell's testimony was, just consider that he admitted on the witness stand that in the twelve to twenty-four hours leading up to the crime he had been smashed out of his mind on crack cocaine, marijuana, and alcohol.

"My mind wasn't there," he said when he was asked why he never notified the police or warned anybody in the store that a murder was planned. He said, "My mind was just about getting high."

When he was asked what time the shooting took place, he replied, "I can't remember people. How am I going to remember time?"

Butts should never have been tried, but he was. A jury recently acquitted him, after only a brief deliberation. But by then he had already spent two years in jail. That's two years lost from a young man's life because of the incompetence—or worse—of the police who investigated this case, and Hynes's office, which prosecuted it.

And the real killer is still at large.

(March 2, 2000)

WHEN THE WEIGHT
OF THE EVIDENCE SHIFTS

Steven Cohen is a former federal prosecutor who has become all but obsessed with a case in New York in which he believes two men are serving long prison sentences for a murder they didn't commit.

A former New York City detective, Robert Addolorato, actually seems tormented by the case. He also believes the prisoners are innocent.

Neither of these men is soft on crime. But they insist that in this particular case, the authorities fouled up. Cohen was adamant: "They've got the wrong guys locked up for this murder."

In the early morning hours of November 23, 1990, two bouncers were shot at the old Palladium nightclub on East Fourteenth Street in Manhattan. One of the bouncers died. A couple of hapless young guys, David Lemus and Olmado Hidalgo, who most likely did not know one another, who didn't even speak the same language (one spoke only English and the other only Spanish), and who insisted they were not at the club when the shooting occurred, were arrested, tried, convicted, and sentenced to twenty-five years to life in prison.

The arrests had not been made immediately. Lemus was picked up nearly two months after the shooting, and Hidalgo nearly a year after. Prosecutors told a jury that the two men had gotten into an altercation with the bouncers, and had shot them after a "friend" of the defendants, Jose Figueroa, had unsuccessfully tried to mediate the dispute.

Cohen and Addolorato had no particular interest in the Palladium matter. But in the course of their own investigation of a drug and extortion gang they essentially "solved" the Palladium case. (Lemus and Hidalgo were already in prison.) A gang member named Joey Pillot admitted that he and a buddy named Thomas Morales had been responsible for the murder, that Morales was the actual shooter, and that neither Lemus nor Hidalgo was involved.

A wealth of evidence has since been marshaled to support that account. Several witnesses have bolstered or corroborated Pillot's version of the shooting. The prosecution's theory about what happened that night suffered a severe blow when it was learned that Figueroa, the "friend" who was supposed to have been acting as a mediator, was nowhere near the Palladium when the shooting occurred. He was in prison.

A man who resembled Figueroa, Richard Feliciano, was at the scene. According to court papers filed by defense lawyers, Feliciano "has indicated that he was, in fact, the mediator, that he witnessed the shooting and that Morales, and not Mr. Lemus and Mr. Hidalgo, shot the bouncers."

Lawyers for Lemus and Hidalgo have pressed hard for a new trial, but have not been successful. Another appeal hearing is scheduled to be held.

The *New York Times* and other news outlets have run stories raising serious questions about the case and detailing new evidence that has emerged, including Joey Pillot's confession. The forewoman of the jury that convicted Lemus and Hidalgo has also reviewed the latest evidence. She now believes the two men were innocent. But prosecutors in the Manhattan district attorney's office continue to fight all efforts to have the convictions overturned.

In an article that appeared in July 2000, Jane Fritsch and David Rohde of the *Times* wrote: "It is difficult to overturn a conviction in New York, even in the face of powerful new evidence. Trial judges and state appeals courts have always been reluctant to reverse a jury's verdict, and in 1996, Congress sharply limited the rights of defendants to take their appeals to federal court."

While officials in the district attorney's office continue to insist that Lemus and Hidalgo are guilty, there seems to be at least a little give in the foundation of their certainty. I talked about the case with

James Kindler, the chief assistant district attorney. He said at one point, "We think that at least Morales—there's been some evidence that we had that Morales may have been involved, yes."

"In the shooting?" I said.

"In the shooting."

That did not mean, said Kindler, that Lemus and Hidalgo were innocent. He said they could all have been involved.

I then asked if the district attorney's office had any evidence that linked Morales even remotely to the two men imprisoned for the murder.

"I believe not," said Kindler.

(January 3, 2005)

AN IMAGINARY HOMICIDE

If you are going to charge three defendants with capital murder for killing a newborn, do you have an obligation to show that the baby really was killed?

Not in Alabama, you don't.

Do you need to show, somehow, that the baby ever existed?

Not in Alabama. Not if the defendants are poor, black, and retarded.

"I mean this thing is just unbelievable," said Rick Hutchinson, a lawyer from the tiny Choctaw County town of Butler, whose client, Medell Banks Jr., is in prison for killing the hypothetical infant.

Back in 1999, Banks's estranged wife, Victoria, was in jail on an unrelated charge when she came up with the idea of claiming she was pregnant, hoping that would get her released, said Hutchinson. Both Medell and Victoria Banks are retarded, Hutchinson said, and they had separated in the mid-nineties.

Victoria Banks was seen by a doctor but would not let him do a pelvic exam. The doctor said he did not think she was pregnant. She was then seen by another doctor, who reported hearing a fetal heart tone but conducted no further tests.

That was enough to get Banks released on bond in May 1999. The following August she was taken back into custody. She did not have a baby and there was no evidence at all that she had given birth.

Had the authorities been duped? Where was the baby?

What the authorities didn't know, and wouldn't find out until later, was that in 1995 Banks had undergone a bilateral tubal ligation—a sterilization procedure in which the fallopian tubes are effectively blocked so that conception cannot occur.

The baffled and increasingly angry investigators began an intense period of interrogation. Medell Banks was brought in, and so was Victoria's sister, Dianne Tucker, who is also retarded. Banks was kept in custody and questioned over many days without the benefit of counsel.

By the time the questioning had concluded, all three individuals had confessed. Yes, they said, a baby had been born and they had killed it.

Hutchinson, the lawyer, said he firmly believed that the interrogators "planted that idea in the minds of these mentally retarded people."

All three were arrested and charged with capital murder. The penalty options upon conviction would be execution or life in prison without parole.

I asked the district attorney, Robert Keahey, what evidence he had that a baby had really been born and killed. He said, "Well, they all told us that."

I asked if that was all.

He said, "Well, the baby wasn't inside of her. It was inside of her when she left the jail, and when they said they killed it, it wasn't inside her. So that's pretty good evidence to us."

There's nothing like a capital murder charge to make you start looking around for an escape route. Incredibly, all three defendants ended up pleading guilty to manslaughter for the death of the hypothetical baby.

But Banks continued to insist he was innocent, and his court-appointed lawyers, Hutchinson and a co-counsel, Jim Evans, would not let the case go. They raised enough money from churches and other charitable sources to have a medical test done on Victoria Banks by a noted fertility expert, Dr. Michael Steinkampf of the University of Alabama School of Medicine.

Dr. Steinkampf determined that the tubal ligation—which all parties agreed had been performed in 1995—had been effective, and that in his opinion Banks could not have become pregnant.

The Alabama Court of Criminal Appeals ruled that "a manifest injustice" had occurred in this case and threw out Medell Banks's guilty plea. He is still in prison, however, serving his fifteen-year sentence and awaiting further court action.

(Victoria Banks is also serving fifteen years, concurrent with a sentence in a separate case. Dianne Tucker has been released from prison but has given up all rights to appeal her manslaughter plea.)

If Keahey has any say (and he does), Medell Banks will remain in prison. The district attorney plans to appeal the ruling to the Alabama Supreme Court.

I asked if there was a chance, in light of the latest evidence and the court's ruling, that he would consider dropping the charges against Banks. He replied, "Not in this lifetime."

(August 15, 2002)

WHEN JUSTICE IS MOCKED

The jovial voice on the other end of the phone was that of Robert Keahey, the district attorney for the First Judicial Circuit of Alabama, which includes the tiny town of Butler in Choctaw County.

Keahey is the prosecutor who brought capital murder charges against three retarded individuals for the murder of an infant, despite the fact that he could not show that the infant had ever existed, much less been killed.

If there was anything about the case that bothered him, he didn't let on. He laughed frequently during the conversation, and it was difficult to resist the impression that he found the whole thing amusing.

All three defendants were black and indigent. It turned out that the woman who supposedly gave birth to the baby in 1999, Victoria Banks, had been sterilized in 1995. But Keahey would not drop the charges. With capital murder indictments looming over them, and the hostility of the local community apparent, all three defendants pleaded guilty to the lesser charge of manslaughter.

I asked Keahey how it was first determined that Banks—who claimed she was pregnant in order to get released temporarily from jail in an unrelated case—was really pregnant.

"She came in weighing about 120 and she left weighing about 160," he said. "And the sheriff saw her grow from a thin woman to a fat woman, with her belly poking straight out and her belly button turned inside out."

"Was there a pregnancy test done?" I asked.

"No," said Keahey, adding, "There was no need for a blood test or anything like that. You could look at her and tell."

This was interesting, because a doctor who observed Banks at the time said he did not think she was pregnant. The doctor wanted to do a pelvic examination, but Banks would not allow it. When a second doctor reported hearing a fetal heart tone, Banks was released on bond.

That was in May 1999. When Banks was taken back into custody the following August, she did not have a baby and there was no evidence that she had given birth.

At that point, Keahey's prosecutorial power went into overdrive. Sol Wachtler, a former New York chief judge, once famously said that grand juries would indict a ham sandwich if a prosecutor wanted them to. Keahey managed to prove that not only can you indict the sandwich, you can convict it, and send it off to prison, too.

After intense and prolonged questioning without the benefit of counsel, Victoria Banks, her estranged husband, Medell, and her sister, Dianne Tucker, were all arrested and charged with murdering a baby that—based on the available evidence—was nothing more than a fantasy.

Keahey said all three defendants confessed to the crime, and that was enough.

I asked if there was any evidence, apart from the defendants' statements, that there ever was a baby.

"We have no physical evidence," he said.

After the three defendants pleaded guilty and were incarcerated for manslaughter, lawyers for Medell Banks raised enough money from churches and other charitable sources for an examination of Banks by a noted fertility expert, Dr. Michael Steinkampf of the University of Alabama School of Medicine. Dr. Steinkampf determined that the bilateral tubal ligation performed in 1995 had been effective, and that in his opinion Banks could not have become pregnant in 1999.

Based largely on that evidence, the Alabama Court of Criminal Appeals recently declared that "a manifest injustice" had occurred in this case and threw out Banks's guilty plea. But he continues to serve his fifteen-year prison sentence while awaiting further court action.

The jovial tone in Keahey's voice changed at the mention of

Dr. Steinkampf. "He thinks he's God!" said the D.A. "Yeah, that's right. He don't believe any of the good, honest, law-abiding Christian people in Choctaw County when they say the woman was pregnant."

I pressed Keahey throughout the interview for any evidence he could offer that the child had ever existed. "They hid it from the rest of the world," he said.

When I asked about the possibility of hospital birth records, he burst out laughing. "She didn't go to a hospital," he said. He laughed harder. "If she had gone to a hospital, that would have made it easy."

(August 19, 2002)

POSTSCRIPT

When Medell Banks's guilty plea to manslaughter was thrown out, the prosecutor threatened once again to bring a capital murder charge against him for the death of the baby that never existed. A complicated plea deal was arranged. In January 2003, Banks entered what is called a best interest plea to a charge of tampering with evidence, which carried a maximum sentence of one year in prison. As he had already served three and a half years, he was released from custody immediately. He does odd jobs from time to time for his lawyer, Rick Hutchinson.

4

THE ULTIMATE PENALTY

NEAR-DEATH EXPERIENCE

"I was in a state of shock," said Ellen Reasonover. "I was terrified."

In December 1983 a jury in St. Louis deadlocked over whether to impose the death sentence on Reasonover, who had been convicted of murdering a gas station attendant. It is believed the vote was eleven to one in favor of the death penalty. A unanimous vote was required for a death sentence to be imposed, so Reasonover's life was spared by a frighteningly thin margin.

It's a good thing, because we now learn that she wasn't guilty. And that's the biggest problem with the death penalty. Sometimes you get the wrong person. One more vote, and Ellen Reasonover would have been shoved unfairly and ignominiously into eternity.

Instead she was sentenced to fifty years in prison without parole, and she served more than sixteen grim years of that sentence before a federal judge recently ruled that she had been improperly convicted, and ordered her released.

I talked to Reasonover last week. She was struggling with some of the technological marvels of the last few years. "I never heard of call-waiting," she said. "And I had to learn what a cell phone is and a pager."

She was twenty-four and the mother of a two-year-old girl when she was arrested. She's forty-one now and her daughter is eighteen.

"I didn't think I would be convicted," Reasonover said. "I thought that when I finally got to trial I was going to explain to the judge that I was innocent, just tell him everything that had happened, and then he was going to let me go home."

Reasonover was convicted of murdering James Buckley, a six-foot-eight-inch gas station employee who was severely beaten and shot seven times with a rifle. Reasonover became a suspect when, after viewing a television report about the murder, she voluntarily contacted the police to offer information that she thought might be helpful. She said she had stopped by the gas station to get some change to use at a nearby Laundromat.

As her latest lawyer, Cheryl Pilate, put it: "There was nothing to tie Ellen to this. She came forward originally as a good citizen to report a suspicious character she'd seen at the gas station, and the next thing she knew they had turned her into their suspect."

The case against Reasonover was based almost entirely on the testimony of two jailhouse snitches she encountered after she was arrested. The snitches, Rose Jolliff and Mary Ellen Lyner, were both heroin junkies with long arrest records. They hit the criminal justice jackpot by testifying that Reasonover had told them in a jail cell that she had committed the crime. Jolliff got cash, and Lyner, who admitted she was "looking for a deal," was spared a lengthy term in the state penitentiary.

"When I first went to prison I was depressed," said Reasonover. "I cried a lot and I couldn't sleep. Then I got a job working at night, cleaning the bathrooms, sweeping and mopping the floors, pulling the trash. So that was a little better."

She said guards constantly propositioned her for sex and, when she refused, sometimes beat her. Fellow inmates taunted her.

She read whatever she could get her hands on and wrote endless letters proclaiming her innocence to people she felt might help—the pope, Nelson Mandela, Presidents Reagan, Bush, and Clinton and their wives. "I even thought about writing to Chelsea," she said.

Years passed. She contacted the Centurion Ministries, an organization in Princeton, New Jersey, that seeks justice for the innocent, and they eventually took up her cause.

In a decision handed down in August 1999, U.S. district judge Jean Hamilton ruled that the case brought against Reasonover was "fundamentally unfair." Two conversations that were secretly recorded by the police and that were favorable to Reasonover's defense were withheld by the prosecution. They came to light at a federal court hearing in June.

Had those conversations been disclosed, Judge Hamilton said, the jury "would have been entitled to find" that Reasonover was "a credible witness whose testimony was corroborated" by the tapes.

Reasonover, who is black, said she understands that the lone holdout against the death sentence was a white woman. "I always wondered who that white lady was that didn't vote to put me to death," she said. "I'd like to meet her so I can thank her."

(August 22, 1999)

DEATH PENALTY VICTIMS

Leighanne Gideon was twenty-six when she witnessed an execution for the first time. Gideon is a reporter for the *Huntsville Item,* in Texas, and part of her job has been to cover executions. Nowhere in the Western world is the death penalty applied as frequently as in Texas. Gideon has watched as fifty-two prisoners were put to death.

In a documentary broadcast on National Public Radio's *All Things Considered,* Gideon says: "I've walked out of the death chamber numb and my legs feeling like rubber sometimes, my head not really feeling like it's attached to my shoulders. I've been told it's perfectly normal—everyone feels it—and after a while that numb feeling goes away. And indeed it does."

But other things linger. "You will never hear another sound," Gideon says, "like a mother wailing whenever she is watching her son be executed. There's no other sound like it. It is just this horrendous wail, and you can't get away from it. . . . That wail surrounds the room. It's definitely something you won't ever forget."

Not much attention has been given to the emotional price paid by the men and women who participate in—or witness—the fearful business of executing their fellow beings. The documentary, titled *Witness to an Execution,* is narrated by Jim Willett, the warden at the unit that houses the execution chamber in Huntsville, where all of the Texas executions take place.

"Sometimes I wonder," Willett says, "whether people really understand what goes on down here, and the effect it has on us."

Fred Allen was a guard whose job was to help strap prisoners to the gurneys on which they would be killed. He participated in 130 executions and then had a breakdown, which he describes in the documentary.

I called him at his home in Texas. He is still shaken. "There were so many," he said, his voice halting and at times trembling. "A lot of this stuff I just want to try to forget. But my main concern is the individuals who are still in the process. I want people to understand what they're going through. Because I don't want what happened to me to happen to them."

Everyone understands that the condemned prisoners have been convicted of murder. No one wants to free them. But this relentless bombardment of state-sanctioned homicide is another matter entirely. It is almost impossible for staff members and others in the death chamber to ignore the reality of the prisoners as physically healthy human beings—men and (infrequently) women who walk, talk, laugh, cry, and sometimes pray. Killing them is not easy.

"It's kind of hard to explain what you actually feel when you talk to a man, and you kind of get to know that person," says Kenneth Dean, a major in the Huntsville corrections unit. "And then you walk him out of a cell and you take him in there to the chamber and tie him down and then, a few minutes later, he's gone."

Jim Brazzil, a chaplain in the unit, recalls a prisoner who began to sing as his final moment approached: "He made his final statement and then, after the warden gave the signal, he started singing 'Silent Night.' And he got to the point, 'Round yon virgin, mother and child,' and just as he got 'child' out, was the last word."

Dave Isay, who coproduced the documentary with Stacy Abramson, said: "It is certainly chilling to hear the process of what goes on, the ritual of the execution. The folks who do these executions are just regular, sensitive people who are doing it because it's their job. And it has an enormous impact on some of them."

The Reverend Carroll Pickett, a chaplain who was present for ninety-five executions in Huntsville before he retired in 1995, told me in a telephone conversation that symptoms of some kind of distress were common among those who participated in the executions. "Sure," he said. "It affects you. It affects anybody."

I asked how it had affected him. "Well," he said, "I think it was a contributing factor to a triple bypass I had about eighteen months later. Just all of the stress, you know? I have to say that when I retired I probably had had as much as I could take."

I asked Fred Allen, who suffered the breakdown, if his views on the death penalty had changed.

"Yes," he said. Then, after a long pause, he said, "There's nothing wrong with an individual spending the rest of his life in prison."

(October 12, 2000)

THE CONFESSION

Earl Washington Jr. was both brain damaged and mentally retarded. He grew up in a hard-drinking, violent family in rural Virginia in the 1960s and '70s. He performed dismally in school and dropped out when he was fifteen. On a good day, his IQ could be measured in the high 60s. On at least one occasion, his score was 57. Reciting the alphabet was too tough for him.

But Earl Washington liked to please. So when he found himself in police custody in 1983 he began telling the cops whatever they wanted to hear. He waived his Miranda rights and confessed to all sorts of crimes, including burglary, rape, and murder. His performance was farcical. He knew nothing about a string of crimes he confessed to, and when eyewitnesses were contacted, they basically rolled their eyes and told the police they had the wrong guy.

But prosecutors went ahead and pinned an awful crime on Earl

Washington anyway. They charged him with the rape and murder of a young woman named Rebecca Williams.

The ever-helpful Washington readily confessed to that crime, too.

There were some problems. Washington said the victim was black. She was white. He said she was short. She was tall. He said he had kicked in the door to her residence. The door had not been damaged. He said he stabbed her two or three times. She had been stabbed thirty-eight times.

None of these outlandish discrepancies deterred the authorities. The only evidence they had was Washington's absurd "confession," but that was enough to bring a capital case against him. At the end of a three-day trial he was convicted and sentenced to death.

Most Americans do not believe the criminal justice system functions this ludicrously. But it does. Frequently.

In 1985 Washington came within nine days of being executed. His lawyers, working frantically, managed to secure a stay. Meanwhile, the use of DNA testing was evolving, and early tests seemed to offer concrete evidence of Washington's innocence. On the basis of that evidence, his death sentence was reduced in 1994 to life in prison.

More sophisticated DNA tests were conducted in 2000, and they showed conclusively that Earl Washington, despite his confession, had not attacked Rebecca Williams.

Washington was pardoned by Governor James S. Gilmore III and was freed from prison in February 2001.

The death penalty is always problematic. I am opposed to it in all cases. But if it is used, it should be reserved for the most blameworthy perpetrators of the most heinous acts. Even when mentally retarded defendants are clearly guilty, it is extremely difficult to determine their level of culpability.

A recent report by Human Rights Watch titled "Mental Retardation and the Death Penalty" mentioned the case of a retarded man convicted of raping and murdering an elderly woman. When asked at his trial to explain why rape was wrong, the defendant struggled to find an answer, finally blurting out, "Maybe it's against her religion." Executing such an individual is not the same as executing Timothy McVeigh.

Beyond that, as the report notes, there is wide acknowledgment among mental health experts that "the mentally retarded's characteristic suggestibility and willingness to please" leads them to confess to crimes they may not have committed, including murder.

It is also difficult, often impossible, for retarded individuals to assist in their own defense. Their memories are often unreliable and they have trouble grasping abstract concepts.

All of this was lost on the governor of Texas, a man named Rick Perry. The Texas Legislature, in an uncharacteristically progressive move, passed a law banning the execution of the retarded. But Governor Perry vetoed it saying there was no need for the law.

It would have been a big deal if Texas—the undisputed champion when it comes to executions in the United States—had decided that it was morally unacceptable to execute retarded individuals. But Governor Perry shrank from that challenge.

The United States will someday ban the execution of the retarded, and probably—in the long term—all other individuals as well. Governor Perry could have given us a big push in that direction, but chose not to.

(June 21, 2001)

TRAPPED IN THE SYSTEM

So what do you do if you've put the wrong man on death row, and you've got the evidence in hand to prove who really committed the murder?

One of the great problems of the American criminal justice system is that this is not an easy call. Once an innocent person is trapped in the system, it's extremely difficult to get him—or her—extricated.

On the evening of April 7, 1997, the proprietor of a convenience store in Bridge City, Louisiana, was shot to death by a holdup man wearing a ski mask. Witnesses said that the gunman ran out of the store and dived through the passenger window of a getaway car. As the driver sped off, the gunman tossed the ski mask out the window.

Two years later a retarded teenager named Ryan Matthews was convicted of the murder and sentenced to death. He's now on death row in the Louisiana state penitentiary in Angola.

Eight months after the murder, and just a half mile from the convenience store, a man named Rondell Love slashed the throat of a woman named Chandra Conley, killing her. Love eventually pleaded guilty to manslaughter and was sentenced to twenty years in prison. So he's also in Angola.

Matthews, who was seventeen when the convenience store murder occurred, has always insisted he had nothing to do with the crime. Love, on the other hand, has reportedly bragged in prison about committing that murder.

You be the judge. Matthews was convicted and sentenced to death despite the fact that DNA tests showed conclusively that tissue samples taken from the killer's mask had not come from him. Attorneys handling Matthews's appeal arranged to have the DNA analysis of those samples compared with an analysis of Rondell Love's DNA. It was a perfect match. The human tissue taken from the mask worn by the killer in the convenience store had come from Love.

Attorney Billy Sothern of the Louisiana Crisis Assistance Center, which is representing Matthews, told me in an interview that the DNA analysis cleared up a troubling discrepancy that had existed from the very beginning. Eyewitnesses had said that the gunman in the convenience store was not very tall, perhaps five-foot-five or five-foot-six, and of medium build. Sheree Falgout, who was standing at the register when the proprietor was gunned down, recalled telling the police that the assailant "was not a large person." Other witnesses concurred.

Ryan Matthews is six feet tall. Rondell Love is five-foot-seven and weighs less than 150 pounds.

What we have here is a major-league miscarriage of justice. The question now is how to correct it.

Sothern and Ryan Matthews's mother, Pauline, have been on a campaign to have Matthews's death sentence lifted and his conviction overturned.

"This is the trifecta in terms of what's wrong with the death penalty," said Sothern. "Ryan was a juvenile at the time of the murder, he's retarded, and he's innocent."

The case is also a quintessential example of the hideous consequences that can result when a killer remains at large because the wrong person has been imprisoned. If Rondell Love had been arrested in a timely fashion for the convenience store murder, Chandra Conley's life would have been spared.

Even at this late date no one knows if the courts and prosecutors in Louisiana will ultimately do the right thing. The state's Supreme Court and the Jefferson County district attorney have agreed that another look at the case is warranted, and a hearing will be held August 11.

"As this will be the first time that Ryan, our legal team, the judge, and the district attorneys will be in the same room, it is very difficult for us to know what will happen in advance," said Sothern.

It's easy to say what should happen. Matthews's conviction should be thrown out as quickly as possible, and the case against Rondell Love should be vigorously pursued. But freeing someone who has been wrongfully convicted is a torturously slow and difficult process, with no guarantee at any time that it will end positively.

"For two years," said Pauline Matthews, "we lived each day with the threat that Ryan was going to die."

Sothern said his client, who had an IQ of 71, suffered additional cognitive impairment during his time on death row. Matthews is subject to seizures that must be controlled by medication. On two occasions, said Sothern, Matthews was not given the required medication, and the result has been long-term brain damage.

(July 14, 2003)

POSTSCRIPT

On August 9, 2004, more than a year after this column was written, prosecutors in Louisiana agreed to drop all charges against Ryan Matthews. His formal release from custody was ordered by the same judge who had sentenced him to death in 1999.

DEATH PENALTY DISSENTERS

Harry A. Blackmun was eighty-five years old and near the end of his tenure on the Supreme Court when he declared in 1994 that he could no longer support the imposition of the death penalty.

This was especially noteworthy because Justice Blackmun was

seen as a staunch "law and order" judge when he was appointed to the court by Richard Nixon in 1970, and he played a significant role in the restoration of capital punishment in the United States in 1976.

But he was a thoughtful man. And what turned him around on the death penalty, after decades of trying to ensure that it was imposed fairly, was his realization that it could never be imposed fairly.

In a solitary dissent from the court's refusal to stay an execution in Texas, Justice Blackmun wrote in February 1994, "The problem is that the inevitability of factual, legal and moral error gives us a system that we know must wrongly kill some defendants, a system that fails to deliver the fair, consistent and reliable sentences of death required by the Constitution."

He said that he and a majority of his colleagues on the court had struggled unsuccessfully for more than twenty years to bring an acceptable level of fairness to the system of capital punishment. But, despite all good-faith efforts, he said, "I feel morally and intellectually obligated simply to concede that the death penalty experiment has failed."

Justice Blackmun could no longer bring himself to roll the dice with a person's life at stake. He would no longer participate in a system that he described as "fraught with arbitrariness, discrimination, caprice and mistake."

"From this day forward," he said, "I no longer shall tinker with the machinery of death."

Justice Blackmun died in 1999.

In January 2000, another unlikely individual stepped forward with concerns about the viability of capital punishment. Governor George H. Ryan of Illinois, a pro–death penalty Republican, imposed a moratorium on executions in Illinois because of his state's "shameful record of convicting innocent people and putting them on death row."

More than a dozen men who had been sentenced to death in Illinois since 1977 eventually were found to have been innocent and were freed.

Anthony Porter was one, and he came frighteningly close to dying for a crime he hadn't committed. Porter was convicted of murdering a young couple in a park in Chicago. He spent sixteen years on death row and came within forty-eight hours of actually being executed. He was released from prison in February 1999, after a group of Northwestern University students, working with their journalism professor, uncovered evidence that showed he was innocent.

Echoing Justice Blackmun, Governor Ryan said, "I cannot support a system which, in its administration, has proven so fraught with error, and has come so close to the ultimate nightmare, the state's taking of innocent life."

The latest voice to be heard on this critical issue was that of Supreme Court justice Sandra Day O'Connor, who is also a supporter of the death penalty. "If statistics are any indication," said Justice O'Connor, in an address to a gathering of lawyers in Minnesota, "the system may well be allowing some innocent defendants to be executed."

With that stunningly understated observation, Justice O'Connor became the second pro–death penalty Supreme Court justice to raise the horrifying specter of innocents being delivered to the death chambers. "Perhaps," she said, "it's time to look at minimum standards for appointed counsel in death cases and adequate compensation for appointed counsel when they are used."

Justice Blackmun would have called that tinkering. He did not believe that the courts could develop procedures that would provide "consistency, fairness and reliability" in the administration of the death penalty.

He was more optimistic, he said, that the Supreme Court would eventually have no choice but to declare the death penalty a failure and abandon it altogether. "I may not live to see that day," he said, "but I have faith that eventually it will arrive."

He concluded his opinion on the 1994 case as follows: "The path the court has chosen lessens us all. I dissent."

(July 9, 2001)

COUNTDOWN TO EXECUTION NO. 300

The war trumps all other issues, so insufficient attention will be paid to the planned demise of Delma Banks Jr., a forty-three-year-old man who is scheduled in about forty-eight hours to become the 300th person executed in Texas since the resumption of capital punishment there in 1982.

Banks, a man with no prior criminal record, is most likely innocent of the charge that put him on death row. Fearing a tragic miscarriage of justice, three former federal judges (including William Sessions, a former director of the FBI) have urged the U.S. Supreme Court to block Wednesday's execution.

So far, no one seems to be listening.

"The prosecutors in this case concealed important impeachment material from the defense," said Sessions and the other former judges, John J. Gibbons and Timothy K. Lewis, in an extraordinary friend-of-the-court brief. They said the questions raised by the Banks case "directly implicate the integrity of the administration of the death penalty in this country."

Most reasonable people would be highly disturbed to have the execution of a possibly innocent man on their conscience or their record. But this is Texas we're talking about, a state that prefers to shoot first and ask no questions at all. Fairness and justice have never found a comfortable niche in the Texas criminal justice system, and the fact that the accused might be innocent is not considered sufficient reason to call off his execution.

(One of the most demoralizing developments of the past couple of years is the fact that George W. Bush has been striving so hard to make all of the United States more like Texas.)

Delma Banks was convicted and sentenced to death for the murder of sixteen-year-old Richard Whitehead, who was shot to death in

1980 in a town called Nash, not far from Texarkana. There was little chance that this would have been a capital case if both the accused and the victim had been of the same race. Or if the accused had been white and the victim black.

But Banks is black, and Whitehead was white, and that's the jackpot combination when it comes to the death penalty. Blacks convicted of killing whites are the ones most likely to end up in the execution chamber. In Texas this principle has been reinforced for years by the ruthless exclusion of jurors who are black.

Just two weeks ago the Supreme Court handed down a ruling that criticized courts in Texas for ignoring evidence of racial bias in a death penalty case. Lawyers in the case noted that up until the mid-1970s prosecutors in Dallas actually had a manual that said, "Do not take Jews, Negroes, Dagos, Mexicans, or a member of any minority race on a jury, no matter how rich or well-educated."

The significant evidence against Banks was the testimony of two hard-core drug addicts. One was a paid informant. The other was a career felon facing a long prison term who was told that a pending arson charge would be dismissed if he performed "well" while testifying against Banks.

The prosecution deliberately suppressed information about its arrangements with these witnesses—information that it was obliged by law to turn over to the defense.

And prosecutors made sure that all the jurors at Banks's trial were white. That was routine. Lawyers handling Banks's appeal have shown that from 1975 through 1980 prosecutors in Bowie County, where Banks was tried, accepted more than 80 percent of qualified white jurors in felony cases, while peremptorily removing more than 90 percent of qualified black jurors.

The strongest evidence pointing to Banks's innocence was physical. He was in Dallas, more than three hours away from Texarkana, when Whitehead was killed, according to the best estimates of the time of death, based on the autopsy results.

Prosecutorial misconduct. Racial bias. Drug-addicted informants. "This is one-stop shopping for what's wrong with the administration of the death penalty," said George Kendall, a lawyer with the NAACP Legal Defense and Educational Fund who is handling Banks's appeal.

If, despite all that is known about this case, the authorities walk Banks into the execution chamber on Wednesday, and strap him to a gurney, and inject the lethal poison into his veins, we will be taking another Texas-sized step away from a reasonably fair and just society, and back toward the state-sanctioned barbarism we should be trying to flee.

(March 10, 2003)

PULL THE PLUG

Delma Banks Jr. had eaten his last meal and, in a controlled panic, was starting to count off the final ten minutes of his life when word came last March 12 that his execution was being postponed because the Supreme Court might want to review his case.

A month later the court decided that yes, it would hear Banks's appeal. That decision should throw a brighter spotlight on a case that embodies many of the important things that are wrong with the death penalty in the United States.

Here are just some of the problems. There is no good evidence that Banks, who was accused of killing a sixteen-year-old boy in a small town in Texas in 1980, is guilty. A complete reading of the record, including facts uncovered during his appeals, shows that he is most likely innocent.

There is irrefutable evidence of gross prosecutorial misconduct. The key witnesses against Banks were hard-core drug addicts who had much to gain from lying. One was a paid informer, and the other was a career felon who was told that a pending arson charge would be dropped if he performed "well" while testifying against Banks. The special incentives given to the two men for their testimony were improperly concealed by prosecutors. Both witnesses have since recanted.

And, as in so many capital cases, the race issue runs through this one like a fatal virus. Banks, who had no prior criminal record and has steadfastly proclaimed his innocence, is black. The victim, the prosecutors, and all the carefully selected jurors were white.

It is time to pull the plug on the death penalty in the United States. Shut it down. It is never going to work properly. There are too many passions and prejudices involved (and far too many incompetent lawyers, prosecutors, judges, and jurors) for it ever to be administered with any consistent degree of fairness and justice.

A Columbia University study released in 2002 documented extraordinarily high percentages of death penalty cases that had been tainted by "egregiously incompetent" defense lawyers, by police officers and prosecutors who had suppressed exculpatory evidence, by jurors who had been misinformed about the law, and by judges and jurors who were biased.

A study on race and the death penalty in the United States by Amnesty International notes the following:

"Since 1976, blacks have been six to seven times more likely to be murdered than whites, with the result that blacks and whites are the victims of murder in about equal numbers. Yet 80 percent of the more than 840 people put to death in the U.S.A. since 1976 were convicted of crimes involving white victims, compared to the 13 percent who were convicted of killing blacks."

The Amnesty report asserts, correctly, that studies have consistently found that the criminal justice system "places a higher value on white life than on black life."

The mishandling of the Banks case by local prosecutors led three former federal judges, including William Sessions, a former director of the FBI, to urge the Supreme Court to intervene and block the execution. "The questions presented in Mr. Banks's petition directly implicate the integrity of the administration of the death penalty in this country," the judges wrote in a friend-of-the-court brief. "The prosecutors in this case concealed important impeachment material from the defense. In addition, the district court found, and the court of appeals agreed, that Mr. Banks received ineffective assistance from his lawyer, at least in the penalty phase of his trial."

None of these issues mattered to the state of Texas, which was ready and oh-so-willing to kill this man at six p.m. on March 12, and is still ready and willing to do so.

When state officials have no qualms about executing people even though there are clear doubts about their guilt and about whether they have been treated fairly by the justice system, it's time to bring the curtain down on their ability to execute anyone.

The Supreme Court will examine just a few very specific aspects of the Banks case. It will not, for example, address the race issue. But the death penalty is a rotten edifice, and you will find terrible problems no matter where you look.

Lying witnesses. Lousy lawyers. Corrupt prosecutors. Racism.

The death penalty is broken and can't be fixed. Get rid of it.

(April 24, 2003)

POSTSCRIPT

On February 24, 2004, the U.S. Supreme Court threw out the death sentence against Delma Banks, ruling that prosecutors had deliberately withheld evidence that would have made the imposition of the death penalty less likely. His lawyers are seeking to have the murder conviction overturned.

PART THREE

BARELY
GETTING BY

5

WHERE DOES THE MONEY GO?

PICKING WORKERS' POCKETS

When I started in the newspaper business I made so little money I had to work part time in my father's upholstery shop to make ends meet. So I'd spend the days chasing stories and struggling with deadlines, and the nights wrestling with beat-up sofas and chairs.

Then the editors at the *Star-Ledger* in Newark began asking me to work overtime on the copy desk, dreaming up headlines and doing some editing. The extra time-and-a-half pay was just enough to keep me solvent and out of the upholstery shop. And the copy desk experience was invaluable.

Now suppose the editors had been able to tell me to work the extra hours on the copy desk without paying me overtime. I couldn't have afforded to do it, and might have left the paper.

The Bush administration, which has the very bad habit of smiling at working people while siphoning money from their pockets, is trying to change the federal Fair Labor Standards Act in a way that could cause millions of workers to lose their right to overtime pay.

The act, one of the last major domestic reform measures of the New Deal, gave Americans the forty-hour workweek and a minimum wage (which began at twenty-five cents an hour in the late 1930s). It wiped out grueling twelve-hour days for many workers and prohibited the use of child labor in interstate commerce.

The act's overtime regulations have not been updated since 1975, and part of what the administration is proposing makes sense. Under existing rules, only workers earning less than $8,060 a year automatically qualify for overtime. That would be raised to $22,100 a year.

But then comes the bad news. Nearly 80 percent of all workers are in jobs that qualify them for overtime pay, which is time-and-a-half for each hour that is worked beyond the normal forty-hour week. The administration wants to make it easier for employers to exempt many of those workers from overtime protection by classifying them as administrative, professional, or executive personnel.

The quickest way to determine who is getting the better of this deal is to note that business groups are applauding the proposed changes, while the AFL-CIO held a protest rally outside the Labor Department.

But this is an administration that could figure out a way to sell sunblock to a night crawler. So the rule changes are being spun as a boon to working people.

"By recognizing the professional status of skilled employees, the proposed regulation will provide them a guaranteed salary and flexible hours," said Tammy McCutchen, the Labor Department's wage and hour administrator.

All spinning aside, I wonder how many Americans really think that working longer hours for less money is a good thing.

A more realistic approach to the issue was offered by the Economic Policy Institute, which found that the proposed changes could ultimately eliminate the right to overtime for 8 million people. That represents an awful lot of cash that would be drawn away from working families.

Unfortunately, this is the kind of thing the Bush administration is committed to—undermining a hard-won initiative of Franklin Delano Roosevelt's that has helped many millions of working Americans for more than six decades. It ain't broke, but George W. Bush is busy fixin' it.

You would think that an administration that has presided over the loss of millions of jobs might want to strengthen the protections of workers fortunate enough to still be employed. But that's not what this administration is about.

Jared Bernstein, a coauthor of the study by the Economic Policy Institute, said, "The new rules are structured in such a way as to create a very strong incentive for employers to exempt workers from overtime protection, primarily by converting hourly workers to salaried workers."

One of the workers who joined Monday's protest at the Labor Department was Bob Adams, a bakery manager at a supermarket chain in Minneapolis–St. Paul.

When I asked him why he had traveled to Washington for the demonstration, he said: "Because I think we have to put a stop to this. There seems to be a systematic assault on the rights of workers by this administration, and this is a perfect example of it. They tried to push this through as quietly as they could."

(July 3, 2003)

CAUGHT IN THE CREDIT CARD VISE

"I'm still paying for groceries I bought for my family years ago," said Julie Pickett.

She meant it literally. Pickett and her husband, Jerry, of Middletown, Ohio, are trapped in the iron grasp of credit card debt. Except for the fact that no one is threatening to damage their kneecaps, they're in the same dismal position as the classic victim of loan-sharking.

People used to get thrown in jail for the very things credit card companies can now do legally. While banks and money markets are paying pittances in interest, it's common for the annual percentage rate on your friendly Visa or Mastercard to approach 30 percent.

This used to be called usury.

Julie Pickett stopped working full time when she had the twins. Jerry Pickett's business hit a downturn at about the same time. The family's credit cards, said Julie Pickett, suddenly loomed as "lifelines" to the daily necessities—food, gas, auto repairs, clothing for the children.

Another child was born, and the credit card debt eventually reached $40,000—an amount (with its perpetually increasing interest) that the Picketts are unable to pay off.

"We had one card that had about an $8,000 balance," Julie Pickett said in an interview. "With interest and late fees, it's now $18,000. The interest when we started out was like 18 percent. But after a year of not paying, it jumped to 28 percent."

Families like the Picketts are indeed responsible for the payment of their debts. But the credit card companies are engaged in one of the many big-time legalized rackets that are flourishing in this age of deregulation. The Picketts are profiled in a report, titled "Borrowing to Make Ends Meet," by a nonpartisan public policy group called Demos: A Network for Ideas and Action.

The economy may have boomed in the last half of the nineties. But over the course of that decade, millions of American families sank deeper and deeper into debt, in large part because of the overuse of credit cards.

"Between 1989 and 2001," the report said, "credit card debt in America almost tripled, from $238 billion to $692 billion. The savings rate steadily declined, and the number of people filing for bankruptcy jumped 125 percent."

Few things are easier than flashing the plastic and saying, "Charge it." And few heads of households, when broke, can resist the urge to use a credit card to buy food for the family or gas up the car to go to work.

In the period studied, the credit card debt of the average family increased by 53 percent. For middle-class families, the increase was 75 percent. For senior citizens, 149 percent. And for very low income families, with annual incomes below $10,000, the increase was a staggering 184 percent.

The theme of the report is that while credit card use is frequently associated with frivolous consumption, the evidence seems to show that more and more Americans are using credit cards to bridge the difficult gap between household earnings and the cost of essential goods and services. Men and women struggling with such structural problems as job displacement, declining real wages, and rising housing and health-care costs have been relying on their credit cards as a way of warding off complete disaster.

At the same time the credit card companies have leapt gleefully into an orgy of exploitation. "Late fees," the report said, "have become the fastest growing source of revenue for the industry, jumping from $1.7 billion in 1996 to $7.3 billion in 2002. Late fees now average $29, and most cards have reduced the late payment grace period from 14 days to zero days. In addition to charging late fees, the major credit card companies use the first late payment as an excuse to cancel low, introductory rates—often making a zero percent card jump to between 22 and 29 percent."

How high can interest rates go? According to Tamara Draut, one of the authors of the study, all of the major credit card issuers are located in states that have no limits on the rate of interest they can charge. (The state where the credit card holder resides is irrelevant.)

And how crazy has the situation become? The Pickett family, which is absolutely unable to pay off the debt it has now, gets offers in the mail to open new credit card accounts every day.

(September 22, 2003)

THE REVERSE ROBIN HOOD

If you wanted a quintessential example of what the Bush administration and its legislative cronies are about, it was right there on the front page of the *New York Times*:

"Tax Law Omits $400 Child Credit for Millions."

The fat cats will get their tax cuts. But in the new American plutocracy, there won't even be crumbs left over for the working folks at the bottom of the pyramid to scramble after.

When House and Senate negotiators met to put the finishing touches to President Bush's tax bill, they coldly deleted a provision that would have allowed millions of low-income working families to benefit from the bill's increased child tax credit.

It was a mean-spirited and wholly unnecessary act, a clear display of the current regime's outright hostility toward America's poor and working classes.

The negotiators eliminated a provision in the Senate version of the tax bill that would have extended benefits from the child tax credit to families with incomes between $10,500 and $26,625. This is not a small group. According to the Center on Budget and Policy Priorities, the families that would have benefited include about 12 million children—one of every six kids in the U.S. under the age of seventeen.

While the tax bill will lavish hundreds of billions of dollars in benefits on people higher up the income scale, it leaves this group of working families very ignominiously behind.

And readers of the *New York Times* learned that another group of some 8 million mostly low-income taxpayers—primarily single people without children—will also be left behind, getting no benefit at all from the president's tax cuts. Forget about trickle-down. The goal of this administration is to haul it up.

The provision to extend the tax credit to more low-income families was the work of Senator Blanche Lincoln, an Arkansas Democrat who noted that half of all taxpayers in her state had adjusted gross incomes of less than $20,000. The full Senate approved the provision, but the negotiators knocked it out at the last minute, behind closed doors.

While the most well heeled Americans are happily inflating their bankrolls, there are families with a total of 16 million children at the low end of the income scale who, for one reason or another, won't get the help they should—their fair share—from this tax bill. About half of all African American and Latino children get no benefit—or only a partial benefit—from the child tax credit, according to the

Children's Defense Fund and an advocacy group called the Children's Research and Education Institute.

When the whistles were blown on the child tax credit outrage, Republican leaders were unable to give a coherent explanation for their action. Some tried to argue that they had had to scrap the provision to keep the total cost of the tax bill from exceeding $350 billion over ten years, their agreed-upon limit.

That was not true. For one thing, the $350 billion limit was a completely arbitrary and largely fictional figure. The true cost of the tax bill over ten years will be closer to a trillion dollars than the deliberately deceptive $350 billion figure that the GOP has chosen to use.

Senator Lincoln's provision, which would have offered a little help to so many people who need it, would have cost only $3.5 billion. Even within the phony $350 billion limit, a slight adjustment in a number of different windfalls for the very wealthy would have opened up sufficient room for this modest tax break.

But to really get a sense of the scandalous nature of this GOP tax cut scam, consider that the House and Senate negotiators also got rid of a number of measures in the Senate bill that would have saved billions of dollars by closing abusive corporate tax structures. The Center on Budget noted the following:

"As the *Washington Post* has reported, the Senate bill 'included provisions to crack down on abusive corporate tax shelters, combat some accounting scams such as those pursued by Enron Corp., prevent U.S. companies from moving their headquarters to post office boxes in offshore tax havens such as Bermuda and limit grossly inflated deferred compensation plans for corporate executives.' "

The savings from those provisions would have been about $25 billion, much more than enough to cover the cost of Senator Lincoln's $3.5 billion attempt to give a bit of a break to several million working families.

(June 2, 2003)

ADMIT WE HAVE A PROBLEM

I suppose there are people who still believe that enormous tax cuts for the very wealthy will lead to the creation of millions of good jobs for working people. In the twilight of his first term, the president, stumping for votes in regions scarred by the demon of unemployment, continues to sing from the tattered pages of his economic hymnbook:

"The economy is strong," he says again and again and again, "and it's growing stronger."

At a riverfront rally under cloudy skies in Davenport, Iowa, Bush told a crowd of five thousand, "We are turning the corner and we're not going back."

In another four years, he says, "The economy will be better."

His tax cuts, he insists, couldn't have been better timed.

The true believers were jolted by the news from the Bureau of Labor Statistics that employers added a meager 32,000 jobs in July. In an economy the size of America's, that's roughly equivalent to no jobs at all.

July's poor job-creation performance was widely described as unexpected. But it's important to keep in mind that it didn't occur in a vacuum and that there is no quick fix coming. American workers are hurting.

"The weak job market continues to put downward pressure on wage growth," said Jared Bernstein, a senior economist at the Economic Policy Institute in Washington. He noted that nominal wage growth on a year-over-year basis has been decelerating even as inflation is increasing, which is bad news for an economy so dependent upon consumer spending.

In a report released by the institute, Bernstein wrote, "These job and wage dynamics erode workers' buying power, and this has negative implications for the strength of the recovery."

Retail sales in July were disappointing, hampered by high gasoline prices and anemic wage growth. And the stock market is in a prolonged swoon.

Despite the rosy rhetoric that comes nonstop from the administration, millions upon millions of American families, including many that consider themselves solidly in the middle class, are in deep economic trouble. The *Wall Street Journal* recently featured a page-one article with the ominous headline: "New Group Swells Bankruptcy Court: The Middle-Aged."

Personal bankruptcy filings in the U.S. are at an all-time high. The *Journal* story focused on "an emerging class of middle-age, white-collar Americans who make the grim odyssey from comfortable circumstances to going broke." Among the villains of this disturbing piece are the unstable job market and staggering amounts of personal debt.

It's getting harder and harder to close our eyes to the growing economic devastation. Elizabeth Warren, a Harvard law professor and coauthor of *The Two-Income Trap: Why Middle-Class Mothers and Fathers Are Going Broke,* wrote in 2003: "This year, more people will end up bankrupt than will suffer a heart attack. More adults will file for bankruptcy than will be diagnosed with cancer. More people will file for bankruptcy than will graduate from college. And, in an era when traditionalists decry the demise of the institution of marriage, Americans will file more petitions for bankruptcy than for divorce."

The Century Foundation, in a recent study, addressed the problem of outstanding debt. For many families borrowing has morphed from a tool that, used judiciously, can enhance their standard of living into a nightmare that threatens to destroy their economic viability.

"Debt burdens," the study said, "are at record levels because families have been stretched to the limit in recent years. With more income going to housing and other rising expenses related to medical care, education, vehicles, child care, and so forth, families are relying on credit as a way to meet everyday needs. Remarkably, a family with two earners today actually has less discretionary income, after fixed costs like medical insurance and mortgage payments are accounted for, than did a family with only one breadwinner in the 1970s."

There is no plan from the administration that I've heard of to brighten this bleak picture of the American economic landscape. The first essential step for anyone serious about a search for solutions would be to recognize and acknowledge the sheer enormity of the problem.

(August 9, 2004)

6

THE VANISHING AMERICAN JOB

OUT THE DOOR

Merry Christmas. Get lost.

That, essentially, was the message Robert Pagein received from his employers—make that former employers—at Verizon Communications.

Pagein, who is married and has a year-old son, was a field technician who had worked for the phone company for four years. One of the lures of the job was its stability. The pay wasn't great, but it was steady. If you were disciplined you could pay your bills, take a vacation every year or so, and put a little aside.

That's the way it works in theory. In reality, Pagein was one of 2,400 Verizon workers in New York who were shown the door just a few days before Christmas. Those workers formed the bulk of a preholiday wave of terminations that claimed the jobs of 3,500 Verizon employees in the Northeast and mid-Atlantic states.

Pagein will not be destitute. His wife is working, and he has a college degree. But the cold-blooded way in which he and his fellow workers were lopped off the employment rolls by Verizon, and the phenomenal gap that exists between the compensation available to the company's ordinary workers and the fabulous, multimillion-dollar packages taken home by executives at the top of the Verizon pyramid, has shaken Pagein's faith in a system he believed in.

"I'm thirty-six years old and grew up in Lefrak City, Queens," he said. "As a working-class guy, I kind of accepted long ago that I wasn't going to make a fortune or anything like that. What I figured was that if I worked hard, if I became a cop or I joined the phone company or something like that, at least I would have a regular working-class or middle-class life. At least you'd make your fifty grand or fifty-five grand a year. The government would take out your taxes, but you'd have something left over."

Pagein's comforting belief in a system that looks out for the ordinary worker evaporated with the arrival of his layoff notice. As a not-so-merry Christmas and then a not-so-happy New Year approached, he found himself thinking more and more about the big bucks—the tens of millions of dollars—being pocketed by top Verizon executives like Ivan Seidenberg and Larry Babbio.

It's one thing to acknowledge that there are inequities in the system, he said. But it's "really tough" to accept that you can be thrown out of work by executives who take extraordinary sums out of a company whether their business decisions are wise or not.

"We were laid off, effective immediately," he said. "'Merry Christmas, thanks for working at Ground Zero and breathing the dust. . . . ' They told us we were heroes, and used the pictures of us at Ground Zero to sell themselves. Now we're out."

Last spring Verizon reported a first-quarter loss of $500 million. The company attributed the loss to a tough economy and a $2.5 billion write-down for bad investments. By the third quarter it was reporting earnings of $4.4 billion. But officials said that the layoffs, the first in the history of the New York telephone company, were inevitable because the economy was still in trouble and competition was increasing.

Company officials said that the total compensation in 2001 for Seidenberg, Verizon's chief executive, was $13.4 million, and for Babbio, $24 million.

Figures released by the Communication Workers of America, which represents the laid-off employees, showed that from 1997 through 2001, Seidenberg collected more than $56 million in salary, bonuses, and stock options, and that Babbio, the company's vice-chairman, collected more than $78 million.

Those numbers were on Pagein's mind as he and his family spent Christmas at his grandmother's home in Flushing. "I kind of Scrooged on the presents," he said. "Everybody knew. It was, like, 'Well, don't expect Robert to bring anything because, you know, he just got laid off.'"

He added: "It's tough to take. These guys took their outrageous, outrageous bonuses, and we're out on the street. I guess you don't notice the inequities so much when you're working because then, at least, you've got something."

Pagein said he would go on unemployment for a while and use that time to look for a different career. "Part of the pain I'm feeling right now has to do with some of the others who were fired," he said. "Some of them were the only income earners in their family. They seem shell-shocked."

(January 1, 2003)

JOBLESS, AND STUNNED

Left behind by the great Republican raid on the national Treasury are folks like Karelia Escobar and Joe Bergmann, middle-aged New Yorkers who have worked most of their lives but now find themselves traveling the anxious paths of the long-term unemployed. With bills mounting and each day bringing a heightened sense of dread, they could use a little help. But the jobless are at the bottom of the economic heap, and the Bush administration's help seems always to go to the top.

Escobar is forty-three and single, and lives in a small apartment in Queens. She has worked for a number of airlines over the past several years, most recently as a ticket agent for TWA. That job vanished with the World Trade Center.

"We were laid off October 14, 2001," she said. "I haven't been able to find work since then. I've applied everywhere. I've gone back to school to improve my computer skills. I've learned another language. I feel very bad because I want to work so I can pay my bills. I've always worked. But now I can't find a job."

That plaintive comment is echoing from coast to coast. Unemployment is rising. And as the millions of jobless Americans (including many in the middle class) exhaust their benefits and run through their savings, they are finding themselves face to face with the horror of destitution.

In a speech delivered in Chicago President Bush said, "I worry about people who are out of work. They need our help." But the hundreds of millions of dollars' worth of "help" that he proposed, mostly in the form of tax cuts, would go overwhelmingly to the princes of the new American plutocracy, not to the likes of Karelia Escobar.

Or Joe Bergmann. Bergmann, who lives in Midtown Manhattan, was a creative director for a firm that did interactive advertising. He was laid off October 2, 2001, and, to his amazement, has been out of work ever since. When I asked if he ever imagined it would be so hard to find a job, he said, "Not at all. There's no way."

Bergmann, fifty-four, is married and has two daughters. His wife works, but her employment outlook, even in the short term, is uncertain. The family has had the benefit of some savings and a bonus Bergmann earned at a previous job. But he does not know what will happen if he doesn't get another job soon.

Bergmann believes that many of the big corporate layoffs could have been avoided. He said, "Companies have been living from quarter to quarter for so long they've lost their long-distance planning—their vision of what the company is going to be like in five years. When there's a downturn, they just get rid of people.

"I don't know if we can change the heart of CEOs into thinking, 'Well, you know, I'm getting $30 million, but I can save some jobs if I give back $15 million and live on just $15 million this year.' They never think like that. And until they begin to think like that, we'll be at their mercy."

Unemployment benefits for Escobar and Bergmann ran out last July. The extension signed by President Bush does not apply to them.

Escobar's situation is extremely precarious. Her savings are gone. She received help from a local charity when her electric service was about to be discontinued.

"I cannot even pay my car insurance," she said. "I have an old car but they've canceled the insurance."

"So you can't drive," I said.

"I can't drive. I'm afraid I'll hit somebody, and then I'll end up with no money, no job, and in jail. I don't want that."

Her biggest concern is February's rent. "I don't have it," she said.

The centerpiece of Bush's latest economic plan is the elimination of taxes on stock dividends, an unconscionable giveaway to the rich at a time when so many working Americans are struggling merely to survive.

The plan contained no job-creation program, no investment in the nation's critical infrastructure needs, and no assistance for the many states sinking in the quicksand of mammoth budget deficits.

Escobar has taken the president's policies somewhat personally. "I'm a Republican and I'm not ashamed to say it," she said. "But I'm very upset that they have done nothing for us."

I asked if she had voted for Bush. "I sure did," she said, then added, "I feel very betrayed."

(January 9, 2003)

YOUNG, JOBLESS, HOPELESS

Chicago

You see them in many parts of the city, hanging out on frigid street corners, skylarking at the malls or bowling alleys, hustling for money wherever they can, drifting in some cases into the devastating clutches of drug selling, gang membership, prostitution, and worse.

In Chicago there are nearly 100,000 young people, ages sixteen to twenty-four, who are out of work, out of school, and all but out of hope. In New York City there are more than 200,000. Nationwide, according to a new study by a team from Northeastern University in Boston, the figure is a staggering 5.5 million and growing.

This army of undereducated, jobless young people, disconnected in most instances from society's mainstream, is restless and unhappy, and poses a severe long-term threat to the nation's well-being on many fronts.

Audrey Roberts, a seventeen-year-old who just recently landed a job at a fast food restaurant on Chicago's West Side, talked to me about some of the experiences she and her out-of-work friends have had to endure.

"The stuff you hear about on the news," she said, "that's our everyday life. I've seen girls get raped, beaten up. I saw a boy get his head blown away. That happened right in front of me. I said, 'Oh my God!' I just stood there." The shooting was over a dice game that was being played one afternoon by boys who had nothing better to do with their time, she said.

It's an article of faith among politicians and members of the media that the recession we continue to experience is a mild one. But it has hit broad sections of the nation's young people with a ferocity that has left many of them stunned.

"I don't think I can take it much longer," said Angjell Brackins, a nineteen-year-old South Side resident. "I get up in the morning. I take a bath. I put on my clothes. I go outside."

She has tried for months to find a job, she said, filling out application after application, to no avail. "I'll do any kind of work if they'll just hire me. It doesn't matter, as long as it's a job."

The report from Northeastern, titled "Left Behind in the Labor Market," found that joblessness among out-of-school youths between sixteen and twenty-four had surged by 12 percent since the year 2000. Washington's mindless response to this burgeoning crisis has been to slash—and in some cases eliminate—the few struggling programs aimed at bolstering youth employment and training.

Education and career decisions made during the late teens and early twenties are crucial to the lifetime employment and earnings prospects of an individual. Those who do not do well during this period seldom catch up to the rest of the population.

"Our ability to generate family stability and safe communities is strongly influenced by this," said Dr. Andrew Sum, director of the Center for Labor Market Studies at Northeastern and the lead author of the study.

When you have 5.5 million young people wandering around without diplomas, without jobs, and without prospects, you might as well hand them T-shirts to wear that say "We're Trouble."

Without help, they will not become part of a skilled workforce. And they will become a drain on the nation's resources. One way or another, the rest of us will end up supporting them.

"It's just heartbreaking," said Jack Wuest, who runs the Alternative Schools Network in Chicago, which commissioned the study. "These kids need a fair shake and they're not getting it."

The Bush administration, committed to a war with Iraq and obsessed with tax cuts for the wealthy, has no interest in these youngsters. And very few others in a position to help are willing to go to bat for them.

In a long series of conversations with young unemployed and undereducated Chicagoans, I did not hear much of anything in the way of aspirations. Whether boys or girls, men or women, those who were interviewed seemed for the most part already defeated. They did not talk about finding the perfect job. They did not talk about being in love and eventually marrying and raising a family. They did not express a desire to someday own their own home.

There was, to tell the truth, a remarkable absence of positive comments and emotions of any kind. There was a widespread sense of frustration, and some anger. But mostly there was just sadness.

(February 6, 2003)

TROUBLE IN BUSH'S AMERICA

While our "What, me worry?" president is having a great time with his high approval ratings and his *Top Gun* fantasies, the economy remains in the tank. And the finances of state and local governments are sinking tragically into ever deeper and ever more unforgiving waters.

You want shock and awe? Come to New York City, where jobs are hard to find and the budget (as residents are suddenly realizing) is a backbreaking regimen of service cuts, tax increases, and that perennial painkiller, wishful thinking.

The biggest wish, of course, is that the national economy will suddenly turn around and flood the city and state with desperately needed revenues. Meanwhile, the soup kitchens and food pantries are besieged.

"This is the worst situation I've been in," said Alfonso Shynvwelski, an unemployed waiter who stood in a long line of people waiting for food at the Washington Heights Ecumenical Food Pantry, on Broadway in upper Manhattan. Shynvwelski, thirty-six, has worked at a number of upscale restaurants, including the Russian Tea Room, which has closed. He's been unemployed for a year.

"It's the first time in my life I've had to look for food this way," he said.

This lament is being heard more and more often in the city, which has an official jobless rate of nearly 9 percent. The real rate is substantially higher, which means that more than one in ten New Yorkers who would like to work cannot find a job.

Last week Local 46 of the Metallic Lathers Union announced that it would allow 200 people to apply for membership, which would mean a shot at high-paying work. The line of applicants began at Third Avenue and Seventy-sixth Street and almost circled the block.

The earliest arrivals waited in line for three days. They slept on the sidewalk.

In George W. Bush's America, jobs get erased like chalk marks on a blackboard. More than 2 million have vanished on Bush's watch. There are now more than 10.2 million unemployed workers in the United States, including 1.4 million who are not officially counted because they've become discouraged and stopped looking.

There are also 4.8 million men and women who are working part time because they can't find full-time jobs.

The high unemployment and sharply reduced social services are having devastating consequences. In some cases people are being driven to destitution. "This is a really spooky time for us," said John Hoffmann, who runs a food pantry and soup kitchen in the Bronx. He's faced with both a surge in demand and, because of government budget cuts, a threat to his financing.

"These are folks who are new to services like ours," Hoffmann said of his latest wave of clients. Many of them are working men and women who are struggling to support their families from one paycheck to the next. When workers in that situation are laid off, they have nothing to fall back on.

Nearly a quarter of a million jobs have been lost in New York City in the past two and a half years. Taxes are going up, and services are going down—and still that is not enough. Similar scenarios are being played out in city and state governments throughout the country. California is trying to borrow its way out of a nightmarish crisis. Texas, already near the bottom nationally in social services, is heading further south.

Two forms of help from the federal government are needed. One is direct assistance to local governments to help alleviate the disastrous budget shortfalls. The other is an economic stimulus program that really works, that boosts the economy and creates jobs through investments in some of the nation's real needs, rather than simply transferring trainloads of money to the wealthy in the form of tax cuts.

Bush has no interest in such remedies. Easing the economic struggles of poor and working families in America is not part of his agenda.

(May 8, 2003)

CAUGHT IN THE SQUEEZE

One of the things President Bush knows best is when to turn on the klieg lights, and when to keep them off.

Recently, with no fanfare, he signed a bill increasing the federal debt limit by nearly a trillion dollars. You don't want a lot of coverage when you're mortgaging the future.

But days later it was high fives all around as Bush signed the third-largest tax cut in history at a grand ceremony in the East Room of the White House.

I suppose if your income is large enough, there is every reason to celebrate. After all, the tax cut could save Dick Cheney $100,000 a year, or more.

But given the economic realities in the United States right now, I thought the East Room celebration was in poor taste. The enormous tax-cut package (which is coupled with budget deficits that are lunging toward infinity) is a stunning example of Bush's indifference to the deepening plight of working people.

The economy has lost more than a half-million jobs already this year, and well over 2 million since payrolls peaked two years ago. More than 8.7 million American men and women are officially counted as unemployed. And that figure is artificially low because it does not count those who have become discouraged and stopped looking for work.

The fallout from the continued hemorrhaging of jobs and the swollen ranks of the unemployed is spreading. The *New York Times* recently had an article about college seniors' putting their dreams on hold because they're graduating into the worst hiring slump in twenty years.

"We definitely picked the wrong time to be graduating from college," said Morgan Bushey, a twenty-one-year-old student at the University of North Carolina. She said she planned to go to France, where she would make about $200 a week teaching English.

The jobs squeeze has other effects. "There's been this notion along the way that if you at least kept your job, you'd be O.K.," said Jared Bernstein, an economist with the Economic Policy Institute, in Washington. "But now this persistent unemployment is taking a toll on the wages of those who are still working."

Wages, when adjusted for inflation, are falling for workers across the board. An analysis of government data by Bernstein and Lawrence Mishel, the institute's president, found that the median weekly paycheck fell 1.4 percent over the past year. All the pay grades above and below the median are also sliding backward. White-collar, blue-collar—workers in all pay grades are taking a hit. Even wage earners in the highest category have seen their pay slip by 1.4 percent.

"When unemployment got down to 4 percent in the late 1990s, you had broad-based wage growth—and it was the first time we'd seen that in decades," said Bernstein. "That's gone."

The president is not calling his tax package the "Windfall for the Wealthy" act, which is what it is. He calls it the "Jobs and Growth" act, which is what it's not. He would like us to believe that "with tax relief will come more jobs for the American people." But that's what he said in the last round of tax cuts, and the American people are still waiting.

In fact, the wait is becoming interminable for some. More and more Americans are joining the ranks of the long-term unemployed, those who are out of work for six months or more. A joint study by the National Employment Law Project and the Economic Policy Institute called long-term unemployment "the scourge of a declining economy," and noted that it is taking its greatest toll among those who have traditionally felt economically secure.

"The reality," said the study, "is that the long-term unemployed are better educated, older and more likely to be professional workers."

What the economy needs is a real stimulus that will create real jobs, not an irresponsible package of tax cuts that will inflate the portfolios of the very wealthy while starving the government of the money needed to pay for essential services and to maintain a safety net for the nation's most vulnerable citizens.

We are closing schools and libraries in America, and withholding lifesaving drugs and medical treatment from the poor. The middle class is struggling ever harder to make ends meet, and reshaping its dreams of the future.

In Washington, they're celebrating.

(May 29, 2003)

NO WORK, NO HOMES

Talk about preaching to the choir. President Bush and his clueless team of economic advisers got together for a summit at the president's ranch in Crawford, Texas. This is the ferociously irresponsible crowd that has turned its back on simple arithmetic and thinks that the answer to every economic question is a gigantic tax cut for the rich.

Their voodoo fantasies were safe in Crawford. There was no one at the ranch to chastise them for bequeathing backbreaking budget deficits to generations yet unborn. And no one was there to confront them with evidence of the intense suffering that so many poor, working-class, and middle-class families are experiencing right now because of job losses on Bush's watch.

After the meeting, Bush said, "This administration is optimistic about job creation."

It's too bad George Akerlof wasn't at the meeting. Akerlof, a 2001 Nobel laureate in economics, has bluntly declared that "the Bush fiscal policy is the worst policy in the last 200 years." Speaking at a press conference arranged by the Economic Policy Institute, Akerlof, a professor at the University of California at Berkeley, said, "Within ten years, we're going to pay a serious price for such irresponsibility."

Also participating in the institute's press conference was Robert Solow, an economist and professor emeritus at M.I.T. who is also a Nobel laureate. He assailed the Bush tax cuts as "redistributive in intent and redistributive in effect."

"There has been a dissipation of the huge budget surplus," he said, "and all we have to show for that is the city of Baghdad."

The president and his advisers could have learned something about the real world if, instead of hanging out at the ranch, they had visited a city like Los Angeles (or almost any other hard-hit American venue) and spent time talking to folks who have been thrown out of work and, in some cases, out of their homes in this treacherous Bush economy.

The job market in California is dreadful. More than a million people are out of work statewide, and there are few signs of the optimism that Bush is feeling. Officials at homeless shelters in Los Angeles, as in other large American cities, are seeing big increases in the number of families seeking shelter because of extended periods of joblessness. The pattern is as depressing as it is familiar: the savings run out, the rent doesn't get paid, the eviction notice arrives.

Tanya Tull, president of Beyond Shelter, in downtown Los Angeles, said the percentage of families in her facility had climbed from about one-third to more than one-half because of the employment crisis. The breadwinners can't find jobs, she said, "so they're losing their housing."

Ralph Plumb, president of the Union Rescue Mission, on Los Angeles's skid row, said his agency, traditionally a haven for homeless men with drug and alcohol problems, is providing shelter for more and more "intact" families. Their problems are not the result of drug or alcohol abuse, or mental impairment. They simply have no money. Forty percent of the people at the mission are there "purely due to economic issues," he said.

Tull and Plumb both said that an important factor in the rise of homeless families had been the "reform" of the welfare system. Destitution is the next stop for people who can't find jobs and can't get welfare.

One of the families at the Union Rescue Mission was featured this week in a front-page article in *USA Today*. William Kamstra, who earned $40,000 a year before losing his job, looks for work each day while his wife, Sue, and their three children spend the day at a library. They sleep at the mission.

"Homelessness in major cities is escalating," the article said, "as more laid-off workers already living paycheck to paycheck wind up on the streets or in shelters."

That story ran one day after a front-page *Wall Street Journal* article that spelled out how sweet just one of the Bush tax cuts has been for those in the upper brackets: "The federal tax cut, which slashed the tax rate on dividends and prompted many companies to increase their payouts, is proving to be a boon for some corporate executives who are reaping millions in after-tax gains."

Some people have reason to be optimistic. It's the best of times, or the worst of times. Depending on your perspective.

(August 14, 2003)

THE WHITE-COLLAR BLUES

I am surprised at how passive American workers have become.

A couple of million factory positions have disappeared in the short time since we raised our glasses to toast the incoming century. And now the white-collar jobs are following the blue-collar jobs overseas.

Americans are working harder and have become ever more productive—astonishingly productive—but are not sharing in the benefits of their increased effort. If you think in terms of wages, benefits, and the creation of good jobs, the employment landscape is grim.

The economy is going great guns, we're told, but nearly 9 million Americans are officially unemployed, and the real tally of the jobless is much higher. Even as the Bush administration and the media celebrate the blossoming of statistics that supposedly show how well we're doing, the lines at food banks and soup kitchens are lengthening. They're swollen in many cases by the children of men and women who are working but not making enough to house and feed their families.

IBM has crafted plans to send thousands of upscale jobs from the United States to lower-paid workers in China, India, and elsewhere. Anyone who doesn't believe that this is the wave of the future should listen to comments made last spring by an IBM executive named Harry Newman: "I think probably the biggest impact to employee relations and to the HR field is this concept of globalization. It is rapidly accelerating, and it means shifting a lot of jobs, opening a lot of locations in places we had never dreamt of before, going where there's low-cost labor, low-cost competition, shifting jobs offshore."

An executive at Microsoft, the ultimate American success story, told his department heads last year to "Think India" and to "pick something to move offshore today."

These matters should be among the hottest topics of our national conversation. We've already witnessed the carnage in manufacturing jobs. Now, with white-collar jobs at stake, we've got executives at IBM and Microsoft exchanging high fives at the prospect of getting "two heads for the price of one" in India.

It might be a good idea to throw a brighter spotlight on some of these trends and explore the implications for the long-term economy and the American standard of living.

"If you take this to its logical extreme, the implications for the entire middle-class wage structure in the United States are terrifying," said Thea Lee, an economist with the AFL-CIO. "Now is the time to start thinking about policy solutions."

But that's exactly what we're not thinking about. Government policy at the moment is focused primarily on what's best for the corporations. From that perspective, job destruction and wage compression are good things—as long as they don't get too much high-profile attention.

"This is a significant problem, much greater than we believed it was even a year ago," said Marcus Courtney, president of the Washington Alliance of Technology Workers, an affiliate of the Communication Workers of America.

Accurate data on the number of jobs already lost are all but impossible to come by. But there is no disputing the direction of the trend, or the fact that it is accelerating. Allowing this movement to continue unchecked will eventually mean economic suicide for hundreds of thousands, if not millions, of American families.

Globalization may be a fact of life. But that does not mean that its destructive impact on American families can't be mitigated. The best thing workers can do, including white-collar and professional workers, is to organize. At the same time, the exportation of jobs and the effect that is having on the standard of living here should be relentlessly monitored by the government, the civic sector, and the media. The public has a right to know what's really going on.

Trade agreements and tax policies should be examined and updated to encourage the creation of employment that enhances the quality of life here at home. Corporate leaders may not feel an obligation to contribute to the long-term well-being of local communities or the nation as a whole, but that shouldn't be the case with the rest of us.

(December 29, 2003)

EDUCATION IS NO PROTECTION

The conference was held discreetly in the Westin New York hotel in Times Square, and by most accounts it was a great success.

The main objections came from a handful of protesters who stood outside in a brutally cold wind waving signs that said things like STOP SENDING JOBS OVERSEAS and PUT AMERICA BACK TO WORK. No one paid them much attention.

The conference was titled "Offshore Outsourcing: Making the Journey Work for Your Corporation." Its goal was to bring executives up to speed on the hot new thing in corporate America, the shipment of higher-paying white-collar jobs to countries with eager, well-educated, and much lower paid workers.

"We basically help companies figure out how to offshore I.T., information technology, and B.P., business process functions," said Atul Vashistha, the chief executive of NeoIT, a California consulting firm that cohosted the conference.

Several big-name corporations had representatives at the conference, including Procter & Gamble, Motorola, Cisco Systems, and Gateway.

Because the outsourcing of white-collar jobs is so controversial and politically charged (especially in a presidential election year), there was a marked reluctance among many of the participants to speak publicly about it. But Vashistha showed no reluctance. He was quick to proselytize.

"These companies understand very clearly that this is a very painful process for their employees and for American jobs in the short term," he said. "But they also recognize that if they don't do this, they will lose more jobs in the future and they won't have an ability to grow in the future."

He said his firm had helped clients ship about a billion dollars' worth of projects offshore last year.

Noting that he is an American citizen who was born in India, Vashistha said he is convinced that outsourcing will prove to be a long-term boon to the U.S. economy as well as the economies of the countries acquiring the exported jobs.

Whether it becomes a boon to the U.S. economy or not, the trend toward upscale outsourcing is a fact, and it is accelerating. In an important interview with the *San Jose Mercury News* last month, the chief executive of Intel, Craig Barrett, talked about the integration of India, China, and Russia—with a combined population approaching 3 billion—into the world's economic infrastructure.

"I don't think this has been fully understood by the United States," said Barrett. "If you look at India, China, and Russia, they all have strong education heritages. Even if you discount ninety percent of the people there as uneducated farmers, you still end up with about three hundred million people who are educated. That's bigger than the U.S. work force."

He said: "The big change today from what's happened over the last thirty years is that it's no longer just low-cost labor that you are looking at. It's well-educated labor that can do effectively any job that can be done in the United States."

In Barrett's view, "Unless you are a plumber, or perhaps a newspaper reporter, or one of these jobs which is geographically situated, you can be anywhere in the world and do just about any job."

You want a national security issue? Trust me, this threat to the long-term U.S. economy is a big one. Why it's not a thunderous issue in the presidential campaign is beyond me.

Intel has its headquarters in Silicon Valley. A *Mercury News* interviewer asked Barrett what the Valley will look like in three years. Barrett said the prospects for job growth were not good. "Companies can still form in Silicon Valley and be competitive around the world," he said. "It's just that they are not going to create jobs in Silicon Valley."

He was then asked, "Aren't we talking about an entire generation of lowered expectations in the United States for what an individual entering the job market will be facing?"

"It's tough to come to another conclusion than that," said Barrett. "If you see this increased competition for jobs, the immediate response to competition is lower prices, and that's lower wage rates."

We can grapple with this problem now, and try to develop workable solutions. Or we can ignore this fire in the basement of the national economy until it rages out of our control.

(January 26, 2004)

DARK SIDE OF FREE TRADE

The classic story of the American economy is a saga about an ever-expanding middle class that systematically absorbs the responsible, hardworking families from the lower economic groups. It's about the young people of each successive generation doing better than their parents' generation. The plotline is supposed to be a proud model for the rest of the world.

One of the reasons there is so much unease among voters this year is the fact that this story no longer rings so true. Books based on its plotline are increasingly being placed in the stacks labeled "fantasy."

The middle class is in trouble. Many middle-class Americans, instead of having the luxury of looking ahead to a brighter future for the next generation, are worried about slipping into a lower economic segment themselves.

This is happening in the middle of an economic expansion, which should tell us that the terrain has changed. In terms of job creation, it's the weakest expansion on record. The multinationals and the stock market are doing just fine. But American workers are caught in a cruel squeeze between corporations bent on extracting every last ounce of productivity from their U.S. employees and a vast new globalized workforce that is eager and well able to do the jobs of American workers at a fraction of the pay.

The sense of anxiety is growing and has crossed party lines. "We are losing the information-age jobs that were supposed to take the place of all the offshored manufacturing and industrial jobs," said John Pardon, an information technology worker from Dayton, Ohio. Pardon described himself as a moderate conservative, a longtime Republican voter who has become "alienated from the Republican Party and the Bush administration" over the jobs issue.

Pardon does not buy the rhetoric of the free-trade crusaders, who declare, as a matter of faith, that the wholesale shipment of jobs overseas is good for Americans who have to work for a living.

"There aren't any new middle-class 'postindustrial' or information-age jobs for displaced information-age workers," he told me. "There are no opportunities to 'move up the food chain' or 'leverage our experience' into higher value-added jobs."

The simple truth, as Pardon and so many others have found through hard experience, is that enormous numbers of well-educated, highly skilled white-collar workers are having tremendous trouble finding the kind of high-level employment they've been trained for and the kind of pay they feel they deserve.

The knee-jerk advocates of unrestrained trade always insist that it will result in new, more sophisticated, and ever more highly paid employment in the United States. We can ship all these nasty jobs (like computer programming) overseas so Americans can concentrate on the more important, more creative tasks. That great day is always just over the horizon. And those great jobs are never described in detail.

These advocates are sounding more and more like the hapless Micawber in *David Copperfield,* who could never be swayed from his good-natured belief that something would "turn up."

We've allowed the multinationals to run wild and never cared enough to step in when the people losing their jobs, or getting their wages and benefits squeezed, were of the lower-paid variety. Now the middle class is being targeted, and the panic is setting in.

No one really knows what to do—not the president, not John Kerry or John Edwards, and most of all not the economists and other advocates who have been so certain about the benefits for American working men and women of unrestrained trade and globalization.

What happens when the combination of corporate indifference and the globalized pressure on jobs and wages becomes so intense it weakens the very foundations of the American standard of living?

The fact that this critically important issue is finally becoming an important part of the national conversation is, to borrow a phrase used in another context by the chairman of the president's Council of Economic Advisers, "a good thing."

Perhaps an honest search for solutions will follow.

(February 20, 2004)

WHO'S GETTING THE NEW JOBS?

A startling new study shows that all of the growth in the employed population in the United States over the past few years can be attributed to recently arrived immigrants. The study found that from the beginning of 2001 through the first four months of 2004, the number of new immigrants who found work in the United States was 2.06 million, while the number of native-born and longer-term immigrant workers declined by more than 1.3 million.

The study, from the Center for Labor Market Studies, at Northeastern University in Boston, is further confirmation that despite the recovery from the recession of 2001, American families are still struggling with serious issues of joblessness and underemployment.

The study does not mean that native-born workers and long-term immigrants are not finding jobs. The American workplace is a vast, dynamic, highly competitive arena, with endless ebbs and flows of employment. But as the study tallied the gains and losses since the end of 2000, it found that new immigrants acquired as many jobs as the other two groups lost, and then some.

Andrew Sum, the director of the center and lead author of the study, said he hoped his findings would spark a long-needed analysis of employment and immigration policies in the United States. But he warned against using the statistics for immigrant bashing.

"We need a serious, honest debate about where we are today with regard to labor markets," said Sum, whose work has frequently cited the important contributions immigrants have made. The starkness of the study's findings, he said, is an indication that right now "there is something wrong."

The study found that the new immigrants entering the labor force were mostly male and "quite young," with more than one-fourth under the age of twenty-five, and 70 percent under thirty-five.

"Hispanics formed the dominant group of new immigrants," the study said, "with migrants from Mexico and Central America playing key roles. Slightly under 56 percent of the new immigrant workers were Hispanic, nearly another one-fifth were Asian, 18 percent were white, not-Hispanic, and 5 percent were black."

Those most affected by the influx of new immigrant workers are young, less well educated American workers, and so-called established immigrants, those who have been in the United States for a number of years.

Simply stated, there are not enough jobs being created to accommodate the wide variety of demographic groups in need of work. With that being the case, and with some employers actively recruiting new immigrants, the inevitable result has been the displacement of previously employed workers, especially in the less-skilled and lower-income categories.

College-educated middle-class workers appear to be holding their own in the current employment environment, although significant numbers are underemployed.

The situation is much bleaker for high school graduates and dropouts, especially for men, both black and white, and teenagers.

The new immigrants are not spread evenly across the United States. The study identified sixteen states that each had 50,000 or more new immigrants in the civilian labor force, ranging from slightly fewer than 55,000 in Colorado and Pennsylvania to 276,000 in Texas, and a high of 555,000 in California.

Sum said he used data from the Bureau of Labor Statistics household survey, as opposed to its payroll survey (which is preferred by many economists), because it includes a number of categories of employment—contract workers, farm labor, and others—that attract substantial immigrant labor but are not monitored by the payroll survey.

But even in the traditional area of manufacturing, for example, the employment of new immigrants has been significant. Referring to the period from 2000 to the fall of 2003, the study said, "Nearly 320,000 new immigrants obtained employment in the nation's manufacturing industries at a time when total wage and salary employment in these industries declined by more than 2.7 million positions."

If we are going to continue to encourage immigration, it's essential that we move once again toward full employment. Let the discussions begin now on how to get there. In the absence of full employment, an ugly face-off between American workers and newly arriving immigrants will be inevitable. That is not something we want or need to see.

(July 23, 2004)

7

CORPORATE VALUES

PURSUING THE CHILDREN

The *New York Times*'s Jack Curry had a story in the sports section about Curt Schilling, a star pitcher with the Philadelphia Phillies who was first introduced to smokeless tobacco when he was fifteen.

In March 1998, Schilling, then thirty-one, was told by a dentist to undergo a biopsy. The dentist was worried that a two-inch lesion across the athlete's lower gums might be cancerous.

Potentially deadly lesions in the mouths of young tobacco chewers are common. Of the 141 major leaguers examined in a voluntary screening program, 83 (including Schilling) had at least one tobacco-related lesion. Biopsies were recommended for fifteen of the athletes.

Schilling, one of the best pitchers in baseball, had a very close call. Jack Curry wrote: "On March 17, doctors told Schilling that he had dysplasia, a condition in which the cells become disorganized—the stage before malignancy."

Schilling, who is married and has two children, stopped chewing tobacco.

Questions about Schilling's brush with catastrophe evoked a chilling response from Alan Hilburg, a spokesman for the Smokeless Tobacco Council, in Washington. Curry quoted him as follows: "It has not been scientifically established that smokeless tobacco causes adverse medical effects."

Got that? Those nasty lesions on the lips, tongues, and gums of smokeless tobacco users may have been caused by toothpaste, or mouthwash, or that most perilous of all oral activities, flossing.

Or maybe they just erupted spontaneously.

When you go to work for the tobacco industry you leave your humanity far behind. Dead customers have to be replaced. So do those who quit the habit after losing various portions of their bodies to the surgeon's knife, or undergoing the tortures of radiation or chemotherapy or both. And then there are the hundreds of thousands who manage to quit each year before cancer catches up with them.

They all have to be replaced with new customers, eager and young. This is not a task for sensitive souls. It's a job for someone who can look at the family of a smokeless tobacco victim who has lost part of his face and say: "It has not been scientifically established . . ."

Despite the many laws outlawing the sale of tobacco products to minors, well over a million kids a year become regular smokers, tobacco chewers, cigar chompers, etc. According to the Centers for Disease Control and Prevention, more than 5 million children currently under the age of eighteen will go on to die from tobacco-related diseases.

In 1997 I mentioned in a column that the U.S. Tobacco Company, the maker of Skoal smokeless tobacco, was planning a forty-city rock tour featuring big-name alternative rock musicians, including Iggy Pop, Tonic, and 60 Ft. Dolls.

It was called the "ROAR Tour."

You don't think they were going after children, do you?

The Campaign for Tobacco-Free Kids, which alerted the media to the tour, likes to quote the former sales representative who commented on the cherry flavoring that was added to Skoal Long Cut a few years ago. "Cherry Skoal," he said, "is for somebody who likes the taste of candy, if you know what I mean."

More than a million boys use smokeless tobacco. Two years ago *Consumer Reports* noted: "Half of the teen-age smokeless tobacco users already have pre-cancerous white patches in their mouths. With continued tobacco use, one in 20 of these lesions will become cancerous in five years."

You won't hear much about that from the likes of Alan Hilburg.

Now the tobacco industry is worried that legislation being considered in Washington will lead to financial disruption and might even drive some firms out of business. Maybe so. A genuine crackdown on the sale of tobacco to minors is bound to hurt because the industry depends so heavily on such sales. Just how heavily was made clear in recently released internal documents from the RJ Reynolds Tobacco Company.

One memo, from 1975, said, "To ensure increased and longer-term growth for Camel filter, the brand must increase its share penetration among the 14–24 age group, which have a new set of liberal values and which represent tomorrow's cigarette business."

(May 3, 1998)

NIKE BLINKS

Let's not be too quick to canonize Nike.

Philip Knight, Nike's multibillionaire chairman and chief executive, managed to generate a lot of positive press in May 1998 when he announced that independent organizations would be allowed to inspect the overseas factories that make his company's products, that he would toughen the health and safety standards in the factories, and that he would crack down on the use of child labor.

There is both merit and a lot of smoke in Knight's initiative.

The admission into the plants of truly independent observers from local nongovernmental organizations would be a great advance. If Knight follows through in good faith on this promise the working conditions in the factories are likely to improve, and it will be substantially more difficult for other large apparel companies to resist similar pledges.

The proposed improvements in health and safety standards, which would bring them in line with standards in the United States, are also important. Footwear factories are equipped with heavy machinery that can cause serious injury, and much of the raw material used in the factories is toxic. Many workers at plants turning out shoes for Nike and other international companies spend their days inhaling dangerous fumes.

Knight's child labor initiative is another matter. It's a smoke screen. Child labor has not been a big problem with Nike, and Philip Knight knows that better than anyone. But public relations is public relations. So he announces that he's not going to let the factories hire kids, and suddenly that's the headline.

Knight is like a three-card monte player. You have to keep a close eye on him at all times.

The biggest problem with Nike is that its overseas workers make wretched, below-subsistence wages. It's not the minimum age that needs raising, it's the minimum wage. Most of the workers in Nike factories in China and Vietnam make less than two dollars a day, well below the subsistence levels in those countries. In Indonesia the pay is less than one dollar a day.

No wonder Knight has billions.

Human rights organizations have been saying that Nike's overseas workers need to make the equivalent of at least three dollars a day to cover their basic food, shelter, and clothing needs.

Medea Benjamin, the director of Global Exchange, a San Francisco–based group that has been monitoring Nike's practices, said, "Three dollars a day for Indonesia, China, and Vietnam would still be a tiny sum, but it would make a significant difference in the lives of the workers."

Nike hasn't been listening.

Knight, in fact, has been trumpeting a recent pay increase that Nike's Indonesian workers received. It was less than three dollars a month. Even with the increase, the workers are making less than one dollar a day.

Nike blinked because it has been getting hammered in the marketplace and in the court of public opinion. As Knight put it, "The Nike product has become synonymous with slave wages, forced overtime, and arbitrary abuse."

You bet. And the company's current strategy is to reshape its public image while doing as little as possible for the workers. Does anyone think it was an accident that Nike set up shop in human rights sinkholes, where labor organizing was viewed as a criminal activity, and deeply impoverished workers were willing, even eager, to take their places on assembly lines and work for next to nothing?

The abuses continue, even as Knight spends untold millions trying to show what a good guy he is. I spoke by phone to a woman in

Vietnam named Lap Nguyen. She was called to my attention by Thuyen Nguyen (no relation), who runs Vietnam Labor Watch, another outfit that keeps a sharp eye on Nike.

Lap Nguyen worked in a factory that made Nikes. She made the mistake of speaking to American television reporters about corporal punishment and other working conditions. Despite an excellent employment history, she found herself demoted from team leader on an assembly line to cleaning the factory's toilets—a task, she said, that made her feel "ashamed."

Lap Nguyen was forced to resign.

Nike's still got a long way to go.

(May 21, 1998)

AMERICA'S LITTLEST SHOOTERS

When's the perfect time to give your child a gun?

That's a difficult question for some parents. Is it when your son is twelve years old? When your daughter is fourteen? You have to be careful. You can't hand out high-powered weaponry willy-nilly. Some children just won't know what to do with it.

Luckily, the National Shooting Sports Foundation, the leading trade association for the gun industry in the United States, has been helpful on this matter. A pamphlet distributed some years ago by the foundation (and which still represents the foundation's philosophy) answers the perplexing question "How old is old enough?"

The pamphlet, *When Your Youngster Wants a Gun,* says:

Age is not the major yardstick. Some youngsters are ready to start at 10, others at 14. The only real measures are those of maturity and individual responsibility.

Does your youngster follow directions well? Is he conscientious and reliable? Would you leave him alone in the house for two or three hours? Would you send him to the grocery store with a list and a $20 bill? If the answer to these questions or similar ones are "yes," then the answer can also be "yes" when your child asks for his first gun.

I say, right on. If little Jimmy can run to the store with a twenty and scamper back with the correct change, then by all means he should have a gun if he wants one. You feel that way, don't you?

This is not a joke. The gun manufacturers and distributors, whatever they are saying about the massacre in Littleton, Colorado, have been aggressively marketing their deadly products to the youth of America for years. They have not done it secretly. Gun ownership has been declining in the United States, and the industry has been openly in the hunt for new young shooters.

"The gun industry needs more customers and the gun lobby needs more contributors," said Josh Sugarmann, director of the Violence Policy Center, a research organization in Washington that favors firearms control.

The center released a study documenting the industry's intensive efforts over several years to recruit teenagers and children into the gun culture. The title of the study, "Start 'Em Young," was taken from an article in the July 1998 issue of *Gun World* magazine that giddily championed the association of children and guns. A photo of an adolescent aiming a cocked revolver was captioned, "The author's son Steve would shoot this .22 single action all day every day if he could."

The article was headlined, "Start 'Em Young: There Is No Time Like the Present."

Apparently no child is too young. A photo in the magazine *Guns and Ammo* shows a little kid with big glasses aiming a big gun with both hands. The awkwardly worded caption reads: "The Freedom Arms Model 1997 chambered in .45 Colt is comfortable to shoot as demonstrated by the author's seven-year-old son. Keep in mind that it is still more powerful than the legendary manstopping .45 ACP."

For those who like a little kiddie porn with their promotion of "manstopping" weapons, consider a magazine ad that showed a smiling little girl, a toddler, in a bathing suit that is tugged up suggestively in the rear. The little girl is holding a machine gun. The copy beneath the photo says: "Short BUTTS from FLEMING FIREARMS."

Fun, huh?

I asked Bob Delfay of the National Shooting Sports Foundation about the group's policies regarding children and guns. He said: "We feel the same way about introducing young people to the recreational use of firearms that we always have. It's not only an appropriate thing to do, it is a desirable and beneficial thing for a responsible adult to introduce a responsible young person to the recreational use of firearms. Many, many beneficial things can come from that, and incidents like Littleton rarely, if ever, come from that."

The foundation, in one of its trade publications, has said to the nation's gun manufacturers: "There's a way to help insure that new faces and pocketbooks will continue to patronize your business: Use the schools. This is where most of your potential down-the-line shooters and hunters now are."

The article concludes: "Schools are an opportunity. Grasp it."

(May 2, 1999)

THE GIFT OF MAYHEM

Toys for tots.

Not.

Forward Command Post is one of the weirder toys being marketed for kids this holiday season. It's essentially a bombed-out dollhouse, complete with smashed furniture, broken railings, and bullet holes in the walls. This twisted variation on a traditional childhood theme is manufactured by a company called Ever Sparkle Industrial Toys and is sold by mainstream retailers, including Toys "R" Us and JCPenney. It's being recommended for children five years old and up.

Forward Command Post is at the top of this year's "Dirty Dozen" list, an annual compilation of "toys to avoid" that is put out by the Lion & Lamb Project, a group in Bethesda, Maryland, that opposes the marketing of violent toys to children. The group noted that the Forward Command Post playhouse "comes with dozens of 'accessories,' including a machine gun, rocket launcher, magazine belt and explosives."

For five-year-olds.

Also on the list is a video game called Burnout 2: Point of Impact. This is an auto racing game—rated appropriate for six-year-olds—that features spectacularly gruesome crashes. An ad showed a man's head smashing through a windshield. "The last thing to go through your mind," the ad says, "will be your behind."

Someone needs to get a grip here, and I don't mean the kids with their hands on the joysticks. Any adult who thinks this stuff is appropriate for a five- or six-year-old is a lunatic.

In terms of their approach to the world, a five-year-old playing with a traditional dollhouse and a five-year-old playing with the ruins of the Forward Command Post are at two fundamentally different starting places.

The biggest-selling video game over the last couple of years has been a PlayStation 2 game called Grand Theft Auto III. It actually carries a voluntary "M" rating, which means it's not recommended for kids under seventeen. But teens have no problem buying M-rated games, and they love the various incarnations of Grand Theft Auto.

This is a game in which all boundaries of civilized behavior have vanished. You get to shoot whomever you want, including cops. You get to beat women to death with baseball bats. You get to have sex with prostitutes and then kill them. (And get your money back.) The game is a phenomenal seller. At close to fifty dollars each, millions of copies are sold annually. The latest version, Grand Theft Auto: Vice City, is expected to be one of the biggest sellers this Christmas.

I don't for a moment think these games should be banned. But I do think that millions of American adults have lost all sense of what are appropriate forms of play for children and teenagers. And the country as a whole behaves as though there is no real-world price to pay for a culture that has so thoroughly desensitized us to violence that it takes a terror attack or a series of suburban sniper killings to really get our attention.

Rockstar Games, which created the Grand Theft Auto series, has come out with another extraordinarily violent game called State of Emergency. It's got rioting in the streets, looting, individual acts of extreme sadism, and, of course, endless gory murders. The player gets to be part of it all, killing and maiming at will.

One online enthusiast said, "You could run down the escalator, then wait at the bottom . . . and watch as you blast some guy or gal's head off, watch them stagger about a bit before they collapse, then pick up their severed head and beat them up with it some more."

A reviewer on Amazon.com called the game "an enjoyable cacophony of senseless violence."

State of Emergency will no doubt be a hot gift item for youngsters this year.

Reading about State of Emergency reminded me of the riots in Los Angeles ten years ago, an explosion of violence and inhumanity that did not strike me at the time as the raw material for fun and games. It still doesn't.

Even now the murderous violence in parts of Los Angeles is so intense that decent residents often feel imprisoned in their homes. Killers have been running amok in the streets. The murder rate is rising. It's not a video game. And it's not fun.

The building blocks of violent behavior are dehumanization and desensitization. The lessons begin at a very early age.

(November 28, 2002)

AN UGLY GAME

Ghettopoly is a board game, based on Monopoly, and it has a lot of people fired up. Marches and protests by people denouncing the game as racist have distributors running for cover. Yahoo and eBay have blocked the sale of the game on their sites, and the Urban Outfitters chain has stopped selling it in stores.

People are outraged—outraged!—that a game would portray inner-city blacks as pimps and hustlers and hos.

Kweisi Mfume, president of the NAACP, has threatened to boycott sellers of Ghettopoly, which he described as "demeaning, repugnant and reprehensible, to say the least."

For the record: Ghettopoly is without question an ugly game that promotes disgusting racial stereotypes. It presents blacks as murderous, thieving, dope-dealing, carjacking degenerates. Instead of the familiar Monopoly pieces, like top hats and thimbles, Ghettopoly players get to move around the board as pimps, machine guns, and rocks of crack cocaine.

So I'm not feeling sorry for David Chang, the game's beleaguered twenty-eight-year-old creator. What I'd like to know is why all this outrage is springing up over a board game when so little is heard in the way of protest about the outlandishly self-destructive behavior that gives rise to a game like Ghettopoly, and which is burying any chance of a viable future for extraordinary numbers of young black men and women, and their children.

How can you march against a game and not march against the real-life slaughter on the streets and in the homes of inner cities across America? Violent crime, ignorance, and disease are carving the very heart out of America's black population.

The president of the Los Angeles Council of Churches, the Reverend Leonard Jackson, told me about the long line of funerals he's had to conduct for young black men and women, and boys and girls. He seemed on the verge of tears. "The young people have more of a chance of dying here in South Central than in a military combat zone," he said.

Instead of using their influence to help stop the slaughter, certain truly twisted elements of the hip-hop culture encourage it, celebrating it in songs that not only glorify murderous violence but also degrade black people to a degree that should leave any sensible person stupefied.

"We dangerous," says one song. "Bitches pay a fee just to hang with us."

Trust me, we've got some problems that are bigger than Ghettopoly. We've got insane young men who take their heavy armament into the street and shoot up the neighborhood, and then go back inside to listen to music that celebrates the act of shooting up the neighborhood. That is not a sign of a healthy culture.

It's not that there's been no protest. Marc Morial, the president of the National Urban League, said in a speech that "too many of our young black males believe that manhood is defined by the ability to injure or damage another man, rather than helping another man."

The Urban League, the NAACP, and many other groups and individuals are trying to address some of the myriad problems facing black America. But the efforts have been too few and too timid. And they haven't been accompanied by the bold, honest, creative, and self-critical thinking that is an absolutely necessary precursor to action that would be effective.

Ghettopoly is a stupid and offensive game. But its reach is nowhere near as vast or as dangerous as the *Lord of the Flies* street culture that is seducing one generation after another of black children, and producing freakish entertainers like Nelly and 50 Cent.

We learned that Nelly, a male rapper from St. Louis, is marketing a new drink called Pimp Juice—aimed, I suppose, at niggaz and hos. The drink was a follow-up to Nelly's hit song of the same name, a song with such immortal lines as "You ain't from Russia, so bitch why you Russian?"

50 Cent has the top album of the year, and one of the hit songs is "P.I.M.P." He brags in the song that he'll have his ho "stripping in the street." Of one of his women, he says, "The last nigga she was with put stitches in her head."

That's not entertainment. That's a symptom.

(October 17, 2003)

PART FOUR

———

BLACK AND WHITE

8

WHAT HAPPENED TO THE DREAM?

THE DREAM IGNORED

The recent tributes to the Reverend Dr. Martin Luther King Jr. have been folded and put away. They'll be hauled out again twenty years from now on the fiftieth anniversary of his death. Whether anyone in the year 2018 will pay attention to what Dr. King really stood for is anybody's guess. I doubt it. The ceremonies will likely be as earnest and as empty as ever. We honor Dr. King but we've never listened to him. The essence of his message has been ignored. He preached nonviolence. He believed strongly in integration. And he died fighting for economic justice for the poor.

It's still a shock to read the eight-column *New York Times* headline of Friday, April 5, 1968: "Martin Luther King Is Slain in Memphis; a White Is Suspected; Johnson Urges Calm."

There would be no calm. Nonviolence was the foundation of Dr. King's philosophy, but the long, long night of extreme violence was already settling over black America when he was killed, and the dark hasn't lifted yet. The losses in the black community over the past thirty years to violent death and to prison have been staggering. Saying good-bye to the young has become the most familiar of rituals.

A great deal has been made of Dr. King's last sermon, delivered in Memphis the night before he died. He seemed to prophesy his own death, and I believed for many years that his anguished expression during that sermon, and especially toward the end, was the natural result of his sensing that he was about to die.

"Like anybody, I would like to live a long life," Dr. King said. "Longevity has its place. But I'm not concerned about that now."

He'd seen the promised land, he said. "And I'm happy tonight. I'm not worried about anything."

But he looked worried and deeply sad. His face was contorted with what appeared to be grief. There was nothing in his expression to suggest that he was happy about anything.

I believe that Dr. King was grieving, but not for himself. I believe he knew he was losing the fight against nonviolence and realized the terrible toll that violence would take on the black community, and the ways in which it would undermine the fight for civil rights. Newark and Detroit had gone up in flames the previous summer. Militants with dashikis but no philosophy were advocating black separatism at the same time that they were applauding the destruction of black neighborhoods. Many of the whites who had enlisted bravely in the civil rights struggle had been sent packing. Dr. King himself was derided as an Uncle Tom.

Dr. King was in Memphis to support a strike by sanitation workers, and violence had marred that effort. "Let us rise up with a greater readiness," Dr. King said. "Let us stand with a greater determination."

The bullet that killed him was fired from a .30-06 Remington rifle. It wrecked his jaw and damaged his spine. And it did incalculable damage to the United States of America.

The eight-column headline in the *Times* on Saturday, April 6,

1968, said: "Army Troops in Capital as Negroes Riot; Guard Sent into Chicago, Detroit, Boston; Johnson Asks a Joint Session of Congress."

It was the worst rioting the country had yet seen. Even as he was being readied for burial, Dr. King's fundamental principles were being betrayed.

The following week *Look* magazine was on the stands with an article that had been written by Dr. King. The article described his plans for a series of demonstrations around the country in support of additional jobs and improved housing for the poor. He vowed that there would be both "Negro and white" participation in the demonstrations, which were designed to help the poor of both races.

"Some of the black power groups have temporarily given up on integration," Dr. King wrote. "We have not. So maybe we are the bridge, in the middle, reaching across and connecting both sides."

He complained about the resources, financial and otherwise, that were flowing to Vietnam, which he described as a "tragic mixup in priorities." He warned whites that racism was a "potentially fatal disease" and he warned blacks that violence and continued rioting "will strengthen the right wing of the country."

But he was dead and no one was listening. Now we honor him. But we're still not listening.

(April 9, 1998)

STARING AT HATRED

How deep is the hatred?

After being sentenced to death in Jasper, Texas, in February 1999, John William King was asked if he had anything to say to the relatives of his victim, James Byrd Jr., a forty-nine-year-old black man who was chained to a pickup truck and dragged along a country road until his body literally was torn apart.

King, a twenty-four-year-old white supremacist, did indeed have something to say. Grinning, he assured all within earshot that Byrd's grieving survivors were welcome to perform a sex act on him.

Most Americans would like to believe that the attack on Byrd was an aberration, that it was so far over the top, so sick and inhumane, that it should not be viewed as representative of a much larger societal problem. The reasoning is more or less as follows: The vast majority of Americans were repelled by the murder, arrests were quickly made, and the legal steps toward the ultimate societal sanction are already being taken. Let's move on.

That attitude presupposes that race hatred and other forms of prejudice and intolerance in America are not nearly as deep or as dangerous as the attack on Byrd might suggest.

A long litany of tragedies tells us otherwise.

Matthew Shepard, a twenty-one-year-old college student in Wyoming, died in the fall of 1998 after he was kidnapped, robbed, tied to a fence, beaten in the head with a .357 Magnum, tortured with cigarettes, taunted as he wept and begged for his life, and finally left alone and helpless in near-freezing temperatures. Authorities said he was murdered, at least in part, because he was gay.

A recent report from the Southern Poverty Law Center in Montgomery, Alabama, which tracks hate crimes and hate groups across the country, is filled with other horrible examples that occurred in the twelve months of 1998.

In February, the report said, a dark-haired young woman named Amy Robinson was abducted in Fort Worth, Texas, and murdered by two white men who used her for target practice. They were reported to have burst out laughing when she died. The original plan, according to one of the men, was "to go out and shoot black folks." Robinson was chosen because the men thought she was biracial. They were mistaken. Robinson was, in fact, white.

In October in Buffalo, New York, a group of black teenagers attacked a forty-one-year-old white man, Gary Trzaska, as he was walking to his car. Trzaska, who was gay, was beaten and stomped to death. Witnesses said they saw the teenagers jumping high in the air so they could land on Trzaska's head with both feet. They said the boys appeared to be gleeful as they killed their victim.

In the spring a group of whites "armed with brass knuckles and chanting 'white power'" attacked Lance Corporal Carlos Colbert, a twenty-one-year-old black Marine, as he left a party in San Diego, California. As many as thirty men joined in the assault. Corporal Colbert was not killed, but his neck was broken. He is paralyzed from the neck down.

In May a racially charged exchange in a bar led to the murder of Mark Dale Butts, a thirty-five-year-old white man. He was beaten to death in a cemetery in Victor, Colorado, by a group of black men and teenagers. A shovel was used in the attack. Authorities said Butts was beaten so hard the handle of the shovel eventually broke.

Morris Dees, the chief trial counsel of the Law Center, said he is surprised by what appears to be the increasing frequency and viciousness of such attacks. They are being committed by whites and blacks, he said. Much of the hatred is fueled by the growing number of organized hate groups and the proliferation of Internet sites devoted to racism, anti-Semitism, homophobia, and other forms of intolerance.

The desire to turn away from a crime as grotesque as the murder of James Byrd in Jasper, Texas, is understandable. Once justice is done, what's the point of wallowing in the hideousness of the crime?

But there is a need to understand the rage and the frustrations and the impulses that lead so many of us to mayhem in the name of some warped sense of superiority, or inadequacy, or fear, or whatever.

Dragging someone to his death behind a truck may be unusual. But torturing, maiming, and killing people because they fit a certain despised profile is an everyday occurrence. We can hardly stop it if we're not even willing to look at it.

(February 28, 1999)

HAUNTED BY SEGREGATION

Tunica County, Mississippi

I was ushered into the modest office of C. Penn Owen Jr., the most powerful plantation owner and all-around operator in this rural county in northern Mississippi.

He spoke slowly. "I'm sure I'll get fair treatment from you," he said. He managed to smile without smiling.

We were in his office on Old Highway 61, an ancient two-lane road that runs beside the Mississippi River. Owen is anxiously trying to cash in on the casino boom in the county. He is already building the first few houses of a large upscale development in an unincorporated area called Robinsonville. But he has some problems. The private homes and rental units he plans for the site have deliberately been priced out of the reach of the overwhelmingly black inhabitants of Tunica.

The buyers will have to come from elsewhere, and by all accounts most of them would be white. Big problem number one: the public schools in Tunica County, woefully neglected for decades, are filled with black students. Owen, in a reference to one of the schools, summed up the matter nicely:

"I think there is some fear and concern about the Rosa Fort campus. The percentages, I guess, would be frightening to some people." In other words, there is no chance the wealthy white families he is trying to lure to his development would be willing to send their kids to the nearly all-black public schools.

Owen thought he had a solution. He planned to have his housing development anchored by a brand-new multimillion-dollar state-of-the-art elementary school. He sold the land for the school to the Board of Education at a cut-rate price, and for a while it looked as if there was going to be a great new school for the spiffy new families coming to Robinsonville.

Except that some black people in the county, many of them desperately poor and tired of doing the backbreaking work in the cotton fields and elsewhere while watching a handful of exploitive whites reap all the benefits, objected. Two local groups, Southern Echo and Concerned Citizens for a Better Tunica County, challenged the plan.

They noted that the county was ordered to desegregate its schools nearly three decades ago by the federal government. Whites responded to that order by pulling their children out of the public schools and setting up a vile system of private academies for white children only. In Tunica County the white academy is called the Tunica Institute of Learning. A large slave bell sits proudly on its front lawn.

Owen and other plantation owners and developers now find their grand plans for Robinsonville jeopardized by the persistence of a segregated system they thought was just fine until now. Because the Tunica school board is operating under a desegregation order, it has to get approval from the Department of Justice, in Washington, before

it can build a new school. Justice officials, after listening to local objections, have refused so far to approve the plan. They noted several
months ago that there "is virtually no student population in Robinsonville" and they agreed that the children moving into Owen's development would most likely be white.

Owen and his allies, frustrated, now insist that there is no chance
the proposed school would be predominantly white. They are prepared to scour the county for black children to enroll in the school.
Owen's houses are not selling very quickly, and one way or another
he needs that school to go up.

Penda Hair, codirector of the Advancement Project, a national
civil rights advocacy organization that is working with the local
groups in Tunica, said black students may be funneled into the
school initially but that they would soon be numerically overwhelmed by white students from the development. "The families
that move there will see it as their neighborhood school," she said.

None of this would have been a problem if whites in Tunica and
the rest of Mississippi had at any time over the last half century
dealt fairly with the black population and with the issue of segregated schools. Bigotry always cuts two ways, which is why Mississippi has for so long been one of the most backward states in the
union.

"I don't know why this race issue has to come into it at all," said
Penn Owen. "When I go into the casinos I see colored people, I see
Hispanics, I see Orientals in very top positions. I don't get it."

(May 16, 1999)

WHERE FEAR RULES THE STREET

Los Angeles

The three men were middle-aged and dressed as if they had just come from church. One pointed toward a tiny makeshift shrine of flickering candles and wilting flowers that had been placed at the curb in front of a run-down house on Budlong Avenue in South Los Angeles, a vast expanse of neighborhoods that has had its name changed from South Central in a futile effort to improve its image.

South L.A. is still a viciously destructive place. Some neighborhoods are so dangerous that residents are reluctant to leave their homes, even in the daytime. The neat residential streets and the palm trees are deceptive. The owner of a fast food restaurant told me, "Out here, you're always in danger."

The shrine on Budlong Avenue marked the spot where Londell Murdock was murdered in the middle of the afternoon the previous Wednesday. Murdock, a thirty-three-year-old custodian who was married and had two children, was shot to death on his way to work. The gunman, who was twenty-two, also shot two women who were standing on a porch nearby. They survived.

"It's bad," said Andy Rooks, the man who had pointed toward the shrine. "People don't want to come out. Those who aren't working, they might run to the store before nine in the morning, then go back home and lock up."

" 'Cause they know these boys will shoot you," said Rooks's friend J. C. Pye.

"If you come out here tonight," said Rooks, "you won't see nobody." He mentioned that there was a library a few blocks down the street that had a small park behind it. "The children used to play in that park all the time," he said. "Not anymore."

The gunmen of Los Angeles, many of them gang members from South and East L.A., have turned their city into the murder capital of America. Los Angeles, which has a population of 3.7 million, led the nation in homicides last year, with 653. New York, with a population of 8 million, had just 584 murders.

On one weekend in the middle of last month, ten people were shot to death in Los Angeles and fifteen others were wounded by gunfire.

The mayhem is concentrated in certain sections of the city, and the result for local residents is heartache, paralyzing fear, and a radically constricted lifestyle. About half of all the murders occur in South L.A., and most of the victims are young. Instead of the normal cycle of children growing up and burying their parents, in South L.A. the parents, with stunning frequency, are burying their children.

It is estimated that over the past twenty years some 10,000 young people have died in L.A.'s violence-ridden neighborhoods. Residents who are convinced that no one in those neighborhoods is safe point to the murder on May 28, 2000, of a twenty-year-old woman named Lori Gonzalez. She was a bystander who was shot in the chest and head when gunfire erupted in the parking lot of a fast food restaurant. Gonzalez was the granddaughter of the Los Angeles police chief at that time, Bernard C. Parks.

"The young people have more of a chance of dying here in South Central than in a military combat zone," said the Reverend Leonard Jackson, the president of the Los Angeles Council of Churches. "To say that there's a climate of fear is understating it."

During an interview in his office at the First African Methodist Episcopal Church of Los Angeles, he noted, "In certain areas you find mothers placing their youngsters in the bathtub to sleep, or having them sleep on the floor, for safety."

He spoke sadly of several killings that had touched members of his congregation, including the murder of a teenage boy who was shot to death several months ago just moments after leaving a service at the church. "He was just standing on the street," said Jackson, "less than two blocks from here."

The minister paused for a moment and an expression of deep sadness crossed his face. "It's time for the community to take a stand," he said. "We're doing what we can here at the church. But this is madness. And I have to tell you, I'm personally devastated by it."

There are many reasons for the chaos in South Los Angeles: parents who have neglected or completely abandoned their young; a ridiculously understaffed police force that has never seriously tried to "protect and serve" the most troubled neighborhoods; the chronic demons of poverty and joblessness.

No one seems to know what to do now. Meanwhile, the dying continues.

(June 9, 2003)

CIVIL RIGHTS, THE SEQUEL

It's been more than thirty years since Whitney Young Jr. died and his name is no longer particularly well known, which is a shame.

Young was the executive director of the National Urban League and one of the big four civil rights leaders of the 1960s, along with Martin Luther King Jr., Roy Wilkins, and James Farmer.

He drowned at the absurdly young age of forty-nine during a visit to Nigeria in 1971. More than 6,000 people attended his funeral at Manhattan's Riverside Church, and thousands more lined the streets of Harlem to view the funeral procession. Young had been a giant in the movement, and it was widely recognized that his death represented a terrible loss.

What was not understood at the time was that an incredible decades-long slide into the horrors of violence and degradation for millions of African American youngsters was already under way. More than three decades later we still haven't stopped the descent.

It is now absolutely normal in many circles for young black men and women (and, for that matter, little black boys and girls) to refer to one another as niggaz and bitches and hos. Doing well in school is frequently disdained as a white thing. Doing time in prison is widely accepted as a black thing, and no cause for shame.

Few people are surprised to hear that a gathering at this party or that club degenerated into the kind of violence we used to associate with the OK Corral. Homicide, drugs, and AIDS are carving the heart out of one generation after another, and suicide among blacks is on the rise.

Just before I sat down to write this column I happened to glance at an article that was on the front page of the *Boston Globe*. Beneath a color photo of a black toddler, the article began: "A 3-year-old girl remained in critical condition last night after a former high school basketball star allegedly ended a shouting match with a woman by spraying her Dorchester house with bullets, hitting the child in the back and severing her spinal cord."

My question is a simple one: When are we going to stop this?

I'm waiting for the mothers and the fathers, the aunts and the uncles, the older brothers and the older sisters to step forward and call a halt to the madness, to say: "Enough! This is not what we're about."

I mentioned Whitney Young Jr. because I had a conversation a few days ago with Marc Morial, the former mayor of New Orleans who has just taken over as head of the Urban League and is hoping to raise its profile to a level comparable to the glory days of the Whitney Young era.

He plans to lay out his agenda in a keynote address to be delivered later this month at the league's annual convention. My suggestion: Hammer home the need to stop the self-destruction that continues to block the advancement of millions of black Americans.

I know there are serious economic problems, particularly the absence of good jobs, that are holding some people back. And I know about the abuses in the criminal justice system and the continuing plague of racism and discrimination. I've written reams about all of these things.

None of them is a good reason for parents to turn their backs on their children, for children to turn their backs on school, for a young man or a young woman to pick up a needle and plunge it into a vein, for a gunman to put a bullet into a rival's head or a neighbor's spine, for blacks to view themselves as niggers and whores, for entertainers to sing of the joys of rape and murder.

The paradox of black life in America over the past half century is that so much real progress and such wholesale tragedy should have occurred in the same place at the same time. The task now is to reinforce the progress and bring the curtain down on the tragedy.

Young leaders like Morial (he's forty-five) and venerable institutions like the Urban League (it's ninety-three) are perfectly positioned to begin the coordinated effort that's needed for this fight, which is the most serious to face black Americans since the demise of legal segregation.

Those who are looking to government to lead this effort are deluded. George W. Bush and Clarence Thomas will not be riding to our rescue.

What's required is nothing less than round two of the civil rights movement, the goal being to create a safe and constructive and nurturing environment in which all black Americans can thrive.

(July 7, 2003)

BREAKING AWAY

Caroline Jhingory had been warned but she was still surprised—and hurt—when some of her lifelong friends turned on her the way they did.

Jhingory is a twenty-two-year-old black woman from Washington, D.C., who went off to college a few years ago. "One of the connections I had with my friends back home was that we had always been sort of aspiring hip-hop artists and things like that," she said. "But we were young, you know, and I eventually woke up from la-la land and realized that I would have to get an education and a job, something a little more concrete than fantasies about the hip-hop underground."

She noticed that when she came home on visits from school, some of her friends treated her differently. "I don't know if it was out of jealousy or resentment or whatever," she said, "but they would actually say to me, 'You're acting white now.' They'd say that. They'd say, 'You act white.' Or, 'You act proper.'"

Jhingory had come face-to-face with the dilemma that many black youngsters encounter as they try to improve their lives by studying, going to college, and making other efforts to escape the swarming tentacles of poverty and ignorance. Old friends and sometimes even relatives may see those courageous efforts as a threat, and react bitterly.

"I knew that it would happen because other friends had told me it would happen," said Jhingory. "But I was surprised that it would happen with friends that I was so close to, people I had grown up with from the time I was maybe six or seven. I actually ended friendships because of comments like that. We just couldn't connect anymore because it was just a really negative situation."

I have no idea what the stats are, but I know this perverse peer pressure to do less than your best in scholarly and intellectual pursuits is holding back large numbers of black Americans, especially black boys and men. The other day I had a long conversation with a fifteen-year-old named David Blocker, who also happens to be from Washington. Until January, when he was expelled, David was a student at the Hyde Leadership Public Charter School.

"We were so lackadaisical," he said. "One-third of our school was failing three or more classes. The pressure from my friends was mostly to chill and, like, do what you want to do. People were not doing their work, just coming to school for fun, coming to school high, just playing sports, not really knowing what school was for."

David said he went right along with the crowd. "It's hard to come in and really do work when everybody is just chillin' and playin' around. If everybody's doing that, then you're going to want to chill and play around, too."

What was interesting was that David took a summer math course at a highly regarded private prep school and got an A-minus. But when he came back to Hyde, which was not as rigorous academically, he promptly failed math.

"I guess I'm responsive to how my environment is," he said.

David's parents have responded by homeschooling him since his expulsion. He said he expected to be enrolled soon in a school in which not only the teachers but also the students take academics more seriously, perhaps outside Washington.

The cultural pressure to behave in ways that are detrimental and even destructive go well beyond the classroom. Several young boys have told me about their desire to gain experience as street hustlers so they can someday cash in as "authentic" gangsta rap stars.

David's older sister, Nomoya Tinch, who lives in Brooklyn and is an intern at *Essence* magazine, said there was a time when she so craved the approval of her peers that she had turned into "this all-out wild child, this ponytail honey who was out there cursing and being bad and just didn't care."

Then comes the flip side: the all-out wild child has to walk onto a college campus or into a professional environment, and suddenly the feelings of inadequacy swell up like a wave that is about to overwhelm you.

These are not small issues. They are the day-to-day reality for millions of people, in most cases good and talented people who have had an already tough road made tougher by self-imposed roadblocks, and bad advice from their peers.

(July 10, 2003)

9

DOUBLE STANDARDS

EMPATHY FOR A KILLER

What if a madman had invaded Andrea Yates's home in suburban Houston and drowned her five children?

It would have been the biggest story in America, with the coverage ranging from the sensational to the hysterical. Every angle would have been pursued. Except one. There would have been no serious attempt to understand the mental state of the killer—to determine, for example, if there were mitigating factors at work. Few would have cared if he suffered from depression or some other mental illness, or if he'd been horribly abused as a child.

And there would have been no hemming and hawing about whether prosecutors in Harris County, Texas, which is fanatical about capital punishment, would seek the death penalty. No question at all. Not in a multiple murder case in which all of the victims were children.

But this case is different. The mother herself has confessed to the killings. And she is not some unkempt, crack-smoking, dark-skinned, ghetto-dwelling stereotype who can easily be bad-mouthed for daring to have had babies in the first place. She's a soccer mom. Or at least she might have been if her kids had lived long enough to play soccer.

Suddenly the nation has a mass killer it can empathize with, identify with, care for, even love. So here's *Newsweek,* in its cover story: "Most mass killers are sociopaths, utterly alienated from other human beings. They are callous or sadistic. Andrea was the opposite: if anything, she apparently cared too much."

More *Newsweek*: "Between caring for her father and her children, it is hard to think that Andrea ever had time for herself."

The tone and the approach of *Newsweek*'s coverage was typical. How could Andrea have done it? What could possibly have driven a nice middle-class suburban mother to drown her five children?

This is the case in which root causes, out of favor for so long, made a comeback. Story after story detailed the struggles Yates had with emotional illness, a demanding husband, an ailing father, the five children. Suddenly it was not only OK, but important, to try to understand what drove the killer to kill.

What's wrong with all of this? Nothing. Yates is a human being and deserves to be seen as such, even as the criminal justice system moves ahead with the procedures designed to hold her accountable for her acts.

The problem is that in most serious criminal cases—capital cases, especially—we seldom treat the accused as human, preferring instead to characterize them as monsters to be dispatched as quickly as possible, regardless of mitigating circumstances. They become "the other," so alien and evil that no one can relate. And that makes them easier to kill.

Craig Haney, a psychology professor and expert on capital litigation at the University of California at Santa Cruz, said of the Yates case, "This is a white, middle-class family. And it's a mother. So all of the sentiment—and I think quite appropriately—is running in the direction of trying to understand why she would do this.

"That kind of empathy, unfortunately, does not often extend to the typical capital defendant who may come from a different racial background, and almost always comes from a different class background than the jury."

One of the many Texas cases in which the background and mental state of the defendant was not sufficiently considered was that of Mario Marquez, who was sentenced to death for the rape and murder of a teenager. Marquez had an IQ of about 65. He was savagely abused throughout his childhood. At times his father would tie him to a tree and beat him with a horsewhip until he passed out. His parents abandoned him to the streets when he was twelve.

Marquez was too limited mentally to talk with his lawyer about the specifics of his case. They talked about animals and the things Marquez liked to draw.

Marquez was executed in 1995.

The closer you look at individual cases, the clearer it is that the government-sanctioned execution of human beings is an inappropriate, inequitable, intolerable penalty.

It was wrong to execute Mario Marquez. It would be wrong to execute Andrea Yates. And it will always be wrong to have one standard of justice for people like Marquez, and another for people like Yates.

(July 5, 2001)

POSTSCRIPT

Andrea Yates was convicted of murder and sentenced to life in prison in March 2002. But the conviction was overturned in January 2005 when an appeals court ruled that a prosecution expert had given false testimony at her trial. A new trial was ordered.

BREATHING WHILE BLACK

A federal appeals court says it's all right, but it's not all right.

Here's the lead paragraph from the *New York Times* story on a decision by the U.S. Court of Appeals for the Second Circuit: "A federal appeals court ruled yesterday that police officers in Oneonta, New York, did not violate the Constitution when they tried to stop every black man in town in 1992 after a woman said she had been robbed in her home by a young black man."

Got that? Every black man in town.

This is New York, mind you, not Mississippi.

After hearing that a black man had committed a crime, the cops went after every black man they saw walking the streets. They dragooned black men and boys (and at least one black woman!) who were trying to use public transportation. They pulled over black guys riding in cars. They went to the State University of New York at Oneonta and got a list of all the black students in the school, and they went after them.

These were all innocent people. The cops never did find the alleged assailant. But that didn't matter. Neither the rights of these individuals nor their humanity mattered. These were black people, and whatever you do to them is all right. They may have been masquerading as human beings, but Oneonta's men in blue (assisted by the state police) could see right through that disguise.

The manhunt began early on the morning of September 4, 1992, when a seventy-seven-year-old woman told police she had been attacked by a burglar. The woman, who was white, said she never saw the man's face but could tell from his arm and hand that he was black. She said she thought he was young because he moved quickly. She said the man had a knife and had cut himself on the hand while struggling with her. He then fled.

A canine unit tracked the scent of the alleged assailant for several hundred yards before losing it. Investigators said the path of the scent pointed toward the university campus. That's all the cops had to go on.

No problem. There weren't all that many black people in Oneonta. Of the 14,000 full-time residents fewer than 500 are black. And only about 2 percent of the 7,500 students at the university are black. So the cops, smart enough to know a black person when they see one, decided to stop every black guy in the town to see if one of them had a cut on his hand.

This went far beyond the problem of driving while black. People were being stopped in Oneonta for breathing while black. Trust me, if some poor guy had innocently cut his finger while slicing a tomato for dinner he would have landed in jail.

The cops never did find their man, but they humiliated a lot of people in the process. In the appeals court's opinion, a three-judge panel of the Second Circuit said: "We are not blind to the sense of frustration that was doubtlessly felt by those questioned by the police during this investigation."

But the panel ruled that this police sweep of blacks in Oneonta was OK, that it was constitutionally permissible, that it was not a violation of the equal protection clause of the Fourteenth Amendment or the Fourth Amendment's prohibition against unreasonable seizures. Never mind the breathtaking totality of the sweep. Never mind that the cops were not considering any other aspect of the so-called description except race. Never mind that this would never have happened to the white residents of Oneonta. The court ruled that the stops were not racially discriminatory because, in the court's view, the cops were acting on a description that included more than just the color of the alleged assailant.

With this ruling, cops are free to harass any and all black people as long as they have in hand a complaint that a black person has committed a crime. If you are black, you are a suspect.

The ruling, which upheld a similar ruling by a lower court, grew out of a lawsuit filed against the Oneonta cops and the state police by several of the people caught up in the sweep. The case against the plaintiffs was argued by lawyers from the office of New York State Attorney General Eliot Spitzer, who had a statutory obligation to defend the state in the suit, but who made it clear that he was uncomfortable with the outcome.

"I read the circuit opinion," he said yesterday. "And I said: 'You know what? We won the case but it makes your skin crawl.'"

(November 4, 1999)

JUSTICE, NEW YORK STYLE

Celeste Goring-Johnson would be considered a soccer mom if she were white and lived somewhere other than Brooklyn. She is forty-two years old, married, and the mother of three children. She's an accountant with the city's Department of Youth and Community Development. Her husband of nearly sixteen years, Richard Johnson, is a train operator for the Transit Authority. The family owns a brownstone on Hancock Street.

On August 21, a Saturday, Celeste Johnson drove two of her children, Elizabeth, fourteen, and Josiah, three, to Kings Highway for a dental appointment.

"I took them inside, then I went back out to put some extra coins in the meter," she said.

She noticed a jewelry store nearby and went in to get ring guards for a couple of her rings. That took less than ten minutes and cost six dollars. She paid and was about to leave the store when the proprietor locked the front door and declared that a diamond ring was missing. He said no one could leave.

Johnson recalled in an interview that there were several other customers and employees in the store. But the owner, Scott Mittleberg, got it into his head that Johnson had stolen the ring.

Thus the nightmare began.

Johnson said she had not stolen anything. Mittleberg asked to search her handbag.

She gave him the handbag and he looked through it. No ring. He said he wanted to search her pockets.

"I didn't want to feel this man on my person," she said. So she told him no.

Mittleberg, according to Johnson, said that if she didn't cooperate he would have to call the police. Johnson thought that was an excellent idea, and told him so.

The police were called. Other customers left the store.

Four officers responded. Mittleberg is reported to have told them that he had a videotape showing that Johnson was the only person who had been near the ring that supposedly was missing. The cops looked at the tape. They searched Johnson, including her pockets. No ring.

Case closed, right?

Not in New York in this day and age. Celeste Goring-Johnson, a solid citizen who has never been in trouble with the law, whose children were waiting at the dentist's for their mother to return, who never in her life imagined that she might be charged with a crime, was turned around, handcuffed, and placed under arrest.

"It was so humiliating," Johnson said. "They took me outside in handcuffs, and by this time people were gathering to watch."

Someone brought the children outside and they saw their mother being hauled toward a police car. An officer asked Johnson if she wanted the children turned over to the police. She said no, they should wait at the dentist's office until their father could pick them up.

This is the kind of city we live in now. It's a city in which a woman who had voluntarily undergone two searches can nevertheless be dragged away in handcuffs, presumably because she was near an item that was reported missing.

Johnson's humiliation was just beginning. She was taken to the 61st Precinct stationhouse, where she was strip-searched. Her mouth was searched. Hands were run all through her hair. She was made to squat, etc. No ring was found.

Case finally closed, right?

Not in this town. Not in this era. Johnson was fingerprinted. Her mug shot was taken. And she was handcuffed to a chair in the stationhouse, where she remained for several hours.

And despite the absence of any evidence whatsoever, she was charged with a crime—petty larceny, a Class-A misdemeanor.

Johnson is being represented by the Manhattan lawyer David Everett. He had her take a polygraph test, which she passed with no trouble. He went to see Mittleberg, who, according to Everett, "acknowledged that he never saw her take the ring."

Everett asked to view the store's videotape of Johnson. He said Mittleberg told him it no longer existed. He had recorded over it.

Meanwhile, the humiliation of Johnson is indelible, and the criminal charge, incredibly, is still pending.

(September 16, 1999)

A MOM'S VINDICATION

Celeste Goring-Johnson, the woman who was arrested, hauled away in handcuffs, and strip-searched because a Brooklyn jewelry store owner suspected she had stolen a diamond ring, will not be prosecuted.

"We are declining to prosecute based on our interview with the complaining witness in which it becomes clear that he did not see the accused take the ring," said Dennis Hawkins, the deputy district attorney in the office of Brooklyn D.A. Charles Hynes.

Johnson, whose ordeal has been described in this column, is a forty-two-year-old mother of three children who has never been in trouble with the law and who insisted all along that she did not take the ring. She was searched by police officers in the jewelry store and was forced to undergo a humiliating strip search at the 61st Precinct stationhouse.

"The ring was not recovered during any of the searches," said Hawkins.

Not only was the ring not found, it turns out that the police put potentially devastating information that cannot now be supported into the arrest report and an accompanying affidavit. The police paperwork said the owner of the jewelry store, Scott Mittleberg, had told police he saw Johnson take the ring from a countertop and slip it into the waistband of her skirt.

But Mr. Mittleberg says he never saw anything like that. He told investigators from the D.A.'s office and he told Johnson's attorney, David Everett, that he did not see Johnson take the ring, and he did not see her slip it into her waistband. He said he believed she had stolen the ring because she was the only one near the counter when he noticed that the ring was missing.

After Johnson was released from custody she contacted a lawyer and submitted to a lie-detector test, which she passed.

So how did the damaging information about an eyewitness account—information that could have resulted in a criminal conviction against an innocent woman—get into official police documents? Did the officer who signed the paperwork, Michael Guinan, deliberately falsify his report? Did he make the information up? Or did he just make an awful mistake?

Or, did the jewelry store owner lie to the police when they showed up at the scene, and then change his story when questioned later by the district attorney's office?

The deputy district attorney, Hawkins, said of the alleged theft: "We know now that the complaining witness is honestly saying, 'No, I didn't see it, but I thought it was her because she was the only person there when it was missing.'"

I asked Hawkins how he could square that with the specific charge in the police report that Mittleberg had seen Johnson slip the ring into her waistband.

"Miscommunication?" he said. "Misunderstanding? I just don't know."

This is a matter that should be investigated by both the police and the district attorney. If Mittleberg made a false accusation to the police, that's a crime. If the police deliberately falsified arrest reports, that's a crime. If the whole thing was a grotesque mistake that resulted in Johnson's being incarcerated and degraded over a period of some six hours, then a full public accounting and an apology should be made.

Marilyn Mode, the spokeswoman for the Police Department, said the matter would be looked into. She said of the jewelry store owner: "He told the police officer, apparently, that he did see her take it. We had no option but to proceed."

She then said she was angry about what she described as the "constant knocking of police officers." She said, "I don't know why we've gotten to the point where the civil rights of police officers have been suspended. That is the worst kind of broad-brush prejudice that we can have."

Everett said he is preparing a lawsuit against the city, charging that Johnson was falsely arrested and imprisoned and that her civil rights were violated.

Johnson, who is very religious, said she was "relieved" that the case was being dropped. But she said some of the damage cannot be undone. "My child saw her mother being dragged off in handcuffs by the police, which I'm sure has burned an image in her mind that she will have for the rest of her life. It's heartbreaking."

(September 20, 1999)

POLICE RESTRAINT

Rachel Ellen Ondersma, a seventeen-year-old high school senior, was stopped by the state police in Grand Rapids, Michigan, early on the morning of November 14, 1998. She had been driving erratically. When she failed a Breathalyzer test, the cops placed her under arrest.

An officer cuffed the girl's hands behind her, put her in the back-seat of a police cruiser, and locked the doors, leaving her alone. What happened after that was captured on a video camera mounted inside the vehicle. And while it would eventually be shown on the Fox television program *World's Wackiest Police Videos*, it was not funny.

The video camera showed a clear view through the windshield of the police cruiser. The microphone picked up the sound of Ondersma sobbing, and then the clink of the handcuffs as she began maneuvering to free herself. She apparently stepped through her arms so that her hands, still cuffed, were in front of her. She then climbed into the front seat of the cruiser, slid behind the wheel, and started the engine. As officers shouted, "Hey! Stop!" she roared off.

With the car hurtling along, tires squealing, Ondersma can be heard moaning, "What am I doing?" and "They are going to have to kill me."

I got a copy of the video and studied it, looking closely at the reactions of the police. Ondersma was almost immediately chased by troopers and officers from the Grand Rapids Police Department. At one intersection a Grand Rapids cop car approached head on. Thinking Ondersma would be forced to stop, the officers opened their doors and were about to hop out. But Ondersma careened into a left turn and sped off.

With several cars chasing her, the drunken teenager roared onto a freeway, where she was clocked at speeds that reached eighty miles per hour. At least two police cars got into the lane in front of her and slowed down while another closed in from the right. "Oh no!" cried Ondersma as she crashed into a concrete median on her left. She seemed boxed in. The video showed cops leaping from their cars and heading toward her.

Ondersma threw the cruiser into reverse, backed up, then lurched forward, plowing into one of the police cars. At that point gunfire can be heard as cops began shooting out her tires. The teenager would not stop. She backed up, then lurched forward again, hitting the cop car one more time. An officer had to leap out of the way to keep from being struck.

Somehow Ondersma, a clear and potentially fatal threat to anyone on the highway, managed yet again to get away. But this time, with at least two tires flat, she could no longer control the vehicle. She crashed into another concrete divider and finally was surrounded.

For me the most astonishing part of the video came next. Ondersma, upset, was pulled from the cruiser. She was not treated roughly. There was no cursing by the police, no ranting and raving, no evidence that the cops were particularly upset at all. One officer said to Ondersma: "Calm down, all right? I think you've caused enough trouble for today."

Every time I watched that video I thought about the incident on the New Jersey Turnpike in April 1998 in which four young men in a van were pulled over by state troopers. Three of the men were black and one was Hispanic. They were not drunk and they were not abusive. But their van did roll slowly backward, accidentally bumping the leg of one of the troopers and striking the police vehicle.

The state troopers pulled their weapons and opened fire. When the firing stopped, three of the four young men had been shot.

I wondered what would have happened if a young black guy had stolen the police cruiser in Grand Rapids and roared off, endangering lives and damaging property for mile after mile. And I wondered if the troopers on the New Jersey Turnpike would have opened fire on the minivan if its occupant had been a young white girl.

I asked Lieutenant Tom Hunt of the Michigan State Police why the troopers had exhibited what I found to be such admirable restraint when dealing with Rachel Ondersma.

He said: "They made the conscious decision to try to put the car out of commission instead of her out of commission. That's how we're trained here."

(May 20, 1999)

TRUTH, LIES, AND SUBTEXT

I've seen drunks, incompetents, and out-and-out lunatics in the newsrooms I've passed through over the years. I've seen plagiarizers, fiction writers, and reporters who felt it was beneath them to show up for work at all.

I remember a police captain who said of a columnist at the *Daily News*: "I didn't mind him makin' stuff up as long as I looked OK. But now he's startin' to tick me off."

I was at NBC when some geniuses decided it was a good idea to attach incendiary devices to a few General Motors pickup trucks to show that the trucks had a propensity to burst into flames. That became a scandal that grew into a conflagration that took down the entire power structure at NBC News.

I've seen schmoozers, snoozers, and high-powered losers in every venue I've been in. Most of these rogues, scoundrels, and miscreants were white because most of the staffers in America's mainstream newsrooms are white. What I haven't seen in all these years was the suggestion that any of these individuals fouled up—or were put into positions where they could foul up—because they were white.

Which brings us to the Jayson Blair scandal. Blair was a *New York Times* reporter who resigned after it was learned that his work contained fabrications and plagiarized passages on a monumental scale. The truth and Jayson Blair inhabited separate universes. If there was a blizzard raging, Blair could tell you with the straightest and friendliest of faces that the weather outside was sunny and warm.

Now this would be a juicy story under any circumstances. But Blair is black, so there is the additional spice of race, to which so many Americans are terminally addicted.

Listen up: the race issue in this case is as bogus as some of Jayson Blair's reporting.

Blair was a first-class head case who was given a golden opportunity and responded by spreading seeds of betrayal every place he went. He betrayed his readers. He betrayed his profession. He betrayed the editors who hired and promoted him. But there was no racial component to that betrayal, any more than there was a racial component to the many betrayals of Mike Barnicle, a columnist who was forced to resign from the *Boston Globe* in 1998 after years of complaints about his work. Although Barnicle is white, his journalistic sins have generally—and properly—been seen as the sins of an individual.

But the folks who delight in attacking anything black, or anything designed to help blacks, have pounced on the Blair story as evidence that there is something inherently wrong with the *Times*'s effort to diversify its newsroom, and beyond that, with the very idea of a commitment to diversity or affirmative action anywhere. And while these agitators won't admit it, the nasty subtext to their attack is that there is something inherently wrong with blacks.

Jayson Blair should have been yanked away from his computer long ago. There had been plenty of warnings. The failure to act on those warnings was a breakdown in management for which the paper is paying a heavy price. I don't want to hear that the devil—in this case a devil named diversity—was to blame.

The idea that blacks can get away with the journalistic equivalent of murder at the *Times* because they are black is preposterous.

There's a real shortage of black reporters, editors, and columnists at the *Times*. But the few who are here are doing fine and serious work day in and day out and don't deserve to be stigmatized by people who can see them only through the prism of a stereotype.

The problem with American newsrooms is too little diversity, not too much. Blacks have always faced discrimination and maddening double standards in the newsroom, and they continue to do so. So do women, Latinos, and many other groups that are not part of the traditional newsroom in-crowd.

So let's be real. Discrimination in the newsroom—in hiring, in the quality of assignments, and in promotions—is a much more pervasive problem than Jayson Blair's aberrant behavior. A black reporter told me angrily, "After hundreds of years in America, we are still on probation."

I agree. And the correct response is not to grow fainthearted or to internalize the views of those who wish you ill. The correct response is to strike back—as hard and as often as it takes.

(May 19, 2003)

10

THE PARTY OF LINCOLN

A SLICK MIX

Philadelphia

It was disheartening to see Colin Powell up there doing his bit to help mask the reality of the GOP, a party that since the 1960s has been relentlessly hostile to the interests of black Americans.

This was on the opening night of the Republican National Convention, but you couldn't tell whether you were at a GOP gathering or the Motown Review. The number of blacks paraded before a national television audience by this nearly all-white convention was incredible. The delegates are about 90 percent white, mostly male, and rigidly conservative. So it was a breathtaking exercise in hypocrisy for them to haul so many blacks before the cameras for the sole purpose of singing, dancing, preaching, and praising a party that has wanted no part of them.

General Powell used some of his time to urge the party to become more inclusive, and chastised it for opposing affirmative action. But he nevertheless was the featured performer in the cynical lineup of blacks and other minorities that was put together in a blatant effort to cast the party as something it is not. If you looked at the stage during this farce, and then turned and looked at the audience, you saw two entirely different worlds.

It's been like that all week—ethnic overkill to mask the party's lack of diversity. J. C. Watts, a black Republican congressman from Oklahoma, was harmonizing one moment with the Temptations, and singing the next with a gospel choir. Other entertainment was provided by rhythm and blues singers, dancing black children, and a fired-up preacher and his exultant congregation.

The makeover artists of the GOP put together a slick mix of race, religion, and culture and used it for all the wrong reasons. It was exploitive and demeaning.

The Republicans still aren't interested in blacks. They are simply trying to present a friendlier, more moderate face to white, middle-class swing voters who have been put off by the party's excesses over the past several years.

If the Republicans really wanted to embrace black voters (and not just black children at photo ops) they would honestly address such things as Dick Cheney's voting record; George W. Bush's campaign appearance at Bob Jones University; George Herbert Walker Bush's use of the disgraceful Willie Horton (let's-scare-the-white-folks) campaign ads; President Bush's cynical selection of Clarence Thomas for the Supreme Court; and the GOP's viciously antiblack southern strategy, which has been a divisive force in American politics for more than thirty years.

If the Republicans were serious they would reassess the many long years they spent attacking programs for children and the elderly and the sick, and demonizing Democrats and liberals for attempting to help minorities and the poor.

But they're not serious. They are engaged in a four-day charade, an exercise in duplicity that includes the shameless theft of the slogan "Leave No Child Behind," which was the registered trademark of the Children's Defense Fund, a favorite GOP target.

George W. Bush says he is a "different" kind of Republican. But different from what? We need to know what it was about the Republican Party of the last several decades that he thinks should be changed.

Does he think Republican policies need to change, or just that Republican candidates should hug more black children?

Republicans have long favored enormous tax cuts that served the dual purpose of providing bonanzas for the wealthy and bleeding the government of funds that could be used to help the less fortunate. Does Mr. Bush think that should change?

Most of the Republicans I spoke with found it difficult to think of anything substantive about their party that should change. Representative John Kasich, a conservative Ohio Republican who is chairman of the House Budget Committee, was typical. "We believe in less government," he said.

I asked what he thought Bush meant when he talked about a "different" kind of Republican.

Kasich looked uncomfortable. "I don't know," he said. "I don't know. You'd have to ask George Bush how he's different."

(August 3, 2000)

RACISM AND THE GOP

Strom Thurmond was screaming, and the crowd was going wild. "There's not enough troops in the army," he said, "to force the southern people to break down segregation and admit the nigra race into our theaters, into our swimming pools, into our schools, and into our homes."

That was in 1948. Thurmond, the governor of South Carolina at the time, was accepting the presidential nomination of the States' Rights Democratic Party, commonly known as the Dixiecrats. The only reason the party existed was to advance the cause of white supremacy. Thurmond and his rabid followers felt that the national Democratic Party wasn't racist enough.

Fast-forward to 2002. Thurmond, who was born in 1902, is still with us and, in some execrable corners of the Republican Party, so are his racist mid-century attitudes. He's a hero to Trent Lott, the Senate Republican leader, who's now stuck in a morass of controversy for his recent ringing endorsement of Thurmond's 1948 campaign.

But Lott is not the only culprit here. The Republican Party has become a haven for white racist attitudes and antiblack policies. The party of Lincoln is now a safe house for bigotry. It's the party of the southern strategies and the Willie Horton campaigns and Bob Jones University and the relentless and unconscionable efforts to disenfranchise black voters. For those who now think the Democratic Party is not racist enough, the answer is the GOP. And there are precious few voices anywhere in the GOP willing to step up and say that this is wrong.

Lott got into trouble when, at a party for Thurmond's hundredth birthday, he told the guests with great emphasis: "I want to say this about my state. When Strom Thurmond ran for president, we voted for him. We're proud of it. And if the rest of the country had followed our lead, we wouldn't have had all these problems over all these years either."

That's the Senate leader of the Republican Party speaking. And despite an apology squeezed out of him by the controversy, that's what Trent Lott believes. He made a similar comment in 1980, after Thurmond had delivered one of his frenzied speeches at a campaign rally for Ronald Reagan. Referring to Thurmond, Lott said: "You know, if we had elected this man thirty years ago, we wouldn't be in the mess we're in today."

Much of the current success of the Republican Party was built on the deliberate exploitation of very similar sentiments. One of the things I remember about Reagan's 1980 presidential run was that his first major appearance in the general election campaign was in Philadelphia, Mississippi, which just happened to be the place where three civil rights workers—Andrew Goodman, Michael Schwerner, and James Chaney—were murdered in 1964.

During that appearance, Reagan told his audience, "I believe in states' rights."

Enough said.

Whenever I think about that appearance I can't help also thinking about my friend Carolyn Goodman, who after all these years still grieves for the loss of her son, Andrew.

One of the controversies that arose during the Reagan presidency concerned Bob Jones University, a religious school in Greenville, South Carolina, that opposed the so-called mingling of the races. Interracial dating and marriage were forbidden. (The ban was lifted in March 2000.)

The GOP bond with Bob Jones was an intense one, despite the fact that a former head of the university, Bob Jones Jr., had engaged in an astonishing series of attacks on Catholics in the 1980s. "The papacy," he said, "is the religion of Antichrist and is a satanic system."

Still, Republican presidential wannabes and other big-time GOP leaders would stumble over each other year after shameful year to appear at the school. George W. Bush (whose brother Jeb and sister-in-law Columba would have been expelled from Bob Jones for having dared to fall in love and marry) was among the GOP biggies who appeared at the school while its racially discriminatory policies were in effect.

There are calls now for the ouster of Trent Lott as the Senate Republican leader. I say let him stay. He's a direct descendant of the Dixiecrats and a first-rate example of what much of his party has become.

Keep him in plain sight. His presence is instructive. As long as we keep in mind that it isn't only him.

(December 12, 2002)

BUSH'S NOT-SO-BIG TENT

George W. Bush, who has compiled the worst jobs creation record since Herbert Hoover, is now also the first president since Hoover to fail to meet with the NAACP during his entire term in office.

Bush and the leadership of the nation's oldest and largest civil rights organization get along about as well as the Hatfields and the McCoys. The president was invited to the group's convention in Philadelphia this week, but he declined.

That Bush thumbed his nose at NAACP officials is not the significant part of this story. The Julian Bonds and Kweisi Mfumes of the world can take care of themselves at least as well as Bush in the legalized gang fight called politics.

What is troubling is Bush's relationship with black Americans in general. He's very good at using blacks as political props. And the props are too often part of an exceedingly cynical production.

Four years ago, on the first night of the Republican convention, a parade of blacks was hauled before the television cameras (and the nearly all-white audience in the convention hall) to sing, to dance, to preach, and to praise a party that has been relentlessly hostile to the interests of blacks for half a century.

I wrote at the time that "you couldn't tell whether you were at the Republican National Convention or the Motown Review."

That exercise in modern-day minstrelsy was supposed to show that Mr. Bush was a new kind of Republican, a big-tent guy who would welcome a more diverse crowd into the GOP. That was fiction. It wasn't long before black voters would find themselves mugged in Florida, and soon after that Bush was steering the presidency into a hard-right turn.

Among the most important props of that 2000 campaign were black children. Bush could be seen hugging them at endless photo ops. He said a Bush administration would do great things for them. He promised to transform public education in America. He hijacked the trademarked slogan of the Children's Defense Fund, "Leave No Child Behind," and refashioned it for his own purposes. He pasted the new version, "No Child Left Behind," onto one of the signature initiatives of his presidency, a supposedly historic education reform act.

The only problem is that, to date, the act has been underfunded by $26 billion. A lot of those kids the president hugged have been left behind.

And why not? They can't do much for him. Michael Moore's *Fahrenheit 9/11* captured a telling presidential witticism. Bush, appearing before a well-heeled gathering in New York, says: "This is an impressive crowd: the haves and the have-mores. Some people call you the elite. I call you my base."

It wasn't really his base. He was in New York, after all. But the comment spoke volumes.

Bush said he was a different kind of Republican, but what black voters see are tax cuts for the very wealthy and underfunded public schools. What they see is an economy that sizzles for the haves and the have-mores, but a harrowing employment crisis for struggling blacks, especially black men. (When the Community Service Society looked at the proportion of the working-age population with jobs in New York City, it found that nearly half of all black men between the ages of sixteen and sixty-four were not working last year. That's a Depression-era statistic.)

In Florida, where the president's brother is governor, and Texas, where the president once was the governor, state officials have been pulling the plug on health coverage for low-income children. The president could use his considerable clout to put a stop to that sort of thing, but he hasn't.

And now we know that Florida was gearing up for a reprise of the election shenanigans of 2000. It took a court order to get the state to release a list of 48,000 suspected felons that was to be used to purge people from the voting rolls. It turned out that the list contained thousands of names of black people, who tend to vote Democratic, and hardly any names of Hispanics, who in Florida tend to vote Republican.

Once their "mistake" was caught, the officials scrapped the list.

Bush plans to address the Urban League convention in Detroit. That would be an excellent time for him to explain to an understandably skeptical audience why he campaigned one way—as a big-tent compassionate conservative—and governed another.

(July 16, 2004)

SUPPRESS THE VOTE?

The biggest story coming out of Florida in the summer of 2004 was the tragic devastation caused by the hurricanes that struck the state. But there's another story from Florida that deserves our attention. State police officers have gone into the homes of elderly black voters in Orlando and interrogated them as part of an odd "investigation" that has frightened many voters, intimidated elderly volunteers, and thrown a chill over efforts to get out the black vote in November.

The officers, from the Florida Department of Law Enforcement, which reports to Governor Jeb Bush, say they are investigating allegations of voter fraud that came up during the Orlando mayoral election in March. Officials refused to discuss details of the investigation, other than to say that absentee ballots are involved. They said they had no idea when the investigation might end, and acknowledged that it may continue right through the presidential election.

"We did a preliminary inquiry into those allegations and then we concluded that there was enough evidence to follow through with a full criminal investigation," said Geo Morales, a spokesman for the Department of Law Enforcement.

The state police officers, armed and in plain clothes, have questioned dozens of voters in their homes. Some of those questioned have been volunteers in get-out-the-vote campaigns.

I asked Morales in a telephone conversation to tell me what criminal activity had taken place.

"I can't talk about that," he said.

I asked if all the people interrogated were black.

"Well, mainly it was a black neighborhood we were looking at, yes," he said. He also said, "Most of them were elderly." When I asked why, he said, "That's just the people we selected out of a random sample to interview."

Back in the bad old days, some decades ago, when southern whites used every imaginable form of chicanery to prevent blacks from voting, blacks often fought back by creating voters leagues, which were organizations that helped to register, educate, and encourage black voters. It became a tradition that continues in many places, including Florida, today.

Not surprisingly, many of the elderly black voters who found themselves face-to-face with state police officers in Orlando are members of the Orange County League of Voters, which has been very successful in mobilizing the city's black vote.

The president of the Orange County League of Voters is Ezzie Thomas, who is seventy-three years old. With his demonstrated ability to deliver the black vote in Orlando, Thomas is a tempting target for supporters of George W. Bush in a state in which the black vote may well spell the difference between victory and defeat.

The vile smell of voter suppression is all over this so-called investigation by the Florida Department of Law Enforcement.

Joseph Egan, an Orlando lawyer who represents Thomas, said: "The Voters League has workers who go into the community to do voter registration, drive people to the polls, and help with absentee ballots. They are elderly women mostly. They get paid like one hundred dollars for four or five months' work, just to offset things like the cost of their gas. They see this political activity as an important contribution to their community. Some of the people in the community had never cast a ballot until the league came to their door and encouraged them to vote."

Now, said Egan, the fear generated by state police officers going into people's homes as part of an ongoing criminal investigation related to voting is threatening to undo much of the good work of the league. He said, "One woman asked me, 'Am I going to go to jail now because I voted by absentee ballot?' "

According to Egan, "People who have voted by absentee ballot for years are refusing to allow campaign workers to come to their homes. And volunteers who have participated for years in assisting people, particularly the elderly or handicapped, are scared and don't want to risk a criminal investigation."

Florida is a state that's very much in play in the presidential election. A heavy-handed state police investigation that throws a blanket of fear over thousands of black voters can only help President Bush.

The long and ugly tradition of suppressing the black vote is alive and thriving in the Sunshine State.

(August 16, 2004)

VOTING WHILE BLACK

The smell of voter suppression coming out of Florida is getting stronger. It turns out that a Florida Department of Law Enforcement investigation, in which state troopers have gone into the homes of elderly black voters in Orlando in a bizarre hunt for evidence of election fraud, is being conducted despite a finding by the department in May 2004 "that there was no basis to support the allegations of election fraud."

State officials have said that the investigation, which has already frightened many voters and intimidated elderly volunteers, is in response to allegations of voter fraud involving absentee ballots that came up during the Orlando mayoral election in March 2004. But the department considered that matter closed last spring, according to a letter from the office of Guy Tunnell, the department's commissioner, to Lawson Lamar, the state attorney in Orlando, who would be responsible for any criminal prosecutions.

The letter, dated May 13, said:

"We received your package related to the allegations of voter fraud during the 2004 mayoral election. This dealt with the manner in which absentee ballots were either handled or collected by campaign staffers for Mayor Buddy Dyer. Since this matter involved an elected official, the allegations were forwarded to F.D.L.E.'s Executive Investigations in Tallahassee, Florida.

"The documents were reviewed by F.D.L.E., as well as the Florida Division of Elections. It was determined that there was no basis to support the allegations of election fraud concerning these absentee ballots. Since there is no evidence of criminal misconduct involving Mayor Dyer, the Florida Department of Law Enforcement considers this matter closed."

Well, it's not closed. And department officials have said that the letter sent out in May was never meant to indicate that the "entire" investigation was closed. Since the letter went out, state troopers have gone into the homes of forty or fifty black voters, most of them elderly, in what the department describes as a criminal investigation. Many longtime Florida observers have said the use of state troopers for this type of investigation is extremely unusual, and it has caused a storm of controversy.

The officers were armed and in plain clothes. For elderly African American voters, who remember the terrible torment inflicted on blacks who tried to vote in the South in the 1950s and '60s, the sight of armed police officers coming into their homes to interrogate them about voting is chilling indeed.

One woman, who is in her mid-seventies and was visited by two officers, said in an affidavit: "After entering my house, they asked me if they could take their jackets off, to which I answered yes. When they removed their jackets, I noticed they were wearing side arms. . . . And I noticed an ankle holster on one of them when they sat down."

Though apprehensive, she answered all of their questions. But for a lot of voters, the emotional response to the investigation has gone beyond apprehension to outright fear.

"These guys are using these intimidating methods to try and get these folks to stay away from the polls in the future," said Eugene Poole, president of the Florida Voters League, which tries to increase black voter participation throughout the state. "And you know what? It's working. One woman said, 'My God, they're going to put us in jail for nothing.' I said, 'That's not true.'"

State officials deny that their intent was to intimidate black voters. Tunnell, who was handpicked by Governor Jeb Bush to head the Department of Law Enforcement, said in a statement: "Instead of having them come to the F.D.L.E. office, which may seem quite imposing, our agents felt it would be a more relaxed atmosphere if they visited the witnesses at their homes."

When I asked a spokesman for Tunnell, Tom Berlinger, about the letter indicating that the allegations were without merit, he replied that the intent of the letter had not been made clear by Joyce Dawley, a regional director who drafted and signed the letter for Tunnell.

"The letter was poorly worded," said Berlinger. He said he spoke to Dawley about the letter, and she told him, "God, I wish I would have made that more clear." What Dawley meant to say, said Berlinger, was that it did not appear that Mayor Dyer himself was criminally involved.

(August 20, 2004)

A CHILL IN FLORIDA

The state police investigation into get-out-the-vote activities by blacks in Orlando, Florida, fits perfectly with the political aims of Governor Jeb Bush and the Republican Party.

The Republicans were stung in the 2000 presidential election when Al Gore became the first Democrat since 1948 to carry Orange County, of which Orlando is the hub. He could not have carried the county without the strong support of black voters, many of whom cast absentee ballots.

The GOP was stung again in 2003 when Buddy Dyer, a Democrat, was elected mayor of Orlando. He won a special election to succeed Glenda Hood, a three-term Republican who was appointed Florida secretary of state by Governor Bush. Dyer was reelected last March. As with Gore, the black vote was an important factor.

These two election reverses have upset Republicans in Orange County and statewide. Moreover, the anxiety over Democratic gains in Orange County is entwined with the very real fear among party stalwarts that Florida might go for John Kerry in the 2004 presidential election.

It is in this context that two of the ugliest developments of the current campaign season should be viewed.

"A Democrat can't win a statewide election in Florida without a high voter turnout—both at the polls and with absentee ballots—of African Americans," said a man who is close to the Republican establishment in Florida but asked not to be identified. "It's no secret that the name of the game for Republicans is to restrain that turnout as much as possible. Black votes are Democratic votes, and there are a lot of them in Florida."

The two ugly developments—both focused on race—were the heavy-handed investigation by Florida state troopers of black get-out-the-vote efforts in Orlando, and the state's blatant attempt to purge blacks from voter rolls through the use of a flawed list of supposed felons that contained the names of thousands of African Americans and, conveniently, very few Hispanics.

Florida is one of only a handful of states that bar convicted felons from voting, unless they successfully petition to have their voting rights restored. The state's "felon purge" list had to be abandoned by Glenda Hood, the secretary of state (and, yes, former mayor of Orlando), after it became known that the flawed list would target blacks but not Hispanics, who are more likely in Florida to vote Republican. The list also contained the names of thousands of people, most of them black, who should not have been on the list at all.

Hood, handpicked by Governor Bush to succeed the notorious Katherine Harris as secretary of state, was forced to admit that the felons list was a mess. She said the problems were unintentional. What clearly was intentional was the desire of Hood and Governor Bush to keep the list secret. It was disclosed only as a result of lawsuits filed under Florida's admirable Sunshine law.

Meanwhile, the sending of state troopers into the homes of elderly black voters in Orlando was said by officials to be a response to allegations of voter fraud in last March's mayoral election. But the investigation went forward despite findings in the spring that appeared to show that the allegations were unfounded.

Why go forward anyway? Well, consider that the prolonged investigation dovetails exquisitely with that crucial but unspoken mission of the GOP in Florida: to keep black voter turnout as low as possible. The interrogation of elderly black men and women in their homes has already frightened many voters and intimidated elderly get-out-the-vote volunteers.

The use of state troopers to zero in on voter turnout efforts is highly unusual, if not unprecedented, in Florida. But the head of the Florida Department of Law Enforcement, Guy Tunnell, who was also handpicked by Governor Bush, has been unfazed by the mounting criticism of this use of the state police. His spokesmen have said a "person of interest" in the investigation is Ezzie Thomas, a seventy-three-year-old black man who just happens to have done very well in turning out the African American vote.

From the GOP perspective, it doesn't really matter whether any-one is arrested in the Orlando investigation, or even if a crime was committed. The idea, in Orange County and elsewhere, is to send a chill through the democratic process, suppressing opposing votes by whatever means are available.

(August 23, 2004)

PART FIVE

———

THE AMERICA OF
GEORGE W. BUSH

11

COMPASSIONATE CONSERVATISM

PUNISHING THE POOR

If you want to see "compassionate" conservatism in action, take a look at Mississippi, a state that is solidly in the red category (strong for Bush) and committed to its long tradition of keeping the poor and the unfortunate in as ragged and miserable a condition as possible.

How's this for compassion? Mississippi has approved the deepest cut in Medicaid eligibility for senior citizens and the disabled that has ever been approved anywhere in the United States. The new policy will end Medicaid eligibility for some 65,000 low-income senior citizens and people with severe disabilities—people like Traci Alsup, a thirty-six-year-old mother of three who was left a quadriplegic after a car accident.

The cut in eligibility for seniors and the disabled was the most dramatic component of a stunning rollback of services in Mississippi's Medicaid program. The rollback was initiated by the Republican-controlled state senate and Mississippi's new governor,

Haley Barbour, a former chairman of the national Republican Party. When he signed the new law, on May 26, Barbour complained about taxpayers having to "pay for free health care for people who can work and take care of themselves and just choose not to."

The governor is free to characterize the victims of the cuts as deadbeats if he wants to. Others have described them as patients suffering from diseases like cerebral palsy and Alzheimer's, and people incapacitated by diabetes or heart disease or various forms of paralysis, and individuals struggling with the agony of schizophrenia or other forms of serious mental illness.

The 65,000 seniors and disabled individuals who will lose their Medicaid eligibility have incomes so low they effectively have no money to pay for their health care. The new law coldly reduces the maximum income allowed for an individual to receive Medicaid in Mississippi from an impecunious $12,569 per year to a beggarly $6,768.

Many of the elderly recipients have Medicare coverage, but their Medicare benefits in most cases will not come close to meeting their overall requirements—which include huge prescription drug bills, doctor visits, and often long-term care.

According to the Mississippi Health Advocacy Program, which is coordinating an effort to somehow maintain the Medicaid coverage: "The people affected are low-income retirees now subsisting on Social Security or other pension benefits and people who have permanent disabilities that prevent them from being able to work."

Jane Powell, a seventy-five-year-old Jackson resident who fears she will be lopped off the program, told reporters she has ten different prescriptions for a variety of ailments, including heart disease and osteoporosis. She worried aloud that if the law is not changed she might someday be found "dead in the street."

While Barbour insists he won't reconsider the matter, a backlash is developing against the cutbacks, which are extreme even for Mississippi.

The Democratic-controlled House opposed the cuts all along but gave in at the last minute. Democratic leaders insisted they were coerced. Technical aspects of the state's Medicaid law have to be renewed every year by the legislature. If they are not, control of the entire Medicaid program can go to the governor. The Democrats said they were afraid that under those circumstances Barbour would have cut services even more.

At the time the bill was signed, the House speaker, Billy McCoy, called it "an absolute sin on society."

Now, with public clamor growing, the House (including most of the Republican members) is attempting to have the law reversed.

Representative Steve Holland, chairman of the House Public Health and Human Services Committee, told me this week: "My heart has been broken and crushed and stomped to pieces over this. I knew this was wrong." He added, "This governor is my friend, but he's a Republican and his mantra is to starve this beast of big government in Mississippi."

I asked Holland if he thought Mississippi had a big government.

"Good God, no!" he said.

(June 11, 2004)

OBLIVIOUS IN D.C.

"Of all the challenges we face, none is more troubling than the fact that thousands of Oregonians—many of them children—don't have enough to eat. Oregon has the highest hunger rate in the nation."

—GOVERNOR TED KULONGOSKI,
in his State of the State address

Those who still believe that the policies of the Bush administration will set in motion some kind of renaissance in Iraq should take a look at what's happening to the quality of life for ordinary Americans here at home.

The president, buoyed by the bountiful patronage of the upper classes, seems indifferent to the increasingly harsh struggles of the working classes and the poor. As Bush moves from fund-raiser to fund-raiser, building the mother of all campaign stockpiles, states from coast to coast are reaching depths of budget desperation unseen since the Great Depression. The disconnect here is becoming surreal. The National Governors Association recently let it be known that the fiscal crisis that has crippled one state after another is worsening, not getting better.

Taxes have been raised. Services have been cut. And the rainy-day funds accumulated in the 1990s have been consumed. If help does not materialize soon—in the form of assistance from the federal government or a sharp turnaround in the economy—some states will fall into a fiscal abyss.

That already seems to be happening in places like California, which has been driven to its knees by a two-year $38.8 billion budget gap, and Oregon, which has seen drastic cuts in public school services and the withholding of potentially lifesaving medicine from seriously ill patients.

Most states have been unable to protect even the most fundamental services from damaging budget cuts.

"Few states have succeeded in exempting high-priority programs such as K-12 education, Medicaid, higher education, public safety, or aid to cities and towns," according to the compilers of the *Fiscal Survey of States*, a report produced jointly by the governors' association and the National Association of State Budget Officers.

Scott Pattison, director of the budget officers' group, said, "If economic conditions remain stagnant or worsen, and if budget shortfalls continue next year, the states will have exhausted many of their options for countering a weak economy."

The budget crisis in California, where an unpopular Democratic governor is politically paralyzed and the Republicans in the state legislature refuse to consider raising taxes, is potentially catastrophic.

Jack Kyser, a public policy economist in Los Angeles told the Associated Press: "People are nervous. There's a real chance for a meltdown that could have rippling effects throughout the nation. This is something of a different magnitude than we've seen before."

The governors' association called the fiscal survey the most accurate gauge of the health of state budgets. Its discouraging findings were released as the president was preparing a fund-raising swing that added millions more to his campaign stockpile, and as the Internal Revenue Service was reporting that the nation's richest taxpayers were accumulating an even greater share of the nation's wealth.

Some Americans are missing meals and going without their medicine, while others are enjoying a surge in already breathtaking levels of wealth. So what are we doing? We're cutting aid to the former while showering government largesse on the latter.

There's a reason those campaign millions keep coming and coming and coming.

A *New York Times* article noted that the wealthiest 400 taxpayers accounted for more than 1 percent of all the income in the United States in 2000, "more than double their share just eight years earlier."

The influence of the wealthy has always been great, but it hasn't always been so cruel. Especially in the past six or seven decades there were many powerful political and civic leaders who looked out for the interests of the less fortunate and pressed their claims for treatment that was reasonably fair.

That's changed. The Bush juggernaut, at least for the time being, is rolling over everything that dares to get in its way. And fairness is not something it is concerned about.

(June 30, 2003)

A STRANGE BUDGET CUT

Say it ain't so, Mr. President.

You might think that with the country gearing up for war this would be the wrong time—absolutely the worst time—to cut federal school aid for the children of men and women in the armed forces.

Nobody would do that, right? Right?

Alas.

Undeterred by the anxiety and hardships faced by youngsters whose parents may be heading overseas, and perhaps into combat, President Bush has proposed substantial cuts in the government's Impact Aid program, which provides badly needed funds to school districts that have a significant number of students from military families.

The program was established during the Truman administration. When a school district is in an area that has military installations or other types of federal property, it is cut off from a range of revenue sources—residential, business, and industrial property taxes, for example—that would have been available if the land and facilities were privately owned and developed. The districts are still obligated, however, to provide schooling for children whose parents are stationed or work at such facilities.

The idea of Impact Aid is to at least partially offset this revenue shortfall. In school districts that serve a large number of military families, Impact Aid is a crucial component of the annual budget.

Case in point: the Virginia Beach public schools. The school system has students whose parents are assigned to Fort Story, the Little Creek Naval Amphibious Base, the Oceana Naval Air Station, and other military installations. It receives about $12 million in Impact Aid. President Bush's budget proposal would cut that by more than half—an estimated $7.5 million, according to the district's superintendent, Dr. Timothy Jenney.

"That would be fairly devastating for us," Dr. Jenney said in an interview. "We're very lean with our operating funds, the lowest per pupil in the area, and certainly well below the state average. So we're not flush with money to begin with. And with the economy right now, people are not predisposed to increasing their taxes."

Under Bush's budget proposal, Impact Aid would continue for youngsters whose parents live on a military base, but not for those whose families live off base. This is a specious distinction that does not take into account the overall deficit in tax revenues and the special needs of military youngsters.

The Virginia Beach school system has more than 26,000 children from military families, the vast majority of them off base. And like military youngsters everywhere, they are living through a traumatic period.

"There's a fair amount of anxiety among our children," said Jenney, "especially at the elementary level, from the kids whose parents are now deployed, or those who hear that their mom or dad has been called up and the deployment is imminent. So we've had to ratchet up all of our comprehensive services—psychological and guidance services—to work with our parents and the community. It's been a burden."

In February 2003 a gung-ho President Bush stood before thousands of sailors at a naval station near Jacksonville, Florida, and declared, "In this challenging period, great tasks lie ahead for the navy and for our entire military."

If that's so, how do you then turn around and tell your military personnel: oh, by the way, we're going to cut the financial support we've been providing for your kids in school?

Virginia Beach is just one of many districts across the country that will be hit hard if the president's proposed cuts actually take effect. They would have to make up tens of millions of dollars in lost federal aid.

Presidents eager for budget savings have frequently proposed cuts in Impact Aid. Congress has almost always resisted. What makes Bush's proposal so potentially devastating is that it comes when he is marshaling the nation for war, when the federal government is running up record budget deficits, when most states are struggling with huge budget deficits of their own, when school districts across the country are already suffering financially, and when both houses of Congress are controlled by the president's party.

Who could imagine that in a wartime atmosphere we would consider leaving the children of the military behind?

(February 20, 2003)

POSTSCRIPT

A strenuous last-ditch effort by a group of U.S. senators that included Edward M. Kennedy managed to derail the president's proposed cuts in the Impact Aid program.

SICK STATE BUDGETS, SICK KIDS

While headlines continue to tell us how great the economy is doing, states across the United States are pulling the plug on desperately needed health coverage for low-income Americans, including about a half-million children.

Even as the Bush administration continues its bizarre quest for ever more tax cuts, the states, which by law have to balance their budgets, are cutting vital social programs so deeply that tragic consequences are inevitable.

The cruel reality is that Americans at the top are thriving at the expense of the well-being of those at the bottom and, increasingly, in the middle.

A new report by the Center on Budget and Policy Priorities shows that thirty-four states have made potentially devastating cuts over the past two years in public health insurance programs, including Medicaid and the very successful children's health insurance program known as CHIP. More cuts are expected this year.

"Almost half of those losing health coverage (490,000 to 650,000 people) are children," the report says. "Substantial numbers of low-income parents, seniors, people with disabilities, childless adults and immigrants are also losing coverage. Cutbacks of this depth in health insurance coverage for low-income families and individuals are unprecedented."

The worst of the cuts are in Texas. "The Lone Star State has adopted deep cutbacks in its State Children's Health Insurance Program that will cause about 160,000 children—one-third of its SCHIP caseload—to lose coverage," the report says.

Texas is also making Medicaid available to fewer pregnant women, a dangerous move that increases the number of women without coverage for prenatal care and the actual deliveries. "All told," the report says, "Texas is eliminating coverage for between 344,000 and 494,000 children and adults. Census data showed that, even before these changes, the percentage of people who were uninsured was higher in Texas than in any other state."

A loss of health coverage frequently leads to a reluctance to seek needed care. "In poor or low-income families, where there is not a lot of disposable income, people will avoid going to the doctor or getting a prescription," said Leighton Ku, one of the authors of the report.

"Certain diseases can then become much more severe. With children, it's likely that they won't get treatment for ear infections, asthma, diabetes—conditions that can ultimately lead to hospitalization."

When treatment can no longer be avoided, the financial consequences can be ruinous. Medical expenses are one of the leading causes of bankruptcy in the United States.

Officials at the Center on Budget and Policy Priorities noted the case of a woman in St. Louis who works but whose annual income is below the poverty line. Under eligibility rules in effect until eighteen months ago, she would have qualified for Medicaid. Under the new rules, she does not.

The woman became ill and was told upon her release from the hospital to seek follow-up care. But without any health insurance, her medical bills have been overwhelming. According to the center, "The woman has occasional abdominal pain but is not getting any treatment. She intends to declare bankruptcy because she cannot pay the $47,000 she owes in medical bills, but so far has been unable to save the funds needed to pay for a bankruptcy filing."

People caught in this kind of squeeze often find themselves "sicker, much poorer, or both," said Robert Greenstein, the center's director.

It seems extremely strange that in the United States of America, the richest, most powerful nation in the history of the world, we are going backward in the twenty-first century in our ability to provide the most fundamental kinds of health care to ordinary people, including children.

The health insurance cutbacks would have been even worse if not for the $20 billion in emergency state aid that was reluctantly approved by the Bush administration and the Republican-led Congress last year. Despite the economic upturn, states are still struggling. They face a collective budget deficit of $40 billion to $50 billion for the coming fiscal year, and there is little sentiment among Republican leaders in Washington for another round of fiscal relief.

Maybe the nation itself needs a doctor. Shoving low-income people, including children, off the health care rolls at a time when the economy is allegedly booming is a sure sign of some kind of sickness in the society.

(January 9, 2004)

HEAVY LIFTING

He's at it again.

President Bush traveled to Nashville to talk about, among other things, compassion, which is a topic this president probably should leave alone. Bush's idea of compassion tends to send a shiver of dread through those who are disadvantaged.

But there he was in Nashville at the National Religious Broadcasters Convention, exhorting his audience to "rally the armies of compassion so that we can change America one heart, one soul at a time."

The president said religious organizations had a responsibility to assist the poor and those who are suffering, and to help alleviate the "artificial divisions" of race and economics.

"I welcome faith to help solve the nation's deepest problems," he said.

If religious leaders take up the challenge they will have to do some awfully heavy lifting, because Bush's domestic policies—instead of easing suffering—are all but guaranteed to provide an ever-swelling stream of people in need of help.

Everywhere you turn, support programs for the poor, the ill, the disabled, and the elderly are under attack. Children's services are being battered. As Bush smiles and talks about compassion, funding for programs large and small is being squeezed, cut back, eliminated.

The day after Bush's upbeat speech to the religious broadcasters, the *New York Times*'s Robert Pear revealed that the administration was proposing a change in federal law that would result in rent increases for thousands of poor people receiving housing aid.

The administration has proposed a restructuring of Medicare that would curtail, rather than enhance, delivery of health services to the elderly.

In the $2.2 trillion budget that Bush sent to Congress last week was an unconscionable proposal that would eliminate after-school programs for 500,000 children. In the arena of bad ideas, that one's a champion. It would result in not just hardship, but tragedy. For one thing, the peak hours for juvenile crime are three p.m. to eight p.m., with the biggest, most dangerous burst coming in the very first hour after school. That is also the time of day when most teenage girls become pregnant.

Bush has proposed cuts in juvenile delinquency programs, public housing assistance, children's health insurance, and on and on. He's even undermined the funding for his own highly touted school reform program, the No Child Left Behind Act.

Senator Edward Kennedy, who had worked closely with the president on the school reform legislation, said yesterday, "As soon as the klieg lights were off and the bunting came down, the Bush administration turned its back on school reform and America's children."

Looming over this calculated assault on programs of crucial importance to millions of Americans is Bush's colossal accumulation of tax cuts for the wealthy and an endless mountain range of federal budget deficits. The ideologues on the right are close to realizing their dream of crippling social services by starving the government of revenues.

Dr. J. Lawrence Aber, director of the National Center for Children in Poverty, at Columbia University, said yesterday:

"These cuts are tearing at what was emerging as a bipartisan consensus at the end of the last administration that the unfinished agenda on welfare reform was to create the work and family supports necessary to continue to help people move from welfare to work."

Tip O'Neill once said of Ronald Reagan, "He has no concern, no regard, no care for the little man of America."

George W. Bush is making the Gipper look like a softy.

Policies that affect the poor and working poor seldom get sustained attention. In an atmosphere of terror and impending war, Bush's approach to social services is getting even shorter shrift than usual. The policies he is attempting to put in place would largely overturn the notion we've had of a federal responsibility for programs to help struggling Americans. Bush would turn much of that responsibility over to the states, which are struggling with backbreaking budget problems of their own that are forcing drastic reductions in state services.

The collective result would be a long-term abandonment of the most needy among us. It's difficult to square that with the idea of compassion, conservative or otherwise.

(February 13, 2003)

NOT SO FRIVOLOUS

Alliance, Ohio

President Bush traveled to Youngstown, Ohio, to talk about health care, and before long he was reprising his complaint about "junk and frivolous" malpractice suits, which he said are discouraging good doctors from practicing medicine.

As he often does, the president called for reforms to make it more difficult for patients to seek compensation and to restrict the amount of damages that could be paid to those who prove they have been harmed. To bolster his argument Bush introduced a local doctor, Compton Girdharry, to an audience at Youngstown State University. Dr. Girdharry, an obstetrician/gynecologist, said he had been driven from a practice of twenty-one years by the high cost of malpractice insurance.

The president praised Dr. Girdharry and thanked him for his "compassion."

If Bush was looking for an example of a doctor who was victimized by frivolous lawsuits, Dr. Girdharry was not a great choice. Since the early 1990s, he has settled lawsuits and agreed to the payment of damages in a number of malpractice cases in which patients suffered horrible injuries.

"It's been four years since my son passed away, and I don't feel any stronger or any happier than the day I lost him," said Lisa Vitale, whose suit against Dr. Girdharry and a hospital was settled out of court.

During an interview in her home in Alliance, Vitale said she went into Alliance Community Hospital on the morning of August 17, 1993, for the delivery of her second child.

Her first delivery had been by Caesarean section, but Vitale said she was told that a vaginal delivery this time would not be a problem. While she was in the delivery room, however, the fetal monitoring strip was not properly checked and, she said, she was left alone and in pain for long periods. Dr. Girdharry stopped by around six p.m. and then went to dinner.

No one noticed that the baby was in serious distress.

Dr. Girdharry blamed the ensuing tragedy on the nurse. Vitale, he told me, "was being monitored by a nurse who was what they call a casual part-time nurse, who was not very well trained in reading fetal monitor strips."

By the time he was called back from dinner, he said, it was "too late" to take the steps, including a Caesarean delivery, that might have prevented permanent injury. The baby was born with severe brain damage. He was unable even to drink from a bottle. He lived six years and four months, requiring nursing care the entire time.

Judy Mays, another patient of Dr. Girdharry, delivered a son by Caesarean section on March 26, 1999. The baby was fine. But, as alleged in a suit filed by Mays, when the incision was closed, a sponge with a cord and a ring attached to it was left inside her.

Mays said she complained repeatedly to Dr. Girdharry about the pain she experienced, which at times was incapacitating. "When I brought it to the doctor's attention," she said, "he told me, 'Well, you just had major surgery. You've got to heal.'"

After four and a half agonizing months, Mays felt a bulging growth beneath the skin, "about the size of a grapefruit."

She was petrified, she said, thinking it was a tumor. She said an associate of Dr. Girdharry ordered tests, including a CAT scan. The sponge was spotted, but by that time it had adhered to her internal organs and her intestines were surrounding it.

Dr. Girdharry told me he began operating to remove the sponge but found the damage was worse than he had expected. Another surgeon was called in to complete the surgery.

Mays said she learned after the surgery that part of her large and small intestines had been removed, and that she probably would have died if the sponge had stayed inside her for another month. The surgery, she said, has left her with a variety of permanent ailments.

These are just two of the cases settled by Dr. Girdharry, who told me that his appearance in Youngstown with President Bush was "a dream come true."

A White House spokesman said the president had not been aware of the problems in Dr. Girdharry's background. "Had this doctor provided that information," the spokesman said, "he would not have been at that event."

(June 18, 2004)

BLISS AND BIGOTRY

I wanted to see this threat to the very foundation of civilization close up.

"We met over a noodle kugel that I made that she liked," said Deborah Gar Reichman.

I nodded. Reichman broke into a wide smile and moved forward in her chair, warming to the topic: her engagement to Shelley Curnow.

I had dropped by their third-floor walk-up in the Carroll Gardens neighborhood of Brooklyn. Very frankly, the two women did not look like revolutionaries. "We're worrying about where to register and arguing with our parents over the guests they want to invite," Reichman said.

President Bush and others are adamant in their contention that allowing two men or two women to wed would imperil the institution of marriage, which Bush described as "the most fundamental institution of civilization." The hard-liners on this issue seem convinced that something awful will be unleashed if gays are allowed to walk down the aisle and exchange vows of everlasting love. The president said the nation "must enact a constitutional amendment to protect marriage in America."

I kept staring at Reichman and Curnow, trying to locate the threat that others perceive in relationships like theirs. But they never came across as menacing. They just looked happy.

"We've been together almost six years now," Reichman said. "We had big crushes on each other right from the beginning."

"We started planning our wedding a year ago," Curnow said.

"We had no idea there was any chance that it might be legal," Reichman said. "We just found a place that we really liked, and it happened to be in Massachusetts. Of course, we want to be legally married. But that issue was never going to stop us. We wanted to have a wedding. We wanted to celebrate with our family and friends the way all our other friends have done, and the way that's been a tradition in our families.

"My family and I wanted to have a Jewish ceremony, and Shelley's OK with that. We found a rabbi that's going to declare us married in the Jewish faith."

"The state sanction is kind of an extra layer, if you will," said Curnow. "If it doesn't happen, we'll still have our wedding."

In a world beset by ignorance and poverty and suffering, a world wracked with wars and terror attacks and ethnic strife of every kind, it seems crazy to be twisting ourselves into knots over the desire of good men and women to transcend the prison of themselves and affirm their love for one another by marrying.

That kind of desire is a good thing, isn't it?

And those of you who are already married, tell the truth: the marriage of Deborah Reichman and Shelley Curnow (planned for May 22) won't make your marriage any weaker, will it?

We should rein in the combative rhetoric on this matter—the references to the "defense" of marriage, the "protection" of the institution, the "threat" to civilization. No one is waging war on marriage. It's just the opposite. This is all about people who are longing to embrace it.

"People talk about the marriage penalty," said Mike Rutkowski, a resident of Yardley, Pennsylvania, who married Tim Harper twenty years ago in a ceremony that is not legally recognized. "I would gladly pay the marriage penalty for the benefits that go with it."

Rutkowski is a grant coordinator, and Harper is a biochemist. They met twenty-two years ago in a church choir.

The opponents of gay marriage are on the wrong side of history. The interests of civilization are not served by driving mature love underground. And the interests of the United States, which is supposed to be the quintessence of a free society, are not served by enshrining bigotry in law.

The other day I saw a photo on my assistant's computer screen of two women in wedding dresses: Joanna Tessler, a Manhattan real estate agent, and Nicoletta Sellas, a psychology intern at the Bronx Psychiatric Center. Their arms are raised high in the air, and they are dancing joyfully in the aftermath of their marriage ceremony in Miami on Valentine's Day. It's an absolutely beautiful photo. The wedding guests are laughing and applauding.

"Bliss" would have been an appropriate caption. Why anyone would want to turn the people in that picture into outlaws is beyond me.

(February 27, 2004)

STOLEN KISSES

In the film *Cinema Paradiso* a priest previews each movie that is to be shown in a small Italian town and orders the removal of all kissing scenes. Near the end of the film, the main character, a man named Salvatore who had been a small boy at the time the priest exercised his powers of censorship, is given a film reel in which all the deleted kisses have been collected and turned into a montage. He watches, profoundly moved, as one couple after another gives physical expression to their mutual love.

In the magic of moviemaking we can sometimes recapture the intimacy that is lost to misguided and intolerant customs and policies. Real life is another matter.

In the United States, many people are still uncomfortable with the idea of two men holding hands (unless it's in a football huddle) or two women kissing. Sex between people of the same gender remains a major taboo. And the notion of gay marriage, viewed as an abomination by a huge swath of the electorate, is threatening to become a decisive element in the presidential campaign.

In a country that is quick to celebrate the rights of the individual and the ideals of freedom, real tolerance is often hard to come by.

One of the particularly absurd arguments against allowing gays to marry is that such a lapse would send us skidding down that dreadful slope to legalization of incest, polygamy, bestiality, and so forth.

In an interview last spring with the Associated Press, Senator Rick Santorum, a Pennsylvania Republican, said we'll be on that slope if the courts even tolerate homosexual acts. Referring to the U.S. Supreme Court's consideration of a challenge to a Texas anti-sodomy law, the senator said, "And if the Supreme Court says that you have a right to [gay] consensual sex within your home, then you have the right to bigamy, you have the right to polygamy, you have the right to incest, you have the right to adultery. You have the right to anything."

That line of thinking reminded me of a passage in Randall Kennedy's book *Interracial Intimacies: Sex, Marriage, Identity, and Adoption.* In a nineteenth-century miscegenation case, a black man in Tennessee was charged with criminal fornication. The man's defense was that the woman, who was white, was his wife. They had been married lawfully in another state.

"That argument," writes Kennedy, "was rejected by the Tennessee Supreme Court, which maintained that its acceptance would necessarily lead to condoning 'the father living with his daughter . . . in lawful wedlock,' " and "the Turk being allowed to 'establish his harem at the doors of the capitol.' "

We have a tendency to prohibit things simply because we don't like them. Because they don't appeal to us. They don't feel quite right. Or we've never done it that way before. And when things don't feel quite right, when they make us uncomfortable, we often leap, with no basis in fact, to the conclusion that they are unnatural, immoral, degenerate, against the will of God.

And then the persecution begins.

I find a special irony in the high level of opposition among blacks to gay marriage. When the U.S. Supreme Court, in the deliciously titled *Loving v. Virginia* case, finally ruled that laws prohibiting interracial marriage were unconstitutional, sixteen states, including Virginia, still had such laws on the books. That was in 1967, at the height of the war in Vietnam and three years after the Beatles had launched their spectacular assault on American-style rock 'n' roll.

In the *Loving* case a mixed-race married couple was charged with violating Virginia's Racial Integrity Act. The judge who sentenced the couple wrote: "Almighty God created the races white, black, yellow, malay and red, and he placed them on separate continents. And but for the interference with his arrangements there would be no cause for [interracial] marriages. The fact that he separated the races shows that he did not intend for the races to mix."

Now we're told that he doesn't want gays to marry. That there is something unnatural about the whole idea of men marrying men and women marrying women. That it's abhorrent to much of the population, just as interracial marriages were (and to many, still are) abhorrent.

We need to get a grip.

(March 1, 2004)

A WAR AGAINST THE CITIES

Amid all the muscle-flexing at the Democratic National Convention in Boston ("my homeland security platform is bigger than yours"), it was impossible to hear more than the merest hint or offhand whisper about the demoralizing decline in the fortunes of America's cities over the past few years. Paralyzed by the war in Iraq, we're in danger of forgetting completely about the struggling cities here at home.

Bill Clinton mentioned the 300,000 poor children being cut out of after-school programs and the increases in gang violence across the country. And he gave cheering delegates a devastating riff on the impending lapse of the ban on assault weapons and White House plans to scrap federal funds for tens of thousands of police officers.

"Our policy," he said, "was to put more police on the street and to take assault weapons off the street—and it gave you eight years of declining crime and eight years of declining violence. Their policy is the reverse. They're taking police off the streets while they put assault weapons back on the street."

But those brief comments were the exception. A clearer sense of the rot that's starting to reestablish itself in America's cities was offered in an article out of Cleveland by the *New York Times*'s Fox Butterfield. "Many cities with budget shortfalls," he wrote, "are cutting their police forces and closing innovative law enforcement units that helped reduce crime in the 1990's, police chiefs and city officials say."

Cleveland has laid off 15 percent of its cops—250 officers. Pittsburgh has lost a quarter of its officers, and Saginaw, Michigan, a third. The Los Angeles County Sheriff's Department has waved good-bye to 1,200 deputies, closed several jails, and released some inmates early. In Houston, police officers are taking up the duties of 190 jail guards who were let go.

This is nuts. We know that low levels of crime and violence are essential if cities are to thrive. Tremendous progress—in some places, like New York, almost miraculous progress—has been made in reducing crime since the crack-crazed, gun-blazing days of the late eighties and early nineties. To even begin rewinding the clock to that time of madness would in itself be an act of madness.

Yet that's what we're doing.

Mayor Martin O'Malley of Baltimore, who cochairs the Task Force on Homeland Security for the U.S. Conference of Mayors, told me in an interview that budgetary horror stories are coming in from police officials all over the country. There are many reasons, he said, including the recession and the weak recovery that followed, the anti-terror obligations that have fallen to the police since September 11, and "the cascading effect" of enormous federal tax cuts at a time when the nation is at war. Local taxes have gone up sharply, and services have had to be cut back even as federal taxes have decreased.

"This is all compounded," Mayor O'Malley said, "by the fact that there is just less money coming in from Washington" for traditional crime-fighting efforts.

Local police, fire, and other agencies have also been affected by the call-up of thousands of military reservists and members of the National Guard. In addition to losing their services, most cities pay the difference between the municipal salaries of these men and women and the substantially lower pay they receive from the military.

In an address to the convention delegates, Mayor O'Malley echoed many other municipal officials when he said police and fire departments are not even getting sufficient help from the federal government to maintain their anti-terror efforts. The first responders, he said, cannot continue to finance their homeland security responsibilities "with increased property taxes and fire hall Bingos."

The crime-fighting difficulties and underfunded homeland security responsibilities are part of a parade of very serious problems that have descended on cities in recent years. Tax cuts for the wealthy and the administration's hard-right ideology have removed much of the social safety net that we managed to weave over the past several decades, leaving us with a swelling population of vulnerable men, women, and children. This has had a disproportionate impact on cities, and the outlook, both short- and long-term, is bleak at best.

These are important issues that could be wrestled with if cities were on anybody's agenda.

But they're not.

(July 30, 2004)

12

HOW GOES THE WAR ON TERROR?

"IT WASN'T A DREAM"

For the first twenty-four-hours—as the horrifying images exploded again and again on television screens across the nation—there was the numbness and the disbelief that accompanies shock. But yesterday, as the rubble that once was the World Trade Center began yielding up its ghastly trove of lifeless flesh, the full measure of the catastrophe began to settle in for New Yorkers.

Exhausted rescue workers were finding it difficult to maintain their composure as they shoveled and clawed their way past bodies and parts of bodies in search of anyone who might still be alive.

"I lost count of all the dead people I saw," said Rudy Weindler, a firefighter who spent twelve mostly fruitless hours looking for survivors in the smoke and the debris.

New York is a city of increasing heartbreak, with no respite in sight. "It is absolutely worse than you could ever imagine," said Weindler.

It was hard to believe that anything could be worse than Tuesday's hideous events, when one atrocity followed another, hour after hour. Among the many people who plunged to their deaths from the upper floors of the World Trade Center were a man and a woman who held hands as they fell.

A shaken police officer, speaking to me by phone on Tuesday afternoon, said, "I saw bodies flying out of windows in clouds of debris. I saw pieces of bodies on the ground. I saw firemen in tears as they listened on the radio to their buddies trapped inside."

I spoke to that same officer on Wednesday and he said, "When I woke up today all I could think was, 'It wasn't a dream.'"

New Yorkers throughout the city felt similarly. They awakened Wednesday to the awful and undeniable realization that the soaring towers of the World Trade Center, and the uncounted thousands of people who perished in their rubble, were really gone.

Senator Charles Schumer was near tears as he spoke on the Senate floor of the vast number of New Yorkers with relatives and friends who are missing. "I know of a call," he said, "someone on the 104th floor who worked for the good firm of Cantor Fitzgerald—we can't find hardly anybody from that firm—who called his parents, told them he loved them, and they haven't heard from him since."

At several locations, friends and relatives of those who are missing have been lining up with photographs and detailed descriptions of their loved ones, hoping that a tattoo on a forearm or a picture of an engagement ring or a distinctive surgical scar will lead to a miracle.

The weather remained gorgeous Wednesday, as if to mock the continuing horror. Sunlight glistened off the roofs of ambulances lined up in military fashion on the West Side Highway. On the East Side, near Bellevue Hospital and the morgue, were some of the large refrigerated vehicles used to transport bodies.

Scores of bodies had been driven to the morgue by midday yesterday. Most of them were believed to be firefighters.

"That's just the beginning, the first small wave," said a rescue worker. "When they really start coming in, I don't see how Bellevue will be able to handle it. I don't think people understand the scope of this yet. Fish companies are calling up, saying, 'What do you need? You need refrigerated trucks? We have them. Where do you want them?' "

The threat of terrorism has always been, for most Americans, an abstraction. But that changed with Tuesday's spectacular televised attack. The toll went far beyond the thousands of lost lives and the destruction of the preeminent symbol of the New York skyline. Our sense of security and much of our innocence was lost as well.

An extraordinary search is under way for anyone connected to what Senator Schumer described as "this dastardly and disgusting act." But at the same time New York is struggling with grievous wounds that will take a very long time to heal.

The city will survive because New York is too big and too ornery to do anything else. But for the moment, this great city grieves. And with its deep sadness that won't soon be eased, it hunts for its dead.

(September 13, 2001)

HIGH-ALTITUDE RAMBOS

Dr. Bob Rajcoomar, a U.S. citizen and former military physician from Lake Worth, Florida, found himself handcuffed and taken into custody in August 2002 in one of the many episodes of hysteria to erupt on board airliners in the United States since the September 11 attacks.

Dr. Rajcoomar was seated in first class on a Delta Airlines flight from Atlanta to Philadelphia on August 31 when a passenger in the coach section began behaving erratically. The passenger, Steven Feuer, had nothing to do with Dr. Rajcoomar.

Two U.S. air marshals got up from their seats in first class and moved back to coach to confront Feuer, who was described by witnesses as a slight man who seemed disoriented. What ensued was terrifying. When Feuer refused to remain in his seat, the marshals reacted as if they were trying out for the lead roles in Hollywood's latest action extravaganza.

They handcuffed Feuer, hustled him into first class, and restrained him in a seat next to Dr. Rajcoomar. The 180 or so passengers were now quite jittery. Dr. Rajcoomar asked to have his seat changed and a flight attendant obliged, finding him another seat in first class. The incident, already scary, could—and should—have ended there. But the marshals were not ready to let things quiet down.

One of the marshals pulled a gun and brandished it at the passengers. The marshals loudly demanded that all passengers remain in their seats, and remain still. They barked a series of orders. No one should stand for any reason. Arms and legs should not extend into the aisles. No one should try to visit the restroom. The message could not have been clearer: anyone who disobeyed the marshals was in danger of being shot.

The passengers were petrified, with most believing that there were terrorists on the plane.

"I was afraid there was going to be a gun battle in that pressurized cabin," said Senior Judge James A. Lineberger of the Philadelphia Court of Common Pleas, a veteran of twenty years in the military, who was sitting in an aisle seat in coach. "I was afraid that I was going to die from the gunfire in a shoot-out."

Dr. Rajcoomar's wife, Dorothy, who was seated quite a distance from her husband, said, "It was really like Rambo in the air." She worried that there might be people on the plane who did not speak English, and therefore did not understand the marshals' orders. If someone got up to go to the bathroom, he or she might be shot.

There were no terrorists on board. There was no threat of any kind. When the plane landed about half an hour later, Feuer was taken into custody. And then, shockingly, so was Dr. Rajcoomar. The air marshals grabbed the doctor from behind, handcuffed him, and, for no good reason that anyone has been able to give, hauled him to an airport police station, where he was thrown into a filthy cell.

This was airline security gone berserk. No one ever suggested that Dr. Rajcoomar, a straight-arrow retired army major, had done anything wrong.

Dr. Rajcoomar, who is of Indian descent, said he believes he was taken into custody solely because of his brown skin. He was held for three frightening hours and then released without being charged. Feuer was also released.

Officials tried to conceal the names of the marshals, but they were eventually identified by a *Philadelphia Inquirer* reporter as Shawn B. McCullers and Samuel Mumma of the Transportation Security Administration, which is part of the U.S. Transportation Department.

The Transportation Security Administration has declined to discuss the incident in detail. A spokesman offered the absurd explanation that Dr. Rajcoomar was detained because he had watched the unfolding incident "too closely."

If that becomes a criterion for arrest in the United States, a lot of us reporters are headed for jail.

Dr. Rajcoomar told me yesterday that he remains shaken by the episode. "I had never been treated like that in my life," he said. "I was afraid that I was about to be beaten up or killed."

Lawyers for the American Civil Liberties Union have taken up his case, and he has filed notice that he may sue the federal government for unlawful detention.

"We have to take a look at what we're doing in the name of security," said Dr. Rajcoomar. "So many men and women have fought and died for freedom in this great country, and now we are in danger of ruining that in the name of security."

(September 23, 2002)

STRATEGIC ADVICE FROM THE PUBLIC

Maude LeFrem, a woman in her sixties, put on a brave face as she waited for a train at the Broadway-Nassau subway stop in lower Manhattan. She, too, had heard the rumors. The terrorists were coming. They had their eyes on the subways. Chemical weapons. Any day now. Any moment.

"I know what they're saying," she said. "Everyone's praying. We don't really know what will happen, but prayer can change things, and I believe that. What am I doing different? I'm praying more, that's all."

It seemed toward the end of last week, with rumors circulating the city like a virus and cops with machine guns patrolling Grand Central Terminal, that the only available response to the hideous issues of the day for people like LeFrem—people outside the power elite— was resignation. You could pray. You could sink into the slough of denial. You could do whatever to try to fend off the paralyzing anxiety. What you couldn't do was change anything.

Most people—in New York and across the nation—felt helpless against the phantomlike forces of terror. And few people believed, despite the ambivalence (or outright opposition) of ordinary Americans to a U.S.-led invasion of Iraq, that anything could be done to divert the Bush administration from its rush to war, and its potentially catastrophic aftermath.

And then, over the weekend, democracy got a desperately needed boost. With temperatures in the twenties and icy winds skimming off the rivers that frame Manhattan, a frosty assemblage of demonstrators for peace and sanity materialized. The protesters kept arriving until their numbers reached 100,000, 200,000, and still they came, chanting, singing, and linking arms symbolically with a huge and remarkable wave of fellow demonstrators across the U.S. and around the globe.

It seemed to me that the most important aspect of the U.S. protests was the demand that, on this crucial issue of war, the Bush administration pay at least some heed to the views, wishes, and feelings of the American people.

And I think the essential view of the protesters (and probably the majority of Americans) is that the United States and its allies should take all possible steps short of war to squeeze Saddam's regime so tight that survival is all but impossible; and that, above all, the United States should be leading a real, all-out war against the forces of Al Qaeda, wherever they may be.

Walt Rostow, one of the ultimate hawks on Vietnam, died recently. He, along with many others, suffered from an optimism about the use of U.S. military force in that conflict that bordered on delusion. In an obituary the *New York Times*'s Todd Purdum quoted Nicholas deB. Katzenbach, an undersecretary of state and attorney general in the Johnson administration, who had argued with Rostow over the efficacy of U.S. bombing.

"I finally understand the difference between Walt and me," said Katzenbach. "I was the navigator who was shot down and spent two years in a German prison camp, and Walt was the guy picking my targets."

President Bush and his hawkish advisers speak blithely about a U.S.-led invasion leading to a garden of democracy blooming in the desert soil of Iraq. I wouldn't reach for my gardening tools too quickly. What the administration has been unwilling to tell the public is the truth about some of the implications of war with Iraq—first and foremost, the bloody horror of men, women, and children being blown to smithereens in the interest of peace, and then the myriad costs and dangers associated with a long-term U.S. military occupation.

As late as last week the administration tried to give the impression that the United States could be in and out of Iraq in as little as two years. That's a case of optimism as dangerous as Walt Rostow's.

As former senator Gary Hart said in a conversation, "Most thoughtful people who don't have a bias here think there is no short-term exit strategy." More realistic, he said, is a U.S. occupation of five to ten years, or longer.

Hart, who was cochairman of a special commission on national security that issued early warnings about the nation's vulnerability to terror attacks, then mentioned the concern expressed again and again by ordinary Americans worried about war with Iraq. "Are we prepared," he asked, "for what I believe are inevitable retaliatory attacks? The answer, I think, is no."

(February 17, 2003)

STAYING IN THE DARK

We never heed the warnings.

When the power failed on August 14, 2003, I was reading a report commissioned by the Council on Foreign Relations that found that even now—two years after the tragic events of September 11, 2001— the United States remains "dangerously unprepared" to cope with another catastrophic terrorist attack.

The blackout that interrupted my reading showed once again how suddenly we can be thrown out of our daily routine and into a widespread emergency. I walked down the ten flights from my office in the *New York Times* Building and out to Times Square, where the bewildered, disoriented throngs, frightened by thoughts of terror, were trying to get their bearings in an environment that had been transformed in an instant.

It seemed that almost everyone had a cell phone and none of them was working. That freaked out a lot of people. The cell phone has emerged as the lifeline of the twenty-first century, the quintessential emergency gadget. It's the one device that's supposed to work when everything else is falling apart.

There were already reports circulating (true, as it turned out) that the blackout extended all the way into Canada and as far west as Ohio. A woman asked a reporter if he thought the entire nation was under attack. The reporter said no, he thought it was just a blackout, like the ones in 1965 and 1977. But bigger, maybe.

The night would bring a reacquaintance with deep silence and flickering shadows and the comfort of listening to baseball on a battery-operated radio. But there was also the disturbing sense (nurtured in the long, dark, humid hours of the night) that much of our trust is misplaced, that in instance after instance the people in charge of crucial aspects of our society are incompetent or irresponsible, or both, and that American lives are far more at risk than they should be because of that.

The enormous, cascading blackout should never have occurred. We knew the electrical grid was in sorry shape, and the experiences of 1965 and 1977 were still in our collective memory. The experts told us again and again to expect a breakdown. Two years ago an official with the North American Electric Reliability Council said, "The question is not whether, but when the next major failure of the grid will occur."

We ignored the warnings, which is what we always do with warnings, and we paid a terrible price. Now we're left wondering what might happen if terrorists were to link their madness to our electric power vulnerabilities.

The report I was reading when the power failed was issued less than two months ago and was titled, "Emergency Responders: Drastically Underfunded, Dangerously Unprepared."

The report acknowledged that some progress against terrorism has been made through the Department of Homeland Security and other federal, state, and local institutions. But it said, "The United States has not reached a sufficient national level of emergency preparedness and remains dangerously unprepared to handle a catastrophic attack on American soil, particularly one involving chemical, biological, radiological, or nuclear agents, or coordinated high-impact conventional means."

The task force that conducted the study was headed by former senator Warren Rudman, a Republican, who, with former senator Gary Hart, a Democrat, wrote two previous important studies that spotlighted the woeful state of our defenses against large-scale terror attacks.

Their first study was issued before the September 11 catastrophe. It predicted a deadly attack, saying, "Americans will likely die on American soil, possibly in large numbers." Their second study was issued last year and it accused the White House and Congress of failing to take the extensive and costly steps necessary to defend against another catastrophic attack, which they said was almost certain to occur.

Now we have yet another warning. If an attack were to occur, the report said, the so-called first responders—police and fire departments, emergency medical personnel, public works, and emergency management officials—are not ready to respond effectively. And one of the reasons is that we won't spend the money or invest the effort necessary to adequately train and equip them.

After the next attack we'll have another study to assess what went wrong. And we won't pay attention to that study either.

(August 18, 2003)

READY OR NOT

More alarm bells. This time they're being rung by a bearded New York physician whose mature, low-key manner (bedside and otherwise) is the farthest you can imagine from alarmist.

Now fifty-nine, Dr. Irwin Redlener has spent many years delivering health care to poor and neglected children throughout the United States. Back in the 1980s he and the musician Paul Simon (in an outstanding collaboration of hip and square) created the Children's Health Fund, which turned specially equipped vans into mobile units that could be driven to wherever the underserved children were.

When the World Trade Center was attacked, Dr. Redlener immediately sent vans from the Children's Health Fund to the triage center that was set up on Manhattan's West Side. That sudden experience of the intersection of medicine and terror led to an entirely new mission.

Dr. Redlener is now one of the key individuals working on the urgent task of developing strategies to care for the sick and wounded in the event of another terrorist attack. He's the founding director of the new National Center for Disaster Preparedness, at Columbia University's Mailman School of Public Health.

At the moment our state of readiness is not good.

"My biggest concern," said Dr. Redlener, "is that now, nearly two years after 9/11, the hospitals and public health systems are absolutely unprepared for another major act of terrorism. There's been very little improvement from two years ago. No one's really even defined what we mean by preparedness."

Extensive steps have been taken to prevent the use of airliners in another September 11–type attack. But Dr. Redlener noted that there is a wide range of potential acts of terror that frontline emergency organizations, hospitals, and the public health system may have to cope with. "We need to be prepared for things like car bombs or a terrorist attack on a nuclear power facility. We need to be prepared for the release of a chemical or biological agent in a public place—a train station, an airport, a sports arena. We need to be prepared for sabotage of major infrastructural systems—bridges, for example, and transportation and communications facilities.

"The health care system has to be ready to respond effectively to any of these emergencies. And right now it's not." A series of recent studies have found that not just the health care system but also critical organizations like police and fire departments and public school systems are dangerously unprepared. A study commissioned by the Centers for Disease Control and Prevention and released just last week by the RAND Corporation found that most emergency workers in the forty cities and towns surveyed "feel vastly underprepared and underprotected for the consequences of chemical, biological or radiological terrorist attacks."

A study prepared for an association that represents school safety officers found that while its members believed their schools were potential "soft targets" for terrorists, they did not feel the schools were prepared to cope with an attack.

Other recent studies have found that most urban hospitals do not have the medical equipment needed to handle the number of patients that would likely result from a bioterrorist attack, and that the federal government's ability to fend off such an attack may well be jeopardized by "a shortage of science and medical experts."

Dr. Redlener and his colleagues at the National Center for Disaster Preparedness are trying to help bring a greater sense of order and effectiveness to the current chaotic state of disaster planning in the United States. They are trying to do this in a kind of think tank–plus atmosphere, combining intensive research with very practical tasks, such as the development and coordination of training programs, specialized curricula, and protocols. (The military has already done important work in this area, and Dr. Redlener said those efforts should be more widely shared.)

"We need national standards and benchmarks for what should be done," Dr. Redlener said. "We need new ways of looking at these problems. This whole issue of preparedness could end up being the ultimate Achilles' heel for America."

(August 25, 2003)

WAKING UP TO THE WAR

The public is catching on. Americans heading into the Fourth of July weekend are increasingly concerned that the war in Iraq, rather than bringing stability to the Middle East and a greater sense of safety here at home, has in fact made the world more dangerous and the United States more vulnerable than ever to terror attacks.

A *Wall Street Journal*/NBC News poll has found that a majority of Americans now believe the war has increased the threat of terrorism. A *New York Times*/CBS News poll found that 47 percent of respondents believe the terror threat has increased, while only 13 percent say it has declined. Thirty-eight percent of the respondents in that poll said the war had not made a difference.

There is a sound basis for the concern. The U.S. invasion and occupation of Iraq has been a gift-wrapped, gilt-edged recruiting tool for Al Qaeda and its offshoots. If Osama bin Laden had personally designed a campaign to expand the ranks and spread the influence of anti-American terrorists, it's hard to imagine him coming up with a better scenario than the U.S. invasion and occupation of Iraq.

"We have created the greatest recruiting tool possible for bin Laden and his ilk," said Bob Boorstin, a national security specialist at the Center for American Progress.

His words echoed the conclusions of the senior Central Intelligence Agency analyst who is the anonymous author of *Imperial Hubris: Why the West Is Losing the War on Terror.* The author, who spent years tracking bin Laden and his followers, said, "There is nothing that bin Laden could have hoped for more than the American invasion and occupation of Iraq."

The fact that this war has made America more, not less, vulnerable to terrorism should be treated as a national scandal. But that is not the kind of story that has the legs of, say, the Monica Lewinsky scandal. Or the O.J. Simpson saga.

We have certainly known since September 11, if not before, that terrorism poses the gravest and most immediate threat to the United States. Instead of marshaling the nation's resources and the support of our allies for a sustained, all-out campaign aimed at destroying Al Qaeda and its offshoots, President Bush launched the war in Iraq and turned that country into a breeding ground for such terrorists.

There were warnings. Recruiting by Al Qaeda and other terrorist groups was already surging in early 2003 in response to the buildup for war with Iraq. On March 16, 2003, three days before the start of the war, the *New York Times* reported:

"In recent weeks, officials in the United States, Europe and Africa say they had seen evidence that militants within Muslim communities are seeking to identify and groom a new generation of terrorist operatives. An invasion of Iraq, the officials worry, is almost certain to produce a groundswell of recruitment for groups committed to attacks in the United States, Europe and Israel."

We now have nearly 140,000 troops in Iraq, with more on the way, and we'll be bogged down there for years to come. The tremendous costs in personnel and money have drained resources needed to combat terror groups around the world and shore up defenses against terror here at home.

Now the public is tiring of the war. A majority of the respondents in both the *New York Times* and the *Wall Street Journal* polls said the war was not worth its cost in American lives.

But there is no sign of the war ending. The so-called handoff of sovereignty was a furtive ritual that was far more symbolic than substantive. Three Marines were killed in a roadside bombing in Baghdad a day after the transfer, and another was killed the next day in Al Anbar, west of Baghdad.

We're holding a terrible hand. There is no exit strategy for American troops in Iraq. There is no plan in our insane tax-cut environment for paying for the war. The U.S. military is stretched dangerously thin, lacking sufficient troops to meet its obligations around the world. Homeland security is deeply underfunded. And with the terror networks energized, the feeling among intelligence experts with regard to a strike in the United States is not if, but when.

(July 2, 2004)

13

MISLEADERSHIP IN IRAQ

WITH EARS AND EYES CLOSED

Washington

It was a weekend of going through the motions. Lip service was still being given to the idea that the war could be stopped. IT'S NOT TOO LATE, read one of the signs displayed on Saturday as tens of thousands of antiwar protesters marched from the Washington Monument to the White House.

Dick Cheney was on television yesterday morning advancing the fiction that "we're still in the final stages of diplomacy." President Bush was meeting in the Azores with his coalition of the hard-of-hearing, the small but stubborn group of men committed to attacking Iraq no matter how wrong or undesirable that might be, or how much outrage it provokes around the world.

We're about to watch the tragedy unfold. The president, who's wanted war with Iraq all along, has been unwilling to listen seriously to anyone with an opposing view. He's turned his back on those worried about the consequences of a split in the transatlantic alliance that has served the world well for better than half a century. He's closed his mind to those who have argued that preemptive warfare will ultimately make the world more—not less—unstable.

Bush has remained unmoved by the millions of protesters against the war who have demonstrated in the United States and around the world. If any one of those millions has had something worthwhile to say, the president hasn't acknowledged it.

Risks? In the president's view this is a war of liberation that, in addition to removing Saddam Hussein and his weapons of mass destruction, will bring democracy to the people of Iraq and lead to a miraculous flowering of democracy throughout the Mideast.

Never mind the secret State Department document (disclosed by the *Los Angeles Times*) that holds just the opposite view—that not only are the prospects for democracy in the region poor, but entrenched economic and social problems are likely to undermine even basic stability for years to come.

President Bush may not see them, but the risks are enormous.

"This is an invasion and a long-term occupation of an Arab country in the midst of the most volatile region of the world," said former representative Tom Andrews of Maine, who has led a particularly well-organized and thoughtful protest group called Win Without War.

The *New York Times* ran a front-page story about warnings from intelligence officials that a U.S.-led invasion and occupation of Iraq would embolden Islamic terrorist organizations around the world, strengthening their recruitment efforts and increasing the likelihood of another strike in the United States.

The president's unwillingness to listen to other voices has extended even to the religious community in the United States. "With the exception of the Southern Baptist Convention, almost every major church in this country has expressed huge reservations about going to war with Iraq," said the Reverend Clifton Kirkpatrick, the chief ecclesiastical officer of the Presbyterian Church.

Kirkpatrick was part of a delegation of religious leaders who met in London in February 2003 with Prime Minister Tony Blair of Britain. The group has developed a proposal that it calls a "possible alternative to war." The proposal calls for, among other things, the indictment of Saddam Hussein as a war criminal by an international tribunal; the use of the current military buildup to support and enforce a "greatly intensified" regime of weapons inspections; the development of a UN plan for the temporary administration of a post-Saddam Iraq; and the creation of a huge international humanitarian effort to address the continued suffering of the Iraqi people.

"We don't claim to be public policy experts, but these are at least contributions that need to be explored much more deeply," said Kirkpatrick.

That hope was soon gone. The Reverend Jim Wallis, editor of the evangelical journal *Sojourners*, headed the delegation that met with Blair and that had been trying to arrange a meeting with Bush. He told me, "I got a call back from the White House saying the president is not scheduling any more meetings."

The president's mind was made up long ago, and all the chatter pro and con was just so much smoke in the wind. Bush will have his war.

The week's end was a time of sadness around the world as people who think that war should always be a last resort lit candles to express their sorrow, their frustration, and, however unrealistically, their last faint flickerings of hope.

(March 17, 2003)

READY FOR THE PEACE?

Now that U.S. strikes against Iraq have begun, we should get rid of one canard immediately, and that's the notion that criticism of the Bush administration and opposition to this invasion imply in some sense a lack of support or concern for the men and women who are under arms.

The names of too many of my friends are recorded on the wall of the Vietnam Memorial for me to tolerate that kind of nonsense. I hope that the war goes well, that our troops prevail quickly, and that casualties everywhere are kept to a minimum.

But the fact that a war may be quick does not mean that it is wise. Against the wishes of most of the world, we have plunged not just into war, but toward a peace that is potentially more problematic than the war itself. Are Americans ready to pay the cost in lives and dollars of a long-term military occupation of Iraq? To what end?

Will an occupation of Iraq increase or decrease our security here at home?

Do most Americans understand that even as we are launching one of the most devastating air assaults in the history of warfare, private companies are lining up to reap the riches of rebuilding the very structures we're in the process of destroying?

Companies like Halliburton, Schlumberger, and the Bechtel Group understand this conflict a heck of a lot better than most of the men and women who will fight and die in it, or the armchair patriots who'll be watching on CNN and cheering them on.

It's not unpatriotic to say that there are billions of dollars to be made in Iraq and that the gold rush is already under way. It's simply a matter of fact.

Back in January, an article in the *Wall Street Journal* noted: "With oil reserves second only to Saudi Arabia's, Iraq would offer the oil industry enormous opportunity should a war topple Saddam Hussein. But the early spoils would probably go to companies needed to keep Iraq's already rundown oil operations running, especially if facilities were further damaged in a war. Oil-services firms such as Halliburton Co., where Vice President Dick Cheney formerly served as chief executive, and Schlumberger Ltd. are seen as favorites for what could be as much as $1.5 billion in contracts."

There is tremendous unease at the highest levels of the Pentagon about this war and its aftermath. The president and his civilian advisers are making a big deal about the anticipated rejoicing of the liberated populace once the war is over. But Iraq is an inherently unstable place, and while the forces assembled to chase Saddam from power are superbly trained for combat, the military is not well prepared for a long-term occupation in the most volatile region in the world.

What's driving this war is President Bush's Manichaean view of the world and messianic vision of himself, the dangerously grandiose perception of American power held by his saber-rattling advisers, and the irresistible lure of Iraq's enormous oil reserves.

Polls show that the public is terribly confused about what's going on, so much so that some 40 percent believe that Saddam Hussein was personally involved in the September 11 attacks. That's really scary. Rather than correct this misconception, the administration has gone out of its way to reinforce it.

I think the men and women moving militarily against Saddam are among the few truly brave and even noble individuals left in our society. They have volunteered for the dangerous duty of defending the rest of us. But I also believe they are being put unnecessarily in harm's way.

As a result of the military buildup, there is hardly a more hobbled leader on earth at the moment than Saddam Hussein. A skillful marshaling of international pressure could have forced him from power. But then the Bush administration would not have had its war and its occupation. It would not have been able to turn Iraq into an American protectorate, which is as good a term as any for a colony.

Is it a good idea to liberate the people of Iraq from the clutches of a degenerate like Saddam Hussein? Sure. But there were better, less dangerous, ways to go about it.

In the epigraph to his memoir, *Present at the Creation,* Dean Acheson quoted a thirteenth-century king of Spain, Alphonso X, the Learned:

"Had I been present at the creation I would have given some useful hints for the better ordering of the universe."

(March 20, 2003)

WHAT IS IT GOOD FOR?

Somewhere George Shultz is smiling.

Shultz, whose photo could appropriately appear next to any definition of the military-industrial complex, was secretary of state under Ronald Reagan and has been a perennial heavyweight with the powerful Bechtel Group of San Francisco, where he previously reigned as president and is now a board member and senior counselor.

Unlike the antiwar soul singer Edwin Starr—who, in an ironic bit of timing, went to his eternal reward just as American ground forces were sweeping toward Baghdad—Shultz knows what war is good for.

And he wanted this war with Iraq. Oh, how he wanted this war. Shultz was chairman of the fiercely prowar Committee for the Liberation of Iraq, which was committed to moving beyond the mere political liberation of the oil-rich country to the all-important and conveniently profitable "reconstruction of its economy."

Under the headline "Act Now; The Danger Is Immediate," Shultz, in an op-ed article in the *Washington Post* in September 2002, wrote: "A strong foundation exists for immediate military action against Hussein and for a multilateral effort to rebuild Iraq after he is gone."

Gee, I wonder which company he thought might lead that effort.

Shultz's Bechtel Group was able to demonstrate exactly what wars are good for. The Bush administration gave it the first big Iraqi reconstruction contract, a prized $680 million deal over eighteen months that puts Bechtel in the driver's seat for the long-term reconstruction of the country, which could cost a hundred billion dollars or more.

Bechtel essentially was given a license to make money. And that license was granted in a closed-door process that was restricted to a handful of politically connected American companies.

When the George Bushes and the George Shultzes were banging the drums for war with Iraq, we didn't hear one word from them about the benefits that would be accruing to corporate behemoths like Bechtel. And we didn't pay much attention to the grotesque conflict of interest engaged in by corporate titans and their government cronies who were pushing young American men and women into the flames of a war that ultimately would pour billions of dollars into a very select group of corporate coffers.

Now the corporations (not just Bechtel by any means) have a lock on Iraq, and U.S. taxpayers are obliged to pay the bill.

Among those in Congress who are beginning to challenge this loathsome process is Senator Ron Wyden, an Oregon Democrat who is one of the lead sponsors of a bipartisan bill that would require a public explanation of any decision to award Iraqi reconstruction contracts without a "fully open, competitive bidding process."

In an interview, he said, "You look at this process, which is secret, limited, or closed bidding, and you have to ask yourself: 'Why are these companies being picked? How's this process taking place, and is this the best use of scarce taxpayer money at a time when seniors can't afford medicine, kids are having trouble getting access to a quality education, and local communities are just getting pounded?' The administration has been keeping the taxpayers in the dark with respect to how this money is being used, and that information ought to be shared."

The blatant war-mongering followed immediately by profiteering inevitably raise questions about the real reasons American men and women have been fighting and dying in Iraq. President Bush told us the war was about weapons of mass destruction and the need to get rid of the degenerate Saddam. There was also talk about democracy taking root in Iraq and spreading like spring flowers throughout the Arab world.

The two things that were never openly discussed, that never became part of the national conversation, were oil and money. Those crucial topics were left to the major behind-the-scenes operators, many of whom are now cashing in.

The favoritism, the secretive method by which the contracts are being awarded, and the arrogant and unconscionable exclusion of the United Nations and even close U.S. allies from significant roles in the administration and reconstruction of Iraq all contribute to the most cynical interpretation of American motives.

The men and women fighting in Iraq, for reasons they felt were noble and unassailable, deserve better.

(April 21, 2003)

DANCING WITH THE DEVIL

Let's see. Who's less patriotic, the Dixie Chicks or Dick Cheney's long-term meal ticket, the Halliburton Company?

The Dixie Chicks were excoriated for simply exercising their constitutional right to speak out. With an ugly backlash and plans for a boycott growing, the group issued a humiliating public apology for "disrespectful" anti-Bush remarks made by its lead singer, Natalie Maines. The Chicks learned how dangerous it can be to criticize the chief of a grand imperial power.

Halliburton, on the other hand, can do no wrong. Yes, it has a history of ripping off the government. And, yes, it's made zillions doing business in countries that sponsor terrorism, including members of the "axis of evil" that is so despised by the president.

But the wrath of the White House has not come thundering down on Halliburton for consorting with the enemy. And there's been very little public criticism. This is not some hapless singing group we're talking about. Halliburton is a court favorite. So instead of being punished for its misdeeds, it's been handed a huge share of the riches to be reaped from the reconstruction of Iraq and U.S. control of Iraqi oil.

A Democratic congressman, Henry Waxman of California, has raised pointed questions about the propriety of rewarding Halliburton with lucrative contracts as part of the U.S. war on terror when the company has gone out of its way to do business in three nations that the United States has accused of supporting terror: Iraq, Iran, and Libya.

In an April 30 letter to Defense Secretary Donald Rumsfeld, Waxman wrote:

> Since at least the 1980's, federal laws have prohibited U.S. companies from doing business in one or more of these countries.

Yet Halliburton appears to have sought to circumvent these restrictions by setting up subsidiaries in foreign countries and territories such as the Cayman Islands. These actions started as early as 1984; they appear to have continued during the period between 1995 and 2000, when Vice President Cheney headed the company; and they are apparently ongoing even today.

According to Waxman, a subsidiary called Halliburton Products and Services opened an office in Tehran, Iran, in February 2000, has done work on offshore drilling projects, and has asserted, "We are committed to position ourselves in a market that offers huge growth potential."

Shareholder complaints since the attacks of September 11, 2001, particularly from the pension funds of the New York City Police and Fire Departments, have prompted Halliburton officials to agree to reevaluate their operations in Iran.

The federal government has been well aware of Halliburton's shenanigans. In his letter to Secretary Rumsfeld, Waxman noted that "Halliburton was fined $3.8 million in 1995 for re-exporting U.S. goods through a foreign subsidiary to Libya in violation of U.S. sanctions." The fine was not enough to stop the company from dancing with the devil. It still has dealings in Libya.

Now, with the U.S. takeover of Iraq, Halliburton has hit the jackpot. It has only recently been made clear that an "emergency" no-bid contract given in March to the Halliburton subsidiary Kellogg Brown & Root covers far more than the limited task of fighting oil well fires. The company has been given control of the Iraqi oil operations, including oil distribution.

"It's remarkable there's been so little attention paid to the Halliburton contracts," said Waxman. In addition to doing business in countries that have sponsored terrorism, the congressman said, Halliburton has been accused of overcharging the U.S. government for work it did in the 1990s. And in 2002 the company agreed to pay a

$2 million settlement to ward off possible criminal charges for price gouging.

"Their reward for that terrible record," said the congressman, "was a secret no-bid contract, potentially worth billions, to run Iraq's oil operations."

Halliburton and its subsidiaries are virtuosos at gaming the system. It's a slithery enterprise with its rapacious tentacles in everybody's pockets. It benefits from doing business with the enemy, from its relationship with the U.S. military when the United States is at war with the enemy, and from contracts to help rebuild the defeated enemy.

Meanwhile, the flag-waving yahoos are hyperventilating over non-issues like the Dixie Chicks.

(May 22, 2003)

THE HALLIBURTON SHUFFLE

Can you spell Halliburton? R-i-p-o-f-f.

War-torn Iraq has been a gold mine for Halliburton, yet another treasure trove of U.S. taxpayer dollars for a company that has no peer in the fine art of extracting riches from the government.

But if you go through some of Halliburton's filings with the Securities and Exchange Commission over the past several years, as I have, you'll see a company that goes to great lengths—literally to the ends of the earth—to escape paying its fair share of taxes to the government that has been so good to it.

Annual reports filed with the SEC since the mid-nineties—when

Dick Cheney took over as chief executive and wrote the game plan for garnering government goodies—showed Halliburton subsidiaries incorporated in such places as the Cayman Islands, Bermuda, Trinidad and Tobago, Panama, Liechtenstein, and Vanuatu.

Vanuatu? Who knew?

Vanuatu is a mountainous group of islands in the South Pacific. Its people support themselves mostly by fishing and subsistence farming. "Additional revenues," according to the *Columbia Encyclopedia*, "derive from a growing tourist industry and the development of Vila the capital as a corporate tax shelter."

Halliburton, in an SEC filing in 2000, duly noted that it had a subsidiary incorporated in Vanuatu called Kinhill Kramer (Vanuatu) Ltd.

The company adamantly denies that its offshore subsidiaries are used to shift income out of the United States. But it's indisputable that somebody is doing a dandy job of limiting Halliburton's tax liability. When I asked how much Halliburton paid in federal income taxes last year, a company spokeswoman, Wendy Hall, said, "After foreign tax credit utilization, we paid just over $15 million to the IRS for our 2002 tax liability."

That is effectively no money at all to an empire like Halliburton. Less than pocket change. Dick Cheney must be having a good laugh over the way his old company, following his road map, is taking the United States for such a ride.

In the early nineties, when Cheney was defense secretary under the first President Bush, he hired the Halliburton subsidiary Brown & Root to determine what military functions could be outsourced to private profit-making companies. Brown & Root came up with myriad ideas in a classified study and was handed a lucrative contract to implement its own plan.

Cheney took over as chief executive of Halliburton in 1995, and the defense contracts just kept on coming. When he returned to government as vice president in 2001, no firm was better positioned than Halliburton to cash in on the billions of dollars in contracts that resulted from the war on terror and the conflict in Iraq.

Halliburton is bound so intimately to the defense establishment it might as well be an adjunct to the military. (Cheney still receives deferred compensation from Halliburton but insists he has no role in the awarding of contracts.)

Halliburton is an organization that has the reach of a multinational and the eyes of a Willie Sutton. Through its subsidiaries, it has done work with countries the United States has accused of supporting terror. It was accused of overcharging the U.S. government for work done in the 1990s, and in 2002 it agreed to pay a $2 million settlement in response to accusations that it had defrauded the government.

The Pentagon is currently examining allegations that the Halliburton subsidiary Kellogg Brown & Root overcharged the government by $61 million for gasoline imported into Iraq from Kuwait. The company acknowledged that at least one employee had participated in a $6.3 million kickback deal with a Kuwaiti company. That money has reportedly been repaid to the government.

What we have here is a private profit-making multinational company with no particular allegiance (other than contractual) to the U.S. government. Nevertheless, through its powerful allies in the government, Halliburton enjoys extraordinary influence over national defense policies and has its own key to the national treasury.

If it's at all grateful, it hasn't shown it. The United States is at war. The government is running record deficits. Money is tight everywhere. But Halliburton won't even kick in its fair share. It continues to benefit from the nation's largesse, while scouring the world for places to shelter as much of its American riches as possible.

(January 30, 2004)

AN INSULT TO OUR SOLDIERS

Tom Davis, a Virginia Republican, is chairman of the House Committee on Government Reform. He tells a story about Sergeant Daniel Romero of the Colorado Army National Guard, who was sent to fight in Afghanistan.

In a letter dated March 23, 2002, Sergeant Romero asked a fellow sergeant: "Are they really fixing pay issues [or] are they putting them off until we return? If they are waiting, then what happens to those who (God forbid) don't make it back?"

As Davis said at a hearing this past January, "Sergeant Romero was killed in action in Afghanistan in April 2002." The congressman added, "I would really like to hear today that his family isn't wasting their time and energy fixing errors in his pay."

As we mobilize troops from around the country and send them off to fight and possibly die in that crucible of terror known as combat, is it too much to ask that they be paid in a timely way?

Researchers from the General Accounting Office, a nonpartisan investigative arm of Congress, studied the payroll processes of six Army National Guard units that were called up to active duty. What they found wasn't pretty.

There were significant pay problems in all six units. A report released last November said, "Some soldiers did not receive payments for up to six months after mobilization and others still had not received certain payments by the conclusion of our audit work."

This is exactly the kind of thing that servicemen and -women, especially those dealing with the heightened anxiety of life in a war zone, do not need. Major Kenneth Chavez of the Colorado National Guard told a congressional committee of the problems faced by the unit he commanded:

"All sixty-two soldiers encountered pay problems. . . . During extremely limited phone contact, soldiers called home only to find families in chaos because of the inability to pay bills due to erroneous military pay."

These problems are not limited to the National Guard. But one of the reasons the Guard has been especially hard hit is that, in the words of another congressman, Christopher Shays, its payroll system is "old and leaky and antiquated," designed for an era when the members of the Guard were seen as little more than weekend warriors.

That system has been unable to cope with widespread call-ups to extended periods of active duty and deployment to places in which personnel qualify for a variety of special pay and allowances, particularly in combat zones.

The GAO report said, "Four Virginia Special Forces soldiers who were injured in Afghanistan and unable to resume their civilian jobs experienced problems in receiving entitled active duty pay and related health care."

The country is asking for extraordinary—in some cases, supreme—sacrifices from the military, and then failing to meet its own responsibility to provide such basic necessities as pay and health care.

"The military knows that it's really blown it," said Shays, who heads a subcommittee of the Government Reform committee. He noted that National Guard and military reserve units were given enhanced roles in the aftermath of the cold war. But the payroll systems (and some other basic functions) were not upgraded accordingly.

"This is a huge problem," he said.

And it is not likely to be solved soon.

"Anything that could be done in the short term is kind of like Band-Aids, things that will hopefully result in fewer errors but will not fix the problem," said Gregory Kutz, who supervised the GAO report. A lasting solution to the pay problems, he said, will require a completely new system.

Defense Department officials insist they are working simultaneously on short-term fixes and the creation of a brand-new system. Patrick Shine, acting director of the Defense Finance and Accounting Service, told me that a forty-nine-step "plan of action" has been developed in response to the GAO report. He said he hoped that a completely new payroll system could be unveiled in the spring of 2005.

I asked how confident he was about the deadline. "Well," he said, "I'll be very honest with you. I don't think we're all that different from private companies, seeing sometimes slippages in schedules."

But he was optimistic, he said.

(March 15, 2004)

NO END IN SIGHT

We're told that President Bush watched the television news coverage of the Iraqi mob that attacked, burned, and mutilated four American civilians in Falluja. I can imagine the fury he must have felt. But I wonder what specific thoughts ran through his mind, and what other emotions he experienced.

Was there any soul-searching, any second thoughts about whether he did the right thing in launching this war, which he thought was all but over last May but which remains with us, with no end to the carnage in sight? With so many now dead, might the president have felt even the mildest of qualms, the faintest flickering of regret while watching the hideous images from Falluja?

If you talk to the troops who have served in Iraq, you can only marvel at their bravery and commitment to duty, and the lack of bellyaching at the difficult hands they were dealt. I've interviewed several servicemen and servicewomen who have returned from the war zone, including some who were horribly wounded, and I've yet to hear one of them utter any variation of the complaint, "Why me?"

But I inevitably come away from these conversations asking the question for them. Why were they ever placed in harm's way in Iraq? The atrocity in Falluja was inexcusable—unconscionable—and those responsible should be tracked down and punished. But even if that happens, the greater tragedy of the war itself will continue indefinitely.

We rode into this wholly unnecessary conflict on the wave of Bush's obsession with Saddam Hussein and Iraq, and we've made a hash of it. Hundreds of Americans and thousands of innocent Iraqis have died for reasons the administration has never been able to coherently explain.

On May 1, 2003, in a fun moment for the commander in chief, Bush sat in the copilot's seat as an S-3B Viking aircraft landed on the deck of the carrier *Abraham Lincoln.* The president was in full flying regalia: flight suit, parachute, water survival kit. "Yes," he told reporters, "I flew it."

The president's giddily choreographed *Top Gun* spectacle was designed to take full public relations advantage of his triumphant announcement that "major combat operations in Iraq" had ended.

He was wrong, of course, just as he was wrong about the weapons of mass destruction, and about the number of troops that would be needed to secure Iraq, and so many other things. In fact, the Bush administration has managed to conceal any and all evidence that it knows the first thing about what it's doing in Iraq.

When the army chief of staff, General Eric Shinseki, dared to say publicly that several hundred thousand troops would be needed to occupy Iraq, he was ridiculed by the administration and his career was brought to a close. When Bush's former Treasury secretary, Paul O'Neill, disclosed that planning for an invasion of Iraq was already under way in early 2001, he was denounced as someone who didn't know what he was talking about. And there's hardly a serious person in the country who is unaware of the administration's sliming of Richard Clarke, who said, among other things, that the war in Iraq had undermined the war against terror.

There were 4,000 Marines stationed near Falluja when the gruesome attack on the civilians occurred. But Marine commanders, as the *New York Times*'s Jeffrey Gettleman reports, decided they would not intervene to stop the mutilation of the bodies. The atrocity unfolded without interference.

On that same day, five soldiers were killed when their convoy rolled over a bomb buried in the road in a town fifteen miles west of Falluja. A major trade show in Baghdad that was supposed to be held to showcase investment opportunities in the new Iraq had to be postponed because of security concerns.

We are mired in a savage mess in Iraq, and no one knows how to get out of it. More than 600 U.S. troops are already dead. The rest of the world has decided that this is an American show, so we're not getting much in the way of help. President Bush won't come clean about the financial costs of the war. His mantra remains: tax cuts, tax cuts.

We're flying blind. There's no evidence that the president or anyone in his administration knows what the next act of this great tragedy will be.

(April 2, 2004)

THE WRONG WAR

Follow me, said the president. And, tragically, we did.

With his misbegotten war in Iraq, his failure to throw everything we had at Al Qaeda and Osama bin Laden, and his fantasy of using military might as a magic wand to "change the world," President Bush has ushered the American people into a bloody and mind-bending theater of the absurd.

Each act is more heartbreaking than the last. Private First Class Keith Maupin, who was kidnapped near Baghdad on April 9, 2004, showed up on a videotape broadcast by Al Jazeera one week later. He was in the custody of masked gunmen and, understandably, frightened.

"My name is Keith Matthew Maupin," he said, looking nervously into the camera. "I am a soldier from the First Division. I am married with a ten-month-old son."

Private Maupin is twenty years old and should never have been sent into the flaming horror of Iraq. Now we don't know how to get him out.

On the same day that Private Maupin was kidnapped, twenty-year-old Specialist Michelle Witmer was killed when her Humvee was attacked in Baghdad. Witmer's two sisters, Charity and Rachel, were also serving in Iraq. All three women were members of the National Guard.

American troops are enduring the deadliest period since the start of the war. And while they continue to fight courageously and sometimes die, they are fighting and dying in the wrong war, which is the height of absurdity.

One of the things I remember from my time in the service many years ago was the ubiquitous presence of large posters with the phrase, in big block letters, KNOW YOUR ENEMY.

This is a bit of military wisdom that seems to have escaped President Bush.

The United States was attacked on September 11, 2001, by Al Qaeda, not Iraq.

All Americans and most of the world would have united behind President Bush for an all-out war against Al Qaeda and Osama bin Laden. The relatives and friends of any troops who lost their lives in that effort would have known clearly and unmistakably what their loved ones had died for.

But Bush had other things on his mind. With Osama and the top leadership of Al Qaeda still at large, and with the United States still gripped by the trauma of September 11, the president turned his attention to Iraq.

Less than two months after the September 11 attacks, according to Bob Woodward's account in his book *Plan of Attack,* President Bush ordered Defense Secretary Donald Rumsfeld to have plans drawn up for a war against Iraq. Bush insisted that this be done with the greatest of secrecy. The president did not even fully inform his national security adviser, Condoleezza Rice, or his secretary of state, Colin Powell, about his directive to Rumsfeld.

Thus began the peeling away of resources crucial to the nation's fight against its most fervent enemy, Al Qaeda.

General Tommy Franks, who at the time was head of the United States Central Command and in charge of the Afghan war, was reported by Woodward to have uttered a string of obscenities when he was ordered to develop a plan for invading Iraq.

President Bush may truly believe, as he suggested at a recent press conference, that he is carrying out a mission that has been sanctioned by the divine. But he has in fact made the world less safe with his catastrophic decision to wage war in Iraq. At least 700 GIs and thousands of innocent Iraqis, including many women and children, are dead. Untold numbers have been maimed and there is no end in sight to the carnage.

Meanwhile, instead of destroying the terrorists, our real enemies, we've energized them. The invasion and occupation of Iraq has become a rallying cry for Islamic militants. Al Qaeda–type terror is spreading, not receding. And Osama bin Laden is still at large.

Even as I write this, reporters from the *New York Times* and other news outlets are filing stories about Marines dying in ambush and other acts of mayhem and anarchy across Iraq. This was not part of the plan. The administration and its apologists spread fantasies of a fresh dawn of freedom emerging in Iraq and spreading across the Arab world. Instead we are spilling the blood of innocents in a nightmare from which many thousands will never awaken.

(April 19, 2004)

"GOOKS" TO "HAJIS"

The hapless Jeremy Sivits got the recent headlines. A mechanic whose job was to service gasoline-powered generators, Specialist Sivits was sentenced to a year in prison and thrown out of the army for accepting an invitation to take part in the sadistic treatment of Iraqi detainees at Abu Ghraib prison.

But there's another soldier in serious trouble to whom we should be paying even closer attention. His case doesn't just call into question the treatment of prisoners by U.S. forces. It calls into question this entire abominable war.

Staff Sergeant Camilo Mejia is a twenty-eight-year-old member of the Florida National Guard who served six harrowing months in Iraq, went home to Miami on a furlough last October, and then refused to return to his unit when the furlough ended.

Sergeant Mejia has been charged with desertion. His court-martial at Fort Stewart, Georgia, began the same day that Specialist Sivits pleaded guilty to the charges against him. If Sergeant Mejia is convicted, he will face a punishment similar to Sivitz's, a year in prison and a bad-conduct discharge.

Sergeant Mejia told me in a long telephone interview that he had qualms about the war from the beginning but he followed his orders and went to Iraq in April 2003. He led an infantry squad and saw plenty of action. But the more he thought about the war—including the slaughter of Iraqi civilians, the mistreatment of prisoners (which he personally witnessed), the killing of children, the cruel deaths of American GIs (some of whom are the targets of bounty hunters in search of a reported $2,000 per head), the ineptitude of inexperienced, glory-hunting military officers who at times are needlessly putting U.S. troops in even greater danger, and the growing rage among coalition troops against all Iraqis (known derisively as "hajis," the way the Vietnamese were known as "gooks")—the more he thought about these things, the more he felt that this war could not be justified, and that he could no longer be part of it.

Sergeant Mejia's legal defense is complex (among other things, he is seeking conscientious objector status), but his essential point is that war is too terrible to be waged willy-nilly, that there must always be an ethically or morally sound reason for opening the spigots to such horror. And he believes that that threshold was never met in Iraq.

"Imagine being in the infantry in Ramadi, like we were," he said, "where you get shot at every day and you get mortared where you live, [and attacked] with RPGs [rocket-propelled grenades], and people are dying and getting wounded and maimed every day. A lot of horrible things become acceptable."

He spoke about a friend of his, a sniper, who he said had shot a child about ten years old who was carrying an automatic weapon. "He realized it was a kid," said Sergeant Mejia. "The kid tried to get up. He shot him again."

The child died.

All you really want to do in such an environment, said Sergeant Mejia, is "get out of there alive." So soldiers will do things under that kind of extreme stress that they wouldn't do otherwise.

"You just sort of try to block out the fact that they're human beings and see them as enemies," he said. "You call them 'hajis,' you know? You do all the things that make it easier to deal with killing them and mistreating them."

When there is time later to reflect on what has happened, said Sergeant Mejia, "you come face to face with your emotions and your feelings and you try to tell yourself that you did it for a good reason. And if you don't find it, if you don't believe you did it for a good reason, then, you know, it becomes pretty tough to accept it—to willingly be a part of the war."

A military court will decide whether Sergeant Mejia, who served honorably while he was in Iraq, is a deserter or a conscientious objector or something in between. But the issues he has raised deserve a close reading by the nation as a whole, which is finally beginning to emerge from the fog of deliberate misrepresentations created by Bush, Rumsfeld, Wolfowitz et al. about this war.

The truth is the antidote to that crowd. Whatever the outcome of Sergeant Mejia's court-martial, he has made a contribution to the truth about Iraq.

(May 21, 2004)

POSTSCRIPT

Sergeant Mejia was found guilty of desertion and sentenced to the maximum allowable punishment: one year in prison, reduction in rank to private, and a bad-conduct discharge.

DID SOMEBODY SAY WAR?

President Bush fell off his bike and hurt himself during a seventeen-mile excursion at his ranch in Crawford, Texas. Nothing serious. A few cuts and bruises. He was wearing a bike helmet and a mouth guard, and he was able to climb back on his bike and finish his ride.

A little later he left the ranch and went to Austin for a graduation party for his daughter Jenna. And then it was on to New Haven, where daughter Barbara was graduating from Yale. Except for the bicycle mishap, it sounded like a very pleasant weekend.

Meanwhile, there's a war on. Yet another U.S. soldier was killed near Falluja yesterday. You remember Falluja. That's the rebellious city that the Marines gave up on and turned over to the control of officers from the very same Baathist army that we invaded Iraq to defeat.

It's impossible to think about Iraq without stumbling over these kinds of absurdities. How do you get a logical foothold on a war that was nurtured from the beginning on absurd premises? You can't. Iraq had nothing to do with September 11. The invasion of Iraq was not part of the war on terror. We had no business launching this war. Now we're left with the tragic absurdity of a clueless president riding his bicycle in Texas while Americans in Iraq are going up in flames.

How bad is the current situation? General Anthony Zinni, the retired Marine Corps general who headed the U.S. Central Command (which covers much of the Middle East and Central Asia) from 1997 to 2000, was utterly dismissive about the administration's "stay the course" strategy in Iraq. "The course is headed over Niagara Falls," he said in an interview with *60 Minutes*, adding, "It should be evident to everybody that they've screwed up."

When the weapons of mass destruction rationale went by the

boards, the administration and its apologists tried to justify the war by asserting that the United States could use bullets and bombs to seed Iraq with an American-style democracy that would then spread like the flowers of spring throughout the Middle East.

Anthony Cordesman, a Middle East expert at the Center for Strategic and International Studies, in Washington, addressed that point in a report titled, *The "Post Conflict" Lessons of Iraq and Afghanistan.*

"At this point," the report said, "the U.S. lacks good options in Iraq—although it probably never really had them in the sense the Bush administration sought. The option of quickly turning Iraq into a successful, free-market democracy was never practical, and was as absurd a neoconservative fantasy as the idea that success in this objective would magically make Iraq an example that would transform the Middle East."

The president's reservoir of credibility on Iraq is bone dry. His approval ratings are going down. Conservative voices in opposition to his policies are growing louder. And the troops themselves are becoming increasingly disenchanted with their mission. Yet no one knows quite what to do. Americans are torn between a desire to stop the madness by pulling the plug on this tragic and hopeless adventure and the belief that the United States, for the time being, may be the only safeguard against a catastrophic civil war.

The president is about to give a speech to lay out his "clear strategy" for the future of Iraq. Don't hold your breath. This is the same president who deliberately exploited his nation's fear of terrorism in the aftermath of September 11 to lead it into the long, dark, starless night of Iraq.

As for the Iraqis, they've been had. We're not going to foot the bill in any real sense for the reconstruction of Iraq, any more than we've been willing to foot the bill for a reconstruction of the public school system here at home. There's a reason why Ahmad Chalabi and the Bush crowd were so simpatico for so long. They all considered themselves masters of the con. They all thought that they could fool all of the people all of the time.

There's a terrible sense of dread filtering across America at the moment, and it's not simply because of the continuing fear of terrorism and the fact that the nation is at war. It's more frightening than that. It grows out of the suspicion that we all may be passengers in a vehicle that has made a radically wrong turn and is barreling along a dark road, with its headlights off and with someone behind the wheel who may not know how to drive.

(May 24, 2004)

14

BODY COUNT

DEATH COMES KNOCKING

The e-mail to John Witmer from his daughter Michelle came on Father's Day in 2003.

"Dear Daddy," it said,

> Happy Father's Day. I love you so much and you can't imagine how often I think of you. I hope you have lots of fun today and that the weather is lovely.
>
> We had a briefing telling us to prepare ourselves as best as possible for what lies ahead. Things like children running out in front of vehicles to try and get them to stop. We have to prepare ourselves to hit people because stopping is not an option. I guess every convoy that's gone up north so far has taken fire or been ambushed. The question of whether we will or not is not even really a question, more like a guess as to when.
>
> These things, as you can imagine, are a lot to take in. I'm

doing my best. I've been a little depressed lately but I'm trying to keep my chin up. I really miss home. Tomorrow will be exactly three months since I got deployed. Wow, time does not fly. Jeez, this letter wasn't supposed to be down. Sorry. Back to the point. Happy Father's Day. I love and miss you so much.

Love, Shelly.

Specialist Michelle Witmer of New Berlin, Wisconsin, survived for nearly ten more slowly moving months in Iraq, until she was cut down by enemy fire in Baghdad on April 9, 2004. She was twenty when she died.

The e-mail was read on camera by her dad in an extremely moving documentary, *Last Letters Home,* which was jointly produced by the *New York Times* and HBO.

In the hourlong program, grieving relatives read aloud from letters, cards, and e-mail sent by troops who died in Iraq, and comment on the ways they've been affected by the loss of their loved ones. The program is not about pro-war or antiwar sentiments, or grand geopolitical visions. It just gives us a glimpse of the searing personal toll that is inevitable in war. I imagine it would be difficult for anyone to see it and not take the war more seriously. Anything that imposes such unmitigated agony should give us pause.

Second Lieutenant Leonard Cowherd III of Culpeper, Virginia, commented in his last letter to his wife, Sarah, about how young so many of the soldiers were, which was interesting because he was only twenty-two himself. He wrote:

> Some of these guys out here, Sarah, they're just kids. I'm not that old myself but I couldn't imagine going through the experiences these guys are going through at the age of eighteen, nineteen, and twenty. If you saw them walking down the street you would think that they belonged in an arcade or at a movie theater doing stuff kids do. Not putting their lives on the line every second of every day.

The Cowherds were married in 2003 and spent only a few months together before Lieutenant Cowherd was shipped to Iraq. He was shot to death in Karbala in May.

A theme that runs through the documentary is the overwhelming sense of dread that grips relatives when their doors are knocked upon by soldiers or Marines in dress uniforms.

"It was the lightest tap on my door that I've ever heard in my life," said Paula Zasadny, the mother of Specialist Holly McGeogh, a nineteen-year-old who was killed by a bomb in Kirkuk.

"I opened the door and I seen the man in the dress greens and I knew. I immediately knew. But I thought that if, as long as I didn't let him in, he couldn't tell me. And then it—none of that would've happened. So he kept saying, 'Ma'am, I need to come in.' And I kept telling him, 'I'm sorry, but you can't come in.' "

As much as possible, the reality of war is kept at a distance from the American people, which is a shame. My own belief is that the pain of war should be much more widely shared. That would help guard us against wars that are unnecessary, and ensure a more collective effort in those that are inevitable.

This documentary takes us a small step toward understanding the awful depth of that pain.

Melissa Givens was told by a chaplain that her husband, Private first class Jesse Givens, who was thirty-four, had drowned when his tank fell into the Euphrates River. Distraught, she insisted that the chaplain was lying. But she said that was OK, because she would never tell anyone that he had lied. She said he could walk away and she would just forget about the whole thing.

Private Givens died on May 1, 2003, the day that President Bush, on the aircraft carrier *Abraham Lincoln*, declared that "major combat operations in Iraq have ended."

(November 12, 2004)

A PRICE TOO HIGH

How long is it going to take for us to recognize that the war we so foolishly started in Iraq is a fiasco—tragic, deeply dehumanizing, and ultimately unwinnable? How much time and how much money and how many wasted lives is it going to take?

At the United Nations, grieving diplomats spoke bitterly, but not for attribution, about the U.S.-led invasion and occupation. They said it has not only resulted in the violent deaths of close and highly respected colleagues, but also galvanized the most radical elements of Islam.

"This is a dream for the jihad," said one high-ranking UN official. "The resistance will only grow. The American occupation is now the focal point, drawing people from all over Islam into an eye-to-eye confrontation with the hated Americans.

"It is very propitious for the terrorists," he said. "The U.S. is now on the soil of an Arab country, a Muslim country, where the terrorists have all the advantages. They are fighting in a terrain which they know and the U.S. does not know, with cultural images the U.S. does not understand, and with a language the American soldiers do not speak. The troops can't even read the street signs."

The American people still do not have a clear understanding of why we are in Iraq. And the troops don't have a clear understanding of their mission. We're fighting a guerrilla war, which the bright lights at the Pentagon never saw coming, with conventional forces.

Under these circumstances, in which the enemy might be anybody, anywhere, tragedies like the killing of Mazen Dana are all but inevitable. Dana was the veteran Reuters cameraman who was blown away by jittery U.S. troops on Sunday. The troops apparently thought his video camera was a rocket-propelled grenade launcher.

The mind plays tricks on you when you're in great danger. A

couple of weeks ago, in an apparent case of mistaken identity, U.S. soldiers killed two members of the Iraqi police. And a number of innocent Iraqi civilians, including children, have been killed by American troops.

The carnage from riots, ambushes, firefights, suicide bombings, acts of sabotage, friendly-fire incidents, and other deadly encounters is growing. And so is the hostility toward U.S. troops and Americans in general.

We are paying a terribly high price—for what?

One of the many reasons Vietnam spiraled out of control was the fact that America's top political leaders never clearly defined the mission there, and were never straight with the public about what they were doing. Domestic political considerations led Kennedy, then Johnson, then Nixon to conceal the truth about a policy that was bankrupt from the beginning. They even concealed how much the war was costing.

Sound familiar?

Now we're lodged in Iraq, in the midst of the most volatile region of the world, and the illusion of a quick victory followed by grateful Iraqis' welcoming us with open arms has vanished. Instead of democracy blossoming in the desert, we have the reality of continuing bloodshed and heightened terror—the payoff of a policy spun from fantasies and lies.

Senator John McCain and others are saying the answer is more troops, an escalation. If you want more American blood shed, that's the way to go. We sent troops to Vietnam by the hundreds of thousands. There were never enough.

Beefing up the American occupation is not the answer to the problem. The American occupation is the problem. The occupation is perceived by ordinary Iraqis as a confrontation and a humiliation, and by terrorists and other bad actors as an opportunity to be gleefully exploited.

The United States cannot bully its way to victory in Iraq. It needs allies, and it needs a plan. As quickly as possible, we should turn the country over to a genuine international coalition, headed by the UN and supported in good faith by the United States.

The idea would be to mount a massive international effort to secure Iraq, develop a legitimate sovereign government, and work cooperatively with the Iraqi people to rebuild the nation.

If this does not happen, disaster will loom because the United States cannot secure and rebuild Iraq on its own.

A UN aide told me: "The United States is the number one enemy of the Muslim world, and right now it's sitting on the terrorists' doorstep. It needs help. It needs friends."

(August 21, 2003)

OUR WOUNDED WARRIORS

Hector Delgado joined the Marines in the spring of 1999. He was at loose ends in his hometown of Selden, New York, and hoped the Marines would give his life some "structure and discipline."

"Did it work?" I asked.

Corporal Delgado shifted his upper body in his wheelchair and laughed. "Oh, absolutely," he said. "One hundred percent."

His enlistment was supposed to have been up last March, and his plans were to pursue a career in law enforcement. He'd taken and passed the test for the New York City Police Department and was due to enter the police academy.

But the United States went to war with Iraq, and Corporal Delgado's enlistment was extended. "They were pretty much preventing people from getting out," he said. "I was disappointed at first. But I had to sit down and really think about who I was, which was a Marine, you know? This was my job."

Corporal Delgado was in the first wave of troops sent to Iraq and was severely injured in April 2003. He was with a convoy of vehicles, including fuel tankers, that had stopped outside Nasiriya. "All the fuel tankers were staged next to each other," he said. "Everyone was trying to sit in between them to get out of the sun because it was like 105 degrees that day.

"There was a lot of heavy equipment around, shaking the ground. And a tanker trailer really isn't all that sturdy in the sand. I had my friend Corporal Gonzalez sitting to my left, and all of a sudden I just started hearing metal crinkling and everybody yelling, 'Get up! Get up!'"

Somehow the supports holding up the tanker, which had been shielding Corporal Delgado and others from the fierce desert sun, gave way.

"It landed on top of me," Corporal Delgado said. "On top of my waist."

He was pinned to the ground, facedown, for twenty-five minutes, remaining conscious the entire time. His pelvis was crushed. His right hip was broken and dislocated. Bones in his left leg and left foot were shattered. His abdominal muscles were crushed, and he suffered nerve damage in both legs.

In one of the great understatements of the twenty-first century, Corporal Delgado, who is twenty-four, said, "It was very painful."

The rescue effort was excruciating. "They came with a forklift to try to lift it up," he said. "But the forklift couldn't do it. So they came over with a crane, and they hooked it up and the crane wasn't working. So they had to take the crane back and get another crane. As soon as they got it up, they pulled me out, and I was in so much pain they just threw me on the stretcher and put me in the medical Hummer and brought me to the medical tent.

"I looked up and saw both my feet were flopped over to the left, and I didn't want to look up again."

Corporal Delgado would learn later that his close friend Corporal Armando Gonzalez, who was right beside him when the tanker fell, was killed instantly. (Corporal Gonzalez, of Hialeah, Florida, was twenty-five. He had married just six months prior to the accident, and in September 2003 his wife gave birth to a son.)

The troops who are selflessly sacrificing their bodies and their dreams in Iraq (as troops always do in war) are not getting a lot of attention here at home. Most of us are busy with other things— presidential politics, Martha Stewart's rise and fall, the use of steroids in baseball.

I was put in touch with Corporal Delgado (and several other Marines who were badly wounded in Iraq) by John Melia, founder of the Wounded Warrior Project (a division of the United Spinal Association), which tries to assist the young men and women who are hurt in the wars they fight for us.

"They come back," he said, "and in many cases they're not the same kids that they were when they left us."

Thousands of U.S. troops have been wounded and injured in Iraq. They have been paralyzed, lost limbs, suffered blindness, been horribly burned, and so on. They are heroes, without question, but their stories have largely gone untold.

If Corporal Delgado is harboring any bitterness, I couldn't detect it. There were times, he said, when he wished he had died beneath the trailer. But he fought his way through the mental distress, just as he is fighting through the physical pain, and his goal is to one day walk again. He'll be discharged from the Marines soon and hopes to find work helping other disabled veterans.

"That's one way I could repay all the people who are helping me now," he said.

(March 12, 2004)

A SOLDIER'S SACRIFICE

Washington

It was about three a.m. and pitch-black when the convoy of U.S. Army trucks, traveling south on Highway 1, turned right and began moving along a rutted dirt road near Bayji, a small town in the Sunni Triangle about twenty-five miles north of Tikrit.

Tyler Hall, a baby-faced twenty-three-year-old sergeant from Wasilla, Alaska, was among the six soldiers in the second truck, which took the brunt of the explosion when the bomb that was buried in the road detonated.

Sergeant Hall puts the matter quite succinctly: "I was blown up in an IED attack on August 22." *IED* stands for "improvised explosive device."

That the sergeant survived at all is incredible. He will never be the same.

"All I remember is, like, sparks," he said during an interview at the Washington headquarters of Disabled American Veterans. "I saw these sparks, and then the whole truck kind of caved in."

The first time he regained consciousness, he was lying on his back in the road. And he remembers, with the dark humor common to troops in combat, a brief John Wayne–like moment.

"My buddy was trying to resuscitate me. He thought I was dead. I came to for a very brief time, and he was about to give me mouth-to-mouth. I said, 'What do you think you're doing, trying to make out with me or something?' And he said, 'Sergeant Hall, you're alive!' And everybody's like, 'Hey, Sergeant Hall's alive!' All I remember after that is hearing the Blackhawk helicopter coming down, and I just lost consciousness from there."

He wouldn't wake up again for another forty-five days.

Sergeant Hall's mother, Kim, who is forty, sat beside him during the interview. From time to time she rubbed salve on the burns that have disfigured both of her son's hands. The sergeant also has a burn across the bridge of his nose. The lower half of his face, which had to be reconstructed because both of his jaws were broken and ten of his teeth were blown out and part of his palate was destroyed, looks surprisingly normal. The surgeons at Walter Reed army hospital seem to have done a good job.

Sergeant Hall also sustained a brain injury, but you can't tell that from talking to him. He's not just lucid—he's bright and funny. (He compared the negotiating process for his enlistment bonus to plea bargaining.) But he tires easily. And he gets headaches.

He also had three bones in his back broken, and his arm was broken, and he lost his left leg below the knee.

This, of course, is what war does to people. It takes the human body and grinds it up like sausage meat.

Sergeant Hall was the most severely wounded victim of the attack. When his mother was informed by phone that he had been hurt, the caller said his death was most likely "imminent."

"He was in the hospital in Germany," Kim Hall said, "and it took me a few days with the visa and everything to get over there. So every night I would call and beg the nurse in the middle of the night to please put the phone by his ear and I would talk to him, even though he was unconscious. I don't know for sure that he heard me, but I like to believe that he did."

Kim Hall recalled a moment at Walter Reed when a decision had to be made about the amputation of Sergeant Hall's leg. She spotted a young man her son knew who was a triple amputee. "He had lost three limbs, and his father was pushing him in the wheelchair, and they were laughing and talking. And I thought, 'You know, if they can do that, well—' I kind of knew then that we would be all right."

Sergeant Hall said he doesn't dwell on his injuries, and he hasn't had to wrestle with bouts of rage or bitterness. "You try to have a good attitude," he said, "because there are other people around you with injuries that are more severe. Even on your worst days, you kind of feel, you know, that if you don't keep a good attitude you're letting down the people around you."

He said he joined the army to earn money for college and to serve his country, and that he didn't regret enlisting.

Kim Hall leaned over and gently rubbed more lotion onto his hands.

Sergeant Hall said he expected he'd be able to run pretty soon. He is looking forward to it. Keeping busy, he said, helps keep his spirits up. He said he felt he was doing pretty well, considering all the "amazing stuff" that had happened to him.

(April 16, 2004)

FROM DREAM TO NIGHTMARE

At least ten more American soldiers died yesterday in George W. Bush's senseless war in Iraq. They died for a pipe dream, which the *American Heritage Dictionary* defines as a fantastic notion or a vain hope. "Pipe dream" originally referred to the fantasies induced by smoking a pipe of opium. The folks who led us into this hideous madness in Iraq, against the wishes of most of the world, sure seem to have been smoking something.

President Bush and his hyperhawk vice president, Dick Cheney, were busy lip-syncing their way through an appearance before the commission investigating the September 11 attacks. If you want a hint of how much trouble the United States is in, consider that these two gentlemen are still clinging to the hope that weapons of mass destruction will be found in Iraq.

Reality was the first casualty of Iraq. This was a war that would be won on the cheap, we were told, with few American casualties. The costs of reconstruction would be more than covered by Iraqi oil revenues. The Iraqi people, giddy with their first taste of freedom, would toss petals in the path of their liberators. And democracy, successfully rooted in Iraq, would soon spread like the flowers of spring throughout the Middle East.

Oh, they must have been passing the pipe around.

My problem with the warrior fantasies emerging from the comfort zones of Washington and Crawford, Texas, is that they are being put to the test in the flaming reality of combat in Iraq, not by the fantasizers but by brave and patriotic men and women who deserve so much more from the country they are willing to defend with their lives.

There is nothing new about this. It seemed to take forever for American leaders to realize that they were lost in a pipe dream in Vietnam. A key government spokesman during a crucial period of that conflict was Barry Zorthian, the public information officer for American forces in Vietnam from 1964 to 1968. In a book published last year, *Patriots: The Vietnam War Remembered from All Sides*, Zorthian is quoted as saying: "We probably could have gotten the deal we ended up with in 1973 as early as 1969. And between 1969 and 1972 we almost doubled our losses. It's easy to second-guess but I've never been convinced that those last 25,000 casualties were justified."

The sad truth about Iraq is that one year after President Bush gaudily proclaimed victory with his *Top Gun* moment aboard the aircraft carrier *Abraham Lincoln*, we don't know what we're doing in Iraq. We don't know where we're heading. We don't know how many troops it will take to get us there. And we don't know how to get out.

Flower petals strewn in our path? Forget about that. The needle on the hate-America meter in Iraq is buried deep in the bright red danger zone. Even humanitarian aid groups have had to hustle American and other non-Iraqi workers out of the country because of fears that they would be kidnapped, shot, or bombed.

A *USA Today*/CNN/Gallup poll found that only a third of Iraqis believe the U.S.-led occupation is doing more good than harm. There is nothing surprising about the poll's findings. The United States primed Iraq with a "shock and awe" bombing campaign, then invaded, and is attempting to impose our concept of democracy at the point of a gun.

Why would anybody think that would work?

Since then we've destroyed countless homes and legitimate businesses and killed or maimed thousands of innocent Iraqi civilians, including many women and children. That was a lousy strategy for winning hearts and minds in Vietnam and it's a lousy strategy now.

Equally unsurprising is the erosion of support for the war among Americans. There's no upside. Casualties are mounting daily and so are the financial costs, which have never been honestly acknowledged or budgeted.

Bush has enmeshed us in a war that we can't win and that we don't know how to end. Each loss of a life in this tragic exercise is a reminder of lessons never learned from history. And the most fundamental of those lessons is that fantasy must always genuflect before reality.

(April 30, 2004)

BUSH'S BLINKERS

Does President Bush even tip his hat to reality as he goes breezing by?

He often behaves as if he sees—or is in touch with—things that are inaccessible to those who are grounded in the reality most of us have come to know. For example, with more than one thousand American troops and more than ten thousand Iraqi civilians dead, many people see the ongoing war in Iraq as a disaster, if not a catastrophe. Bush sees freedom on the march.

Many thoughtful analysts see a fiscal disaster developing here at home, with the president's tax cuts being the primary contributor to the radical transformation of a $236 billion budget surplus into a $415 billion deficit. The president sees, incredibly, a need for still more tax cuts.

The United States was attacked on September 11, 2001, by Osama bin Laden and Al Qaeda. The president responded by turning most of the nation's firepower on Saddam Hussein and Iraq. When Bush was asked by the journalist Bob Woodward if he had consulted with former President Bush about the decision to invade Iraq, the president replied: "He is the wrong father to appeal to in terms of strength. There is a higher father that I appeal to."

In October 2003 the Jaffee Center for Strategic Studies at Tel Aviv University said in a report:

"During the past year Iraq has become a major distraction from the global war on terrorism. Iraq has now become a convenient arena for jihad, which has helped Al Qaeda to recover from the setback it suffered as a result of the war in Afghanistan. With the growing phenomenon of suicide bombing, the U.S. presence in Iraq now demands more and more assets that might have otherwise been deployed against various dimensions of the global terrorist threat."

There are consequences, often powerful consequences, to turning one's back on reality. The president may believe that freedom's on the march, and that freedom is God's gift to every man and woman in the world, and perhaps even that he is the vessel through which that gift is transmitted. But when he is crafting policy decisions that put people by the hundreds of thousands into harm's way, he needs to rely on more than the perceived good wishes of the Almighty. He needs to submit those policy decisions to a good hard reality check.

Here's one good reason why:

Dr. Gene Bolles spent two years as the chief of neurosurgery at the Landstuhl Regional Medical Center in Germany, which is where most of the soldiers wounded in Iraq are taken. Among his patients was Private First Class Jessica Lynch. In an interview posted on the Web site AlterNet.org, Dr. Bolles was asked: "What kind of cases did you treat in Landstuhl? And these were mostly kids, right?"

He said: "Well, I can call them that since I'm sixty-two years old. And they were eighteen, nineteen, maybe twenty-one. They all seemed young. Certainly younger than my children. As a neurosurgeon I mostly dealt with injuries to the brain, the spinal cord, or the spine itself. The injuries were all fairly horrific, anywhere from the loss of extremities, multiple extremities, to severe burns. It just goes on and on and on. As a doctor myself who has seen trauma throughout his career, I've never seen it to this degree. The numbers, the degree of injuries. It really kind of caught me off guard."

If you're the president and you're contemplating a war in which thousands of deaths and tens of thousands of these kinds of injuries will take place, you have an obligation to seek out the best sources of information and the wisest advice from the widest possible array of counselors. And you have an absolute obligation to exercise sound judgment based upon facts, and not simply faith.

In a disturbing article in the *New York Times Magazine*, the writer Ron Suskind told of a meeting he'd had with a senior adviser to the president. The White House at the time was unhappy about an article Suskind had written.

According to Suskind, "The aide said that guys like me were 'in what we call the reality-based community,' which he defined as people who 'believe that solutions emerge from your judicious study of discernible reality.'" The aide told Suskind, "That's not the way the world really works anymore. We're an empire now, and when we act we create our own reality."

Got that? We may think there are real-world consequences to the policies of the president, real pain and real grief for real people. But to the White House, that kind of thinking is passé. The White House doesn't even recognize that kind of reality.

(October 22, 2004)

PARALYZED, A SOLDIER ASKS WHY

Dale City, Virginia

Sunlight was pouring through the doorway to the furnished basement of the neat two-story home on Reardon Lane. The doorway had been widened to accommodate the wheelchair of Army Staff Sergeant Eugene Simpson Jr., who was once a star athlete but now, at age twenty-seven, spends a lot of time in his parents' basement, watching the large flat-screen television.

I asked the sergeant whether he ever gets depressed. "No," he said quickly, before adding, "I mean, I could say I was sad for a while. But it didn't really last long."

Sergeant Simpson's expertise is tank warfare. But the army is stretched thin, and the nation's war plans at times have all the coherence of football plays drawn up in the school yard. When Sergeant Simpson's unit was deployed from Germany to Iraq, the tanks were left behind and the sergeant ended up bouncing around Tikrit in a Humvee, on the lookout for weapons smugglers and other vaguely defined "bad guys."

He said he felt more like a cop than a soldier.

One evening in April 2004, Sergeant Simpson was the passenger in the lead vehicle of a four-vehicle convoy on a routine patrol in Tikrit. "It was a little housing area," he said. "We were just there to show a presence."

Iraqi soldiers were in the second vehicle of the convoy.

"I looked back and the Iraqi truck had stopped for some reason," Sergeant Simpson said.

He waved the driver forward, but the truck remained motionless. "That was odd," he said. "They wouldn't follow us. Then I happened to look down between two houses and I saw an Iraqi guy standing in the alley with like a remote control key for a car. And that was odd because there were like no cars in the whole little housing area."

Sergeant Simpson had been taught that key remotes can be used by insurgents to set off explosives. "So I knew right then something was wrong, and I raised up my gun to fire at him. But before I could get my weapon all the way up he pushed the button."

The bomb hidden in the road exploded with terrific force just a few feet from Sergeant Simpson.

"When I saw the explosion go off, I tried to jump back into the center of the Humvee for more protection," he said. "Everything went in slow motion for about fifteen seconds. I saw scrap metal and dust and everything flying by me, and I felt it hitting me all in my legs and my back. It felt like hot metal burning my skin everywhere."

The driver of the Humvee fired at the attacker, who vanished. Sergeant Simpson was in agony. "It hurt so bad, I couldn't cry," he said.

The sergeant's spinal cord had been severed. On the short drive back to their home camp, he felt as if he was dying. "I would open and close my eyes," he said, "and all I could see was my family."

Sergeant Simpson is paralyzed from the waist down. He said he remembers hearing, as he was airlifted from Baghdad back to Germany, the moans and the cries and the weeping of the many other wounded soldiers on the plane. And he remembers the grief of the severely wounded soldiers in the military hospital in Landstuhl, where most of the evacuees from Iraq are taken. He saw amputees, and soldiers who were paralyzed or had suffered brain damage or other crippling injuries.

"Some of them never wanted anybody to come into their room," he said. "They never wanted to talk to anybody. The ones with the lesser injuries—you know, maybe got shot in the arm, that kind of thing—they were more upbeat."

Sergeant Simpson is married to a German woman, Shirley Weber, and they have two children. He is trying to get his family into the United States, but the red tape is formidable. "The separation from them—that's the hardest thing to deal with," he said.

His feelings about the military, at the moment, are ambivalent. "Of course, I still wish I could walk and still be in the military," he said. "That's what I love to do."

But when I asked if he still loved the military itself, he paused and then said:

"Not as much. That's basically because we were over there, all these young guys, doing our jobs, but we really didn't know why we were there. I ask myself, 'What was our purpose?' And to this day I still can't figure out our purpose for being there."

He said he accepted his obligation, as a soldier, to fight. He is not resentful. But he would have appreciated a little more clarity about what he was fighting for.

(October 15, 2004)

LETTING DOWN THE TROOPS

Not long ago I interviewed a soldier who was paralyzed from injuries he had suffered in a roadside bombing in Iraq. Like so many other wounded soldiers I've talked to, he expressed no anger and no bitterness about the difficult hand he's been dealt as a result of the war.

But when I asked this soldier, Eugene Simpson Jr., a twenty-seven-year-old staff sergeant from Dale City, Virginia, whom he had been fighting in Iraq—who, exactly, the enemy was—he looked up from his wheelchair and stared at me for a long moment. Then, in a voice much softer than he had been using for most of the interview, and with what seemed like a mixture of sorrow, regret, and frustration, he said: "I don't know. That would be my answer. I don't know."

We have not done right by the troops we've sent to Iraq to fight this crazy, awful war. We haven't given them a clear mission, and we haven't protected them well. I'm reminded of the famous scene in *On the Waterfront* when Terry Malloy, the character played by Marlon Brando, tells his brother: "You shoulda looked out for me a little bit. You shoulda taken care of me just a little bit."

The thing to always keep in mind about our troops in Iraq is that they were sent to fight the wrong war. America's clearly defined and unmistakable enemy, Osama bin Laden's Al Qaeda, was in Afghanistan. So the men and women fighting and dying in Iraq were thrown into a pointless, wholly unnecessary conflict.

That tragic move was made worse by the failure of the United States to send enough troops to effectively wage the war that we started in Iraq. And we never fully equipped the troops we did send. The people who ordered up this war had no idea what they were doing. They were wildly overconfident, blinded by hubris and a dangerous, overarching ideology. They thought it would be a cakewalk.

In May 2003, President Bush thought the war was over. It had barely begun. Many thousands have died in the long and bloody months since then. Even now, Dick Cheney, with a straight face, is calling Iraq "a remarkable success story."

One of the worst things about the management of this war is the way we've treated our men and women in uniform. The equipment shortages experienced by troops shoved into combat have been unconscionable. Soldiers and Marines, in many cases, have been forced to face enemy fire with flak jackets from the Vietnam era that were all but useless, and sometimes without any body armor at all. Relatives back home have had to send the troops such items as radios and goggles, and even graphite to keep their weapons from jamming.

One of the most ominous signs about the war is the growing disenchantment of the troops. They've spent too much time on the most dangerous roads in the world without the proper training, without up-to-date equipment, without the proper armor for their vehicles, and without the support they feel they should be getting from their Iraqi allies.

The *Times*'s Edward Wong, after a series of interviews with Marines in the Sunni-dominated city of Ramadi, wrote:

"They said the Iraqi police and National Guard are unhelpful at best and enemy agents at worst, raising doubts about President Bush's assertion that local forces would soon help relieve the policing duties of the 138,000 American troops in Iraq. The marines said they could use better equipment from the Pentagon, and they feared that the American people were ignorant of the hardships they faced in this desiccated land."

Several members of an Army Reserve unit refused a direct order to deliver fuel along a dangerous route in Iraq. They said their trucks were not armored and were prone to breaking down. An example of the kind of catastrophe they were seeking to avoid came just a week later, when forty-nine unarmed and otherwise unprotected Iraqi soldiers were attacked and killed in cold blood in a remote region of eastern Iraq.

This has been a war run by amateurs and incompetents. Whatever anyone has felt about the merits of the war, there is no excuse for preparing so poorly and for failing to see, at a minimum, that the troops were properly trained and equipped.

The United States has the most powerful military in history, yet it is bogged down in a humiliating quagmire in a country that was barely functional to begin with. We've dealt ourselves the cruelest of hands in Iraq. We can't win this war and, tragically, we don't know how to end it.

(October 29, 2004)

HOW MANY DEATHS WILL IT TAKE?

It was Vietnam all over again—the heartbreaking head shots captioned with good old American names: *Jose Casanova, Donald J. Cline Jr., Sheldon R. Hawk Eagle, Alyssa R. Peterson.*

Eventually there'll be a fine memorial to honor the young Americans whose lives were sacrificed for no good reason in Iraq. Under the headline "The Roster of the Dead," the *New York Times* ran photos of the first thousand or so who were killed. They were sent off by a president who ran and hid when he was a young man and his country was at war. They fought bravely and died honorably. But as in Vietnam, no amount of valor or heroism can conceal the fact that they were sent off under false pretenses to fight a war that is unwinnable.

How many thousands more will have to die before we acknowledge that President Bush's obsession with Iraq and Saddam Hussein has been a catastrophe for the United States?

Joshua T. Byers, Matthew G. Milczark, Harvey E. Parkerson III, Ivory L. Phipps.

Fewer and fewer Americans believe the war in Iraq is worth the human treasure we are losing and the staggering amounts of money it is costing. But no one can find a way out of this tragic mess, which is why that dreaded word from the Vietnam era—*quagmire*—has been resurrected. Most Washington insiders agree with Senator John McCain, who said he believes the United States will be involved militarily in Iraq for ten or twenty more years.

To what end? You can wave good-bye to the naïve idea that democracy would take root in Iraq and then spread like the flowers of spring throughout the Middle East. That was never going to happen. So what are we there for, other than to establish a permanent military stronghold in the region and control the flow of Iraqi oil?

The insurgency in Iraq will never end as long as the United States is occupying the country. And our Iraqi "allies" will never fight their Iraqi brethren with the kind of intensity the United States would like, any more than the South Vietnamese would fight their fellow Vietnamese with the fury and effectiveness demanded by the hawks in the Johnson administration.

The Iraqi insurgents—whether one agrees with them or not—believe they are fighting for their homeland, their religion, and their families. The Americans are not at all clear what they're fighting for. Saddam is gone. There were no weapons of mass destruction. The link between Saddam and the atrocities of September 11 was always specious and has been proven so.

At some point, as in Vietnam, the American public will balk at the continued carnage, and this tragic misadventure will become politically unsustainable. Meanwhile, the death toll mounts.

Elia P. Fontecchio, Raheen Tyson Heighter, Sharon T. Swartworth, Ruben Valdez Jr.

One of the reasons the American effort in Iraq is unsustainable is that the American people know very little about the Iraqi people and their culture, and in most cases couldn't care less. The war in Iraq was sold as a response to September 11. As it slowly dawns on a majority of Americans that the link was bogus, and that there is no benefit to the United States from this war, only endless grief, the political support will all but vanish.

(This could take a while. In a poll done for *Newsweek* magazine, 42 percent of the respondents continue to believe that Saddam Hussein was directly involved in the September 11 attacks.)

We've put our troops in Iraq in an impossible situation. If you are not permitted to win a war, eventually you will lose it. In Vietnam, for a variety of reasons, the United States never waged total war, although the enemy did. After several years and more than 58,000 deaths, we quit.

We won't—and shouldn't—wage total war in Iraq either. But to the insurgents, the Americans epitomize evil. We're the crazed foreigners who invaded their country and killed innocent Iraqi civilians, including women and children, by the thousands. We call that collateral damage. They call it murder. For them, this is total war.

President Bush never prepared the nation for the prolonged violence of this war. He still hasn't spoken candidly about it. If he has an idea for hauling us out of this quagmire, he hasn't bothered to reveal it.

The troops who are fighting and dying deserve better.

(September 10, 2004)

THIS IS BUSH'S VIETNAM

Arlington, Virginia

The rows of simple white headstones in the broad expanses of brilliant green lawns are scrupulously arranged, and they seem to go on and on, endlessly, in every direction.

It was impossible not to be moved. A soft September wind was the only sound. Beyond that was just the silence of history, and the collective memory of the lives lost in its service.

Nearly 300,000 people are buried at Arlington National Cemetery, which is just across the Potomac from Washington. Recently I visited the grave of Air Force Second Lieutenant Richard VandeGeer. The headstone tells us, as simply as possible, that he went to Vietnam, that he was born January 11, 1948, and died May 15, 1975, and that he was awarded the Purple Heart.

His mother, Diana VandeGeer, who is seventy-five now and lives in Florida, tells us that he loved to play soldier as a child, that he was a helicopter pilot in Vietnam, and that she longs for him still. He would be fifty-six now, but to his mother he is forever a tall and handsome twenty-seven.

Richard VandeGeer was not the last American serviceman to die in the Vietnam War, but he was close enough. He was part of the last group of Americans killed, and his name was the last of the more than 58,000 to be listed on the wall of the Vietnam Memorial in Washington. As I stood at his grave, I couldn't help but wonder how long it will take us to get to the last American combat death in Iraq.

Lieutenant VandeGeer died heroically. He was the pilot of a CH-53A transport helicopter that was part of an effort to rescue crew members of the *Mayaguez,* an American merchant ship that was captured by the Khmer Rouge off the coast of Cambodia on May 12, 1975. The helicopter was shot down and half of the twenty-six men aboard, including Lieutenant VandeGeer, perished. (It was later learned that the crew of the *Mayaguez* had already been released.)

The failed rescue operation, considered the last combat activity of the Vietnam War, came four years after John Kerry's famous question, "How do you ask a man to be the last man to die for a mistake?"

Although he died bravely, Lieutenant VandeGeer's death was as senseless as those of the 58,000 who died before him in the fool's errand known as Vietnam. His remains were not recovered for twenty years—not until a joint operation by American and Cambodian authorities located the underwater helicopter wreckage in 1995. Positive identification, using the most advanced DNA technology, took another four years. Lieutenant VandeGeer was buried at Arlington in a private ceremony in 2000.

The Vietnam Veterans of America Foundation put me in touch with the lieutenant's family. "I'm still angry that my son is gone," said Diana VandeGeer, who is divorced and lives alone in Cocoa Beach. "I'm his mother. I think about him every day."

She said that while she will always be proud of her son, she believes he "died for nothing."

Lieutenant VandeGeer's sister, Michelle, told me she can't think about her brother without recalling that the last time she saw him was on her wedding day, in May 1974. "He looked so handsome and confident," she said. "He wanted to change the world."

Wars are all about chaos and catastrophes, death and suffering, and lifelong grief, which is why you should go to war only when it's absolutely unavoidable. Wars tear families apart as surely as they tear apart the flesh of those killed and wounded. Since we learned nothing from Vietnam, we are doomed to repeat its agony, this time in horrifying slow motion in Iraq.

Three more Marines were reported killed in the latest news reports from Iraq. Kidnappings are commonplace. The insurgency is growing and becoming more sophisticated, which means more deadly. Ordinary Iraqis are becoming ever more enraged at the United States.

When the newscaster David Brinkley, appalled by the carnage in Vietnam, asked Lyndon Johnson why he didn't just bring the troops home, Johnson replied, "I'm not going to be the first American president to lose a war."

George W. Bush is now trapped as tightly in Iraq as Johnson was in Vietnam. The war is going badly. The president's own intelligence estimates are pessimistic. There is no plan to actually win the war in Iraq, and no willingness to concede defeat.

I wonder who the last man or woman will be to die for this colossal mistake.

(September 17, 2004)

PART SIX

———

HERBERT'S HEROES

15

A ROLL CALL FOR OUR TIME

THE BEST OF AMERICA

Astronauts speeding in from outer space, forty miles above the earth, sixteen minutes from touchdown . . .

We don't pay much attention to our astronauts until calamity strikes. And yet the grief that accompanies the spectacular loss of these brave strangers, men and women with unfamiliar names like David M. Brown and Laurel Clark, is extraordinary.

The posthumous television images of the smiling, healthy, enthusiastic crew of the space shuttle *Columbia* touch feelings that are usually reserved for those much closer to us. They're very difficult to watch.

For Americans, in some sense, it's like watching the loss of our better selves. The astronauts may not get a tremendous amount of attention under ordinary circumstances, but they are the last unspoiled American heroes. They have not been laid low by scandal or exposed as phonies. They carry none of the taint of bad faith that clings so stubbornly to so many in politics, the world of business, and the media. Their motives, as far as we can tell, are still pure. They have come to embody whatever remains of the American ideal.

Dr. Clark, a navy flight surgeon, had been conducting life-science experiments aboard the *Columbia*. The experiments were part of a wide range of studies by the crew that were aimed at improving the health and safety of humans on Earth and in space.

At a time when much of the world is gripped by the oppressive fear of war and terror, the crew of the *Columbia* was devoting its considerable talent to work that was creative, cooperative, and constructive. Theirs was a mission of peace.

General Omar Bradley, a hero of World War II, delivered a speech in Boston in 1948 that is remarkably appropriate for the violent and chaotic world of today. "The world has achieved brilliance without wisdom," he said, "power without conscience. Ours is a world of nuclear giants and ethical midgets. We know more about war than we know of peace, more about killing than we know about living."

Americans today are not just struggling with forces that are wildly uncertain and dangerous. We're also struggling, on a variety of fronts, with doubts about the direction and the soundness of our national mission. There is a uniform commitment to fighting terror, but public support for an invasion of Iraq varies considerably from week to week. Bitter arguments are raging over civil rights, civil liberties, and immigration policies. And there is nothing close to a consensus on the fairness of the nation's tax policies and social welfare programs.

Mixed with the anxiety over war and terror and the threat posed by a weak domestic economy is an underlying feeling that this great and powerful nation could—as Jack Kennedy contended—do better, that its ideals are still important, and that you court real danger if you continue giving them short shrift.

When our attention is drawn to the astronauts, even in the midst of tragedy, we are pleased to see them as powerful symbols of the most admirable aspects of American life. They are not superhumans.

The *Columbia* disaster showed that they're fragile like the rest of us. But they hold in trust for us the spirit of adventure and exploration and decency and accomplishment that is so important to our view of ourselves as Americans.

No one wants to look in the mirror and see something low or mean. The astronauts help save us from that.

President Bush praised the crew of the *Columbia* for its "service to all humanity." He said, "These astronauts knew the dangers and they faced them willingly, knowing they had a high and noble purpose in life."

That was not hyperbole, but the simple truth.

Some time will go by and the press of world events will cause the astronauts and all they represent to slip again from our consciousness, which is too bad. It would be so much better if this terrible tragedy could somehow prompt a renewed commitment to America's "high and noble" ideals and aspirations. One quick example: the nation's great wealth and good fortune could be used to build a sparkling new generation of schools to educate the millions upon millions of young people whose talents and energy will have to be called upon if the United States is to continue to flourish.

That is one way in which we could honor the astronauts whose lives—and tragic deaths—remind us of our own deeply held aspirations, our ideals, those aspects of ourselves that we admire most.

(February 3, 2003)

REESE AND ROBINSON

Pee Wee Reese, the great Brooklyn Dodgers shortstop, is being treated for lung cancer in Venice, Florida. Wish him well. He's seventy-eight and has already had to fight off prostate cancer. He is also recovering from a broken hip. "He's battling like hell," said a friend, "but those late innings can be tough."

Back in the 1940s and '50s, when major league baseball began tiptoeing into the chilly waters of racial integration, Pee Wee Reese was one of the guys willing to take a stand against the inhumane behavior of narrow-minded nitwits and racial degenerates, both on and off the field.

He was an unlikely supporter of integration of any kind. He had grown up in the Jim Crow atmosphere of Louisville, Kentucky. He signed with the Dodgers at a time when many ballplayers thought black people had been specially designed by the Almighty to shine their shoes and carry their bags. He served in the navy, which was ultrawhite during World War II. Everything in Reese's early environment told him that black people were alien and lesser beings. He had never shaken hands with a black person in his life.

On his way back from service in the South Pacific, Reese was informed that the Dodgers had hired a "nigger" ballplayer, and not only that—the "nigger" was a shortstop. The writer Roger Kahn, who would later become a close friend, noted that Reese had plenty of time aboard ship to ponder this issue. Reese wondered what would happen if he lost his job to this new player, Jackie Robinson. How would his friends react if he were beaten out by, you know, a colored guy?

There was nothing about the situation to like. But Reese decided, before the ship docked in San Francisco, that in his mind at least the issue would be strictly about playing ball, and not about race.

During the spring of 1947, when it was obvious that the Dodgers were planning to bring Robinson up from their Montreal farm club, several of Reese's teammates circulated a petition. As Kahn recalled, in a conversation this week: "It said, essentially, 'If you bring up the nigger, trade us. We won't play.' "

Reese, a southerner, was considered a lock to sign. But he declined. He didn't make a big deal of it. He just refused to sign.

"The momentum for the petition stopped right there," said Kahn.

As it turned out, when the Dodgers brought Robinson up later in the year, they put him at first base. (He would later play second.) Reese was secure at short. But Robinson wasn't secure anywhere. The black man in the bright white Dodgers uniform was a full-time target of all manner of abuse. Pitchers ignored the strike zone and threw directly at his head. Base runners tried to gouge him with their spikes. People spat at him, threw garbage at him. Fans and opposing ballplayers tried to outdo one another with their epithets.

One day, in Cincinnati, when the abuse had reached a fever pitch, Reese decided he had had enough. The Dodgers were on the field, and the players in the Reds' dugout were shouting obscenities at Robinson. Fans were booing and cursing Robinson, who was standing at first and trying amid the chaos and the rising heat of his own anger to concentrate on the game. Reese called time. And in a gesture that has become famous, he walked across the infield to Robinson, placed a hand on his shoulder in a very public display of friendship, and offered him a few words of encouragement.

"It gets my vote," said Kahn, "as baseball's finest moment."

Reese and Robinson eventually became very close. So close, in fact, that Reese could needle Robinson in ways that others didn't dare try. Robinson was often difficult to get along with, and Reese once told him, "You know, Jack, some of these guys are throwing at you because you're black. But others are doing it because they just don't like you."

Kahn remembered another time when someone had threatened to

shoot Robinson if he played in an exhibition game in Atlanta. Robinson took the field anyway. Reese sidled over, in the midst of tremendous tension, and said, "Do me a favor, Jack?" Robinson said, "Yeah, what?" Reese said, "Don't stand too close to me. We don't know what kind of a shot this guy is."

Harold Henry "Pee Wee" Reese. When a guy needed a friend, he was right there.

(March 14, 1997)

POSTSCRIPT

Pee Wee Reese died on August 14, 1999.

THE GOOD TIMES

Willie Mays was on the phone, telling a story about himself and Joe DiMaggio that went back nearly half a century.

The Giants were playing the Yankees in the World Series in 1951. Mays, a precocious twenty-year-old rookie, was in center field for the Giants. His hero, the graceful and already legendary DiMaggio, was thirty-six and playing his final games in center for the Yanks.

The Giants had just pulled off a miracle, coming from far behind the Dodgers in mid-August to tie them at the end of the regular season and then beat them in the playoffs, the final devastating blow being the most famous home run in history, Bobby Thomson's ninth-inning, pennant-winning blast into the lower left-field stands of the Polo Grounds off the Dodger reliever Ralph Branca.

So now Mays was in the World Series with his idol.

"When we were kids growing up in the South we would always pick one guy to emulate," said Mays. "Ted Williams was the best hitter, but I picked Joe to pattern myself after because he was such a great all-around player. I felt if you could hit and play good defense, like he did, and if you could run and throw—if you could do all those things—then you could be in baseball a long time."

I had called Mays, my favorite player when I was a kid, to congratulate him on a lifetime achievement award he received from *New York* magazine. One of the first things he mentioned was that his thoughts were with DiMaggio, who was eighty-four and fighting for his life in a hospital in Hollywood, Florida.

"I never told this to anybody," said Mays, "but Joe hit a home run at the Polo Grounds in that series, and I knew that was his last year, so I was happy for him even though I was playing against him. So what I did was, I started clapping. And you just didn't do that in New York. But there I was standing in the outfield for the Giants clapping for Joe as he's rounding the bases."

I looked it up. DiMaggio had been struggling in the series. Age and injuries had chipped away at his magnificent skills. He was hitless in the first three games. The home run, a two-run shot, came in game four, which the Yankees won, 6–2. They won the series as well, four games to two.

I tried to imagine what it would have been like if that World Series had been covered the way big-time sports events are covered now. At least some of the cameras would have been locked on the Giants' rookie in center field. Over the years we would have seen, again and again, the Say Hey Kid applauding as the Yankee Clipper trotted out his last home run.

Mays and DiMaggio. There is not a sane fan anywhere who will dispute that they were two of the greatest ballplayers ever to lace up a pair of cleats.

Mays was sixty-seven and admitted that a few ailments had slowed him some. He had a lifetime contract with the Giants but he didn't travel as much as he used to. He'd had a cataract operation and some problems with an ear but said he feels fortunate.

"You've got to take care of all those things," he said. "The older you get, sometimes they get out of whack."

I remember as a child walking with my parents into the enormous horseshoe-shaped structure that was the Polo Grounds, and feeling as if I had stepped into Emerald City. All I wanted in that glorious expanse of green was a glimpse of Willie. And there he was, all afternoon, and on many an afternoon to come, drifting easily under a long fly ball and putting it away with a basket catch. And there he was, stealing second base and brushing the dirt from the bright white uniform, and then promptly stealing third. And there he was, with that beautiful swing, sending the ball high and deep, deep to left, and over the fence.

How good was he? *New York* magazine notes that Mays hit 124 more home runs than Mickey Mantle, drove in 366 more runs than DiMaggio, and stole 155 more bases than the two of them combined. The sportswriter Jim Murray once wrote that "he should play in handcuffs to even things out a bit."

The afternoons moved more slowly in those days, and the summers seemed to last a little longer. It seemed as if all the men wore hats. And life could not be better if Willie went four for four.

Willie Mays was laughing on the other end of the phone. He seemed to agree. "Those were good times, man," he said.

(December 10, 1998)

A DESIGNATED HERO

The streak came to an end in mid-July in Cleveland beneath the blazing, bluish lights of Municipal Stadium. The crowd was enormous, 67,468, which at the time was the largest ever to have seen a night baseball game.

Joe DiMaggio came to the plate four times. He grounded sharply to deep third base and was thrown out by the terrific Ken Keltner. He walked. He hit another sharp grounder to third and was thrown out again by Keltner. In the eighth inning, with the bases loaded, he hit into a double play. The incredible fifty-six-game hitting streak was over, but a mythic American hero had been born.

The headlines the next day, July 18, 1941, suggested why. The sports pages were all about the streak. But an article at the top of page one in the *New York Times* began as follows:

> Germany's second offensive against Soviet Russia appeared last night to have reached its full fury as both sides reported violent engagements along the entire front. In Berlin, where the High Command said that the Red Army was desperately throwing its last reserves into a battle of 9,000,000 men, the official news agency reported that German forces had taken the key city of Smolensk, on the road to Moscow.

Next to that was a headline that said: "Konoye Forming Cabinet in Tokyo; Fascist Cast Seen."

Next to that was a story about the beginning of the second wave of the military draft in the United States. And below that was a story about Charles Lindbergh, who, in a letter to President Franklin Roosevelt, denied having any link to the Axis powers.

It was, to say the least, a harrowing time. Less than five months after Joe D. went 0-for-3 in Cleveland, the Japanese would bomb Pearl Harbor.

Joe DiMaggio was tall, handsome, splendidly talented, and a champion. He was modest and came from a humble background. He was tough, and yet he was elegant, both on the field and off. He had class. Americans, still nursing the wounds of the Depression, and now faced with a world war, could use a guy like Joe. He wasn't a middle-aged, over-the-hill rascal, like the retired Babe Ruth. And he wasn't tainted, like Lindbergh.

DiMaggio carried himself like a hero. A teammate, Vernon (Lefty) Gomez, was quoted by the writer Maury Allen as saying, "He knew what the press and the fans and the kids expected of him, and he was always trying to live up to that image. That's why he couldn't be silly in public like I could, or ever be caught without his shirt buttoned or his shoes shined. He knew he was Joe DiMaggio and he knew what that meant to the country."

DiMaggio's career, which ran from 1936 to 1951, coincided with the creation of the colossus that came to be known as postwar America. He embodied the yearning, the anxieties, the willingness to struggle endlessly, the unwillingness to accept failure, and the ultimate resounding triumphs of the men and women of that era. The great DiMaggio, as a character in Hemingway would call him, became the designated hero of the colossus, the preeminent god of this secular creation myth.

DiMaggio played the role to perfection. He was quiet and kept his defenses up. He never let the real DiMaggio steal a scene from the idealized hero. He stifled himself. He was aloof, private, at times reclusive. He smoked three packs of Camels a day. He had stomach problems. He was human. But when he trotted onto the field or otherwise appeared in public, he was almost perfect.

After he retired he met and married the goddess of the myth. It was a mismatch made in Heaven. When the marriage ended after only nine months, Joe was distraught and never really recovered. And Marilyn was already lost.

As the fifties became the sixties and the seventies and so on, Joe D. became the embodiment not of the nation's hopes and fears and triumphs but of its memories. And after a while the memories were only pleasant ones. The frightening headlines have faded and almost disappeared, replaced by reminiscences of glorious seasons and simpler times.

The wind blew hard and brutally cold through the South Bronx on March 8, 1999, the day Joe DiMaggio died. The flag at Yankee Stadium, snapping in the wind, was lowered to half-staff. The people who stopped by to pay their respects didn't have much to say. They knew. The United States needed a hero, and Joe DiMaggio was good enough to oblige.

(March 10, 1999)

RIDING TO FREEDOM

It was an old gag, and so corny it would make you groan. The evil white restaurant owner in the heyday of the civil rights movement would announce defiantly: "We don't serve Negroes here!" And the leader of the well-mannered sit-in contingent would reply amiably: "That's all right. We don't eat them."

When James Farmer would tell that story he would throw his

head back and erupt in a sonic boom of laughter. You couldn't help but laugh with him. You had no choice.

I talked to Farmer in the summer of 1995. He was seventy-four years old and blind and lived alone in a house in Fredericksburg, Virginia. Illness had forced the recent amputation of his right leg. "That's the one," he said, "that I used to use for kicking butts." He turned loose that old familiar laugh and over the phone I could imagine his head rearing back in delight.

Farmer is mostly forgotten now, which is worse than a shame, it's tragic. He was one of the Big Four civil rights leaders of the midcentury—men who led a movement that changed this country and influenced much of the world. The others, Martin Luther King Jr., Roy Wilkins, and Whitney Young, are all dead. Of the four, only Dr. King's name resonates with the young, and even then the thoughts are hazy. I talked to a high school kid some years ago who thought that Dr. King had worked for Al Sharpton.

James Farmer was dedicated and heroic in a way that is difficult to imagine today. Again and again he put his life on the line in the fight for freedom for black Americans. In 1963 a mob of Louisiana state troopers armed with guns, cattle prods, and tear gas closed in on Farmer, who had had the temerity to organize demonstrations in the town of Plaquemine. The troopers hunted him door-to-door.

"I was meant to die that night," Farmer once said. "They were kicking open doors, beating up blacks in the streets, interrogating them with electric cattle prods."

A funeral home director had Farmer "play dead" in the back of the hearse, which carried him along back roads and out of town.

Two years earlier, Farmer, who had helped found the Congress of Racial Equality on Gandhian principles of nonviolence, organized the freedom rides, one of the decade's most perilous civil rights efforts. The Supreme Court had banned segregation in interstate travel facilities but its rulings were virtually ignored in the South. The freedom riders, an interracial group of men and women, mostly college age, boarded buses in Washington, D.C., and headed for Mississippi, determined to make desegregation a reality.

It was—at times, literally—an ordeal by fire. One of the buses was destroyed in a firebombing. The freedom riders were attacked and viciously beaten by Klan-led mobs. Some of the riders suffered permanent injuries; many were jailed. Farmer himself spent forty days in jail in Mississippi.

"In the end, it was a success," Farmer said, "because Bobby Kennedy had the Interstate Commerce Commission issue an order, with teeth in it, that he could enforce, banning segregation in interstate travel. That was my proudest achievement."

Farmer believed that two grave errors were made, even as the civil rights movement was racking up its stunning successes. The first was the almost uniform tendency to confuse segregation with racism. That encouraged the mistaken belief that dismantling the apparatus of legal segregation was in some sense the equivalent of decreasing the poisonous levels of racism in the society.

The second error in some ways followed from the first. "We did not do any long-range planning," said Farmer. "So we were stuck without a program after the success of our efforts, which included passage of a civil rights bill and voting rights legislation. We could have anticipated the backlash that followed. We could have asked ourselves what the jobs prospects would be for blacks in the seventies, the eighties, the nineties, and later on. By and large we didn't do that, except for affirmative action. We should have had a plan."

I spoke to Farmer not long before the Fourth of July, a day to celebrate freedom in America. I'm told the country is starved for heroes. Well, one was living quietly in Fredericksburg, Virginia.

(June 28, 1995)

POSTSCRIPT

James Farmer died on July 9, 1999.

A MUSCULAR IDEALISM

Sargent Shriver is eighty-eight years old, which is all the proof we need that time is flying. That he is not better known is a scandal.

Mention his name now, especially to young people, and you will most likely get a blank stare. His daughter, the TV personality Maria Shriver, who is the wife of Arnold Schwarzenegger and thus the First Lady of California, is much better known.

Yet the author of a new biography of Shriver plausibly suggests that this idealistic and indefatigable man—who created and led the Peace Corps, founded Head Start, created the Job Corps and Legal Services for the poor, gave us Volunteers in Service to America, and was president and chairman of the Special Olympics—may have directly affected more people in a positive way than any American since Franklin Roosevelt.

Shriver came out of an era when it was considered shameful for able-bodied men to run and hide when the nation was at war. He was a heroic naval officer who served in the Pacific in World War II. The book *Sarge: The Life and Times of Sargent Shriver,* by Scott Stossel, gives us a glimpse of the reality of war in its description of a harrowing sea battle that erupted off Guadalcanal on the night of November 14, 1942:

> The foremast was hit. Electrical fires erupted continuously, all around Shriver. Whole gun crews were killed by flying shells. The ship began to slow down, and more Japanese rounds ripped across the deck, killing an officer in the radar plotting room. Three rounds exploded in another battle station, killing a half dozen more men. Steam lines were severed, and the hot, hissing steam scalded numerous sailors. Ladders between decks got knocked out, making putting out fires and attending to the growing scores of wounded much more difficult. Shriver himself was wounded when metal shrapnel from an explosion lodged

itself in his shoulder, a wound for which he was later to be awarded a Purple Heart.

Shriver, who has been married to John F. Kennedy's sister Eunice for more than fifty years, led the talent hunt for the new breed of public servants that staffed the Kennedy administration. You had to search hard, he felt, because those most suited for public office very often don't seek it.

The idea for the Peace Corps came up almost offhandedly during an address by Kennedy in the 1960 campaign. After the election the president asked Shriver to study the feasibility of such a program. Shriver has joked that he was the logical choice to create and lead the Peace Corps because everyone was sure it would be a disaster, and "it would be easier" for the president to fire his brother-in-law than anybody else.

A young Bill Moyers, who joined Shriver at the Peace Corps and eventually became its deputy director, said a crucial component of the corps was Shriver's deep commitment to the idea of America "as a social enterprise . . . of caring and cooperative people."

The Peace Corps turned out to be the signature success of Kennedy's New Frontier.

In 1964, as head of the Office of Economic Opportunity in the Johnson administration, Shriver came across studies that showed connections between poor nutrition, lower IQ scores, and arrested social and emotional development. He wondered whether early childhood intervention "could have a beneficial effect on the children of poor people." Head Start followed in incredibly short order.

There seemed to be no end to the man's restlessness, energy, curiosity, creativity, and optimism. Those qualities never waned through wars, assassinations, political setbacks, or personal disappointments.

I recently spoke with Shriver by phone. "I think I'm one of the luckiest guys in history," he said. "From the time I was, say, seventeen to the time I'm eighty-eight, I have been exposed to a galaxy of wonderful people, to challenging situations, to worldwide problems, sometimes to weaknesses and sometimes to strengths. And we made an effort during that time to find out what was true, and what was needed by way of improvement."

Shriver's commitment to public service has always seemed both joyous and total. In 1994, he told graduating students at Yale, his alma mater, to break all their mirrors. "Yes, indeed," he said, "shatter the glass. In our society that is so self-absorbed, begin to look less at yourself and more at each other. Learn more about the face of your neighbor, and less about your own."

(April 23, 2004)

GET WELL, GEORGE

Nineteen-sixty-four was the year the sixties really began. The earliest years of the decade were for the most part an extension of the conventional, cold-war, black-and-white fifties. Dwight Eisenhower was president through 1960, which was the year the U-2 reconnaissance pilot Francis Gary Powers was shot down over Soviet territory. When John F. Kennedy was inaugurated in 1961, the men participating in the ceremony wore morning coats and top hats.

For a decade known for its excitement, the sixties got off to a decidedly slow start. Doo-wop music was still around in the early sixties. And dreamy songs of widely varying quality—"Moon River," "Where the Boys Are"—were among the biggest hits. It was a quiet time. The average annual salary was $4,700, and a favorite pastime was bowling.

There was no reason to think radical changes were brewing when

1964 debuted. The nation was still in shock and still in mourning over the murder of Jack Kennedy the previous November. The tranquilizer Valium was catching on. Mary McCarthy had a best seller with *The Group.* Herbert Hoover, Douglas MacArthur, and Cole Porter were still alive. *Bonanza* and *Candid Camera* were big hits on television.

And then in February, suddenly and without warning, the Beatles were upon us.

The word this week from overseas is that George Harrison, the so-called quiet Beatle, has suffered another setback in his fight against cancer. Harrison is fifty-eight. He is said to be frail and fatigued from the disease and the treatment.

He is also, apparently, indomitable. "I am feeling fine," he said in a prepared statement. And he apologized for any grief he may have caused his fans. "I am really sorry," he said, "for the unnecessary worry."

If you spend just a little time reflecting on the Beatles you come away astonished by the changes they wrought (or came to symbolize) in what seemed like a split second of real time. They blew in like a sudden storm and permanently altered the cultural landscape. One night they were singing to an audience of shrieking teenyboppers on that quintessential 1950s television program *The Ed Sullivan Show,* and in the next instant, it seemed, the Sullivan era had been left behind and the sixties had blossomed in brilliant, even blinding color.

It wasn't just the music. The Beatles were a perfectly placed, perfectly timed phenomenon. Their charm and spontaneity, insouciance and offbeat humor, and above all their easy acceptance of life's myriad pleasures sliced right through the already fraying bonds of the uptight fifties and early sixties.

For better or worse, they helped get us to where we are now. They spread the word to a massive generation of largely inhibited young people that it was all right to have fun.

There was no need to take anything too seriously. When a

reporter asked John Lennon what he would do when Beatlemania subsided, he replied, "Count the money."

Ringo, commenting on a trip to Florida, said, "Now, this was just the most brilliant place I'd ever been to. People were lending us yachts, anything we wanted."

Within a year or two the sixties that most people remember—some with fondness, some with loathing—were well under way, and the most dominant cultural framing was provided by the Beatles. People dressed differently, wore their hair differently, danced differently, and approached that treacherous triumvirate of sex, drugs, and rock 'n' roll with an openness that surely had been accelerated by John, Paul, George, and Ringo.

The fun, as people soon learned, was laced with madness and a fair amount of tragedy. (Among other things, drugs took their toll on the decade and played a significant role in the Beatles' lives.) You get a sense of the breakneck pace of events when you consider that George was only twenty-seven when the Beatles officially broke up in 1970.

More than three decades later it seems a miracle that so much should have happened in so short a time. The music remains remarkable, often beautiful, including George's "Something," "Here Comes the Sun," and "While My Guitar Gently Weeps."

As for George's fans—well, they are worried. But no one's looking for an apology. They just wish him well.

(July 12, 2001)

POSTSCRIPT

George Harrison died on November 29, 2001.

KEEPING THE BLUES ALIVE

"The sun's gonna shine in my back door some day. The wind's gonna rise and blow my blues away."

—TOMMY JOHNSON

The United States Senate has declared (with unintended irony) that 2003 is the "Year of the Blues." It has urged the president to issue a proclamation to that effect.

It's very difficult to overstate the cultural importance of the blues, which have been around about one hundred years, were crucial to the overall development of jazz, and gave birth about a half century ago to a boisterous new music called rock 'n' roll.

The blues, powerful and bitter and mean and hopeful and funny, grew out of the brutally degraded condition of black Americans in the early decades of the twentieth century. The music was like a salve to the raw wounds of men and women working literally like slaves in the cotton fields and cornfields of the Mississippi Delta, or struggling against the dire poverty and grotesque racism of other Deep South venues, or trying to survive on domestic and janitorial work in the unforgiving environs of the industrial North.

These were lives condemned to poverty and tragedy and desperation. Opportunities were few, and life expectancies were pathetically short. And yet the people endured. The blues provided the sound track.

"I got to keep moving," sang Robert Johnson, perhaps the greatest bluesman of them all. "I got to keep moving, blues falling down like hail, blues falling down like hail. . . . And the day keeps 'minding me, there's a hellhound on my trail, hellhound on my trail, hellhound on my trail."

Now hold on to your hats, folks, because that music is about to make a comeback.

The filmmaker Martin Scorsese and some of his associates are raising the curtain on a dandy project. "This is special," Scorsese said in an interview.

Scorsese and six other directors, including Wim Wenders, Mike Figgis, and Clint Eastwood, are nearing completion of seven feature-length films about the blues. Excerpts from five of the films were shown at the Sundance Film Festival.

All seven films will be shown on PBS as the centerpiece of an even bigger project called "Year of the Blues." This will include a thirteen-part public radio series on the history of the blues, a companion book of rarely seen archival material, and a traveling blues exhibition and education program that the sponsors hope will reach up to 5 million children.

The "Year of the Blues" will begin more or less officially with a benefit concert at Radio City Music Hall in New York.

The film project began about five years ago when Scorsese was the executive producer on a concert film with Eric Clapton in which footage of blues musicians from the past was used. From that, said Scorsese, "came the idea of doing a series of films that would honor the history of the blues."

The films are not straight narratives or documentaries but rather what Scorsese calls "interpretive, personal looks at the blues." "The idea," he said, "was to take the archival footage, and then to take journeys, interpretive looks at the blues, and create an awareness for young people that, first, this is an art form, and then to understand how it happened, where it came from and how it continues."

Scorsese's film, *From Mali to Mississippi*, is not yet finished. "I hope to complete it by March," he said. It goes all the way back to the antecedents of the blues on "the banks of the Niger River in Mali" and then follows the progression of the music to the cotton fields and juke joints of the Mississippi Delta.

The blues somehow flourished in those fields of oppression and went on to nurture nearly every form of popular American music that followed.

In his book *Deep Blues,* Robert Palmer describes a visit he made in 1979 to the Mississippi Delta home of Joe Rice Dockery, who had inherited from his father the remnants of a plantation on which an astonishing number of great blues musicians had lived and played.

Dockery had grown up on the plantation but had never heard the music. "None of us gave much thought to this blues thing until a few years ago," he said. "In other words, we never heard these people sing. We were never the type of plantation owners who invited their help to come in and sing for parties. I wish we had realized that these people were so important."

(January 20, 2003)

LOVING RAY CHARLES

Sing the song, children . . .

In the summer of 1962, when John Kennedy was president, Ed Sullivan was the CEO of Sunday-night television, and the word *Beatles* still sounded to most Americans like a reference to insects, the airwaves were all but overwhelmed by Ray Charles's soaring country ballad "I Can't Stop Loving You."

It was an amazingly popular song. But it was almost a hit by, of all people, Tab Hunter, not Ray Charles. That's right, Tab Hunter, a champion ice-skater and one of the blandest pop stars it's possible to imagine.

Charles recorded the song first, on the now-legendary album *Modern Sounds in Country and Western Music.* But neither he nor the executives at ABC–Paramount Records, which put out the album, expected the song to be a hit. For one thing, an earlier version by Don Gibson had gone nowhere. But disc jockeys started playing it, people loved it, and Tab Hunter pounced. He put out a single that copied the Ray Charles album version almost note for note.

ABC had to scramble to put out its own single. In his book *Ray Charles: Man and Music,* Michael Lydon described ABC's frantic effort to shorten the album version and get it distributed as a single. He quoted the arranger Sid Feller: "If Tab Hunter's record had gotten any more head start, Ray's record would have been lost. Even though Hunter was copying us, people would have thought we were copying him."

Once Ray's single was available, said Feller, "Tab Hunter was finished."

I was in a taxi in Boston heading to Logan Airport, when I heard on the radio that Ray Charles had died.

For someone who had grown up with his music, as I had, who had gyrated to it in moments of fierce adolescent ecstasy, and listened to it with the volume turned low on some of those nights that no one should have to go through, it was like hearing about the death of a close friend who was both amazingly generous and remarkably wise.

Even as youngsters in the late fifties and sixties, my friends and I knew that Ray was special. He had a shamanistic quality. We understood that his music, like life, was both spiritual and profane. And we reveled in the fact that it was also unquestionably subversive.

"I Got a Woman," which debuted in the Eisenhower era and remained a force in the popular-music culture for years, had an irresistible gospel feeling that moved with tremendous power toward a culmination that couldn't be anything but sexual.

Whether he intended to or not, Ray had opened fire on two very distinct cultures at one and the same time: the white-bread mass culture that was on its guard against sexuality of any kind (and especially the black kind), and the black religious community, which felt that gospel was the Lord's music and thus should be off limits to the wild secular shenanigans that Ray represented.

But here's the thing. Ray Charles's music has touched so many people so deeply for so many decades precisely because it is religious. Listen to the way he transforms "America the Beautiful" from an anthem to a hymn. Listen to the joyous call-and-response of "What'd I Say?" or the slow, majestic lament of "Drown in My Own Tears."

Ray's music envelops the willing listener in a glorious, ritualistic expression of the sweet and bitter mysteries of life without the coercion, hypocrisy, or intolerance that is so frequently a part of organized religion.

It transcends cultures. It transcends genres—gospel, rhythm and blues, jazz, rock 'n' roll, country, pop. At its best, it is raw and beautiful and accessible, a gift from an artist who bravely explored regions of the heart and soul that are important to all of us.

Comparing himself to the early rock 'n' rollers, Ray said, "My stuff was more adult, filled with more despair than anything you'd associate with rock 'n' roll."

Maybe that's why so many people were surprised to hear last week that he was only seventy-three. In the obituary in the *New York Times*, Jon Pareles and Bernard Weinraub wrote, "Even in his early years he sounded like a voice of experience, someone who had seen all the hopes and follies of humanity."

My friends and I all felt we knew him. He seemed as familiar as someone who'd actually hung out with us. An old friend. And it's hard whenever an old friend slips away.

(June 14, 2004)

CONCLUSION

WHAT KIND OF AMERICA
DO WE WANT TO LIVE IN?

Some years ago a Gallup poll found that 60 percent of Americans were unable to name the president who ordered the nuclear attack on Japan. Thirty-five percent did not know that the first atomic bomb had been dropped on Hiroshima. One-fourth did not even know that Japan had been the target of a nuclear attack.

A more recent Gallup poll found that only 35 percent of Americans believed that evolution was a "scientific theory well-supported by evidence." I had a conversation once with a woman who didn't know that Gerald Ford had been president of the United States until she saw him on television at a golf outing with Bill Clinton and George H. W. Bush. A poll taken in 2004 found that a third of George W. Bush's supporters believed weapons of mass destruction had been found in Iraq.

We've got some work to do. Of all the forces arrayed against Americans, collectively and individually, I can't think of an enemy more treacherous or implacable than entrenched ignorance. Al Qaeda struck on September 11, 2001, and we ended up in a dreadful, pointless, soul-destroying war in Iraq, which had nothing to do with the attack. A general public with a stronger grasp of the major issues facing the United States might not have been so easily led by deceitful public officials into support for this war. Wholly unnecessary, the war has killed tens of thousands and left us with American military hospitals in Germany and Washington that look like scenes out of Dante, their wards filled with frightened GIs struggling with the agony of paralysis, lost limbs, disfigurement, and lives of radically narrowed promise.

At home, the nation confronts enormous issues that, for better or worse, will shape the quality of all American lives in the coming decades. How is it possible in an increasingly globalized, and therefore increasingly competitive world, to provide the high-quality employment that is essential to sustain a world-class consumer society? How long can we continue to pay the backbreaking costs, in dollars and lives, of our overwhelming dependence on foreign oil? What are the alternatives? What are the implications of our massive federal budget deficits? Can anything substantial be done about the tens of millions of Americans who lack health insurance coverage? What is to become of Social Security?

If the United States is to reestablish the great promise of the postwar era, the public will have to become much better informed about these and many other extremely complex issues. Too many individuals are blind to the forces that buffet their lives and mold the destinies of their children. Suburban couples shouldering a crushing debt load should have some understanding of why a household with two wage earners today has less disposable income than a family with a single breadwinner in the 1970s. Inner-city families struggling to carve out a better future for their children need to be aware that the prevailing public policy is to shift college aid away from lower-income youngsters and toward their better-off peers.

The great task of the American people today is to turn around a giant ship of state that has sailed off in a radically wrong direction. But that can't be done by a largely uninformed population. Ignorance is indeed blissful—but the bliss is experienced by those who reap the colossal benefits of exploiting the millions of Americans who are unaware, naïve, undereducated, or otherwise out of touch with what is really going on.

The government is being stripped of its assets, and breathtaking amounts of treasure are being transferred via tax cuts and other schemes from ordinary Americans to those who are already very wealthy. Economic inequality in the United States is greater than in any other advanced industrial society, but rather than moving to correct that imbalance, we are busy dismantling the programs that offer even a modicum of security to those who are not rich. I recently read in the same edition of the *New York Times* an article about the continued "bare-knuckled tactics" used to fight labor unions across the South and an analysis showing that nearly every leading Republican proposal to privatize a portion of Social Security would require deep cuts in benefits for future retirees.

All of this is taking place in front of the supposedly wide-open eyes of the American electorate. Either the citizens of our country favor massive giveaways to the rich and a fist to the face of working people, or they are not quite up to speed on what is happening in this society, and what should be done about it.

A well-informed electorate is crucial to the well-being of an enormous, teeming, complex, and democratic country like the United States. Voting a vague preference every four years for one candidate or another, perhaps for the nominee with the nicest smile or the smoothest delivery, is not enough. Ignorance allows the unscrupulous elements—in government, in the marketplace, in the criminal justice system, and elsewhere—to triumph. It invites exploitation. It's a virus that, left untreated, kills.

"There are more fools than knaves in the world," said Samuel Butler, "else the knaves would not have enough to live upon."

We should be waging an all-out war against ignorance, but we're not. The politicians offer us ever more simplistic (and frequently devious) solutions to ever more complex problems. Religious zealots opposed to the teaching of evolution are pushing for changes in high school science texts. "Nationally," as Gary Orfield, a Harvard professor and author of *Dropouts in America*, has pointed out, "only about two-thirds of all students—and only half of all blacks, Latinos and Native Americans—who enter ninth grade graduate with regular diplomas four years later."

Among the saddest and most self-defeating attitudes I've ever come across is the idea held by many African American youngsters that doing well in school is somehow a "white thing," and therefore something to be shunned.

There are no quick or easy solutions to the manifold problems confronting the United States in these critical predawn hours of the twenty-first century. But for those of us who are genuinely concerned about the problems and are looking for ways to engage them effectively, it is imperative to figure out ways to enlighten much larger numbers of ordinary people about their importance. Improving the public schools and expanding awareness across college campuses are obvious starting points. But many other approaches should be tried as well: creative uses of the media, gatherings and forums that encourage the widest possible participation, new types of organizations designed to energize and heighten the consciousness of those who have wandered too long in the stultifying fields of unawareness. This will take a long time, and such an effort will likely be met by many bitter disappointments. But it is essential. I have spoken to too many men and women who not only cannot name the chief justice of the United States, but can't explain the function of the Supreme Court.

Ask a question about the steroid scandal in professional sports and you'll get chapter and verse. Ask about the separation of powers and likely as not you'll get a blank stare.

Even the fundamental freedoms enshrined in the Bill of Rights are poorly understood. A nationwide poll by the *Chicago Tribune* on attitudes toward free speech found that sizable minorities of Americans "would choose to muzzle all kinds of expression," including political commentary. Nearly half of those polled believed there should have been government-imposed restraints on the news coverage of the scandal at Abu Ghraib prison in Iraq. Twenty percent believe the media should be prohibited from doing stories that suggest the war is not going well. Thirty-five percent believe that members of a presidential administration should be legally barred from criticizing the administration for a period of time after they leave.

As I said, we've got work to do.

Another critical step for those who are committed to bringing real change to America is to get across the idea that while voting is crucially important, it is not enough. Many Democratic voters were dispirited when John Kerry lost to George W. Bush in the 2004 election. I wrote in a column that they should get over it, that caving in to feelings of helplessness and depression should not be an option when the country was speeding toward an abyss. I suggested they take a more active role in changing the society. Do what you can, I said. Talk to your neighbors. Call or write your elected officials. Circulate petitions. Attend meetings. Protest. Run for office. Support good candidates who are running for office. Volunteer to work in their campaigns. Register people to vote. Reach out to the young and the apathetic. Raise money. Stay informed, and help others stay informed. We need to think of the potential public component of our lives as well as their private aspect. As Barbara Jordan said, "The stakes are too high for government to be a spectator sport."

Americans have to decide what kind of country we want to live in. Is it to be one in which an alliance of powerful corporate interests and their lackeys in government wage an unrelenting war against the weak? Is it to be one in which we invade other nations on the basis of specious rationales and with an insufficient number of troops, who are themselves improperly trained and dangerously ill-equipped? Is it to be a country in which the government claims the right, in the name of national security, to incarcerate people indefinitely, in secret, without charge, and without the right to legal counsel?

If that is the kind of country we want, we've got it. But if we want a different America, one closer in spirit and in fact to its celebrated ideals, then it's time to face up to the reality of how far we've strayed, and to join the very strenuous effort to turn the ship of state around. Frederick Douglass told us that "power concedes nothing without a demand." Reclaiming the United States from those who have established a government of, by, and for the rich is doable, but only with an extraordinary collective effort. That effort would be especially difficult because it would require the enthusiastic participation of men and women who have many important shared interests but have allowed themselves to be divided along fault lines of party affiliation, religion, geography, ethnicity, gender, sexual orientation, cultural preferences, educational background, and so on. The power crowd exploits these differences and laughs all the way to the bank, or to the White House.

When President Bush talks about his desire to create an "ownership society," I can't help thinking that he means a society in which all of us will ultimately be on our own. That is not an America that can remain viable. As the world grows ever more complex, we become ever more dependent on one another, just as nations around the world are more interdependent. We've seen in Iraq the catastrophe that can result from going it alone.

So any strategic plan for a better future will have to include a radically heightened awareness of the issues, increased civic participation, and a recognition that traditional fault lines of prejudice and fear must be overcome and a genuine collective effort undertaken.

Turning the ship of state around will require the help of all hands.

ACKNOWLEDGMENTS

Always there are too many people to thank, especially when you work at a world-class institution like the *New York Times*. The talent, expertise, and other resources available to a writer at the *Times* are immense. They stretch literally around the globe. So my gratitude extends across an extremely broad front.

But I would like to offer specific, very special thanks to my assistant, the incomparable Johanna Jainchill, whose help with this book was invaluable; to my former assistants Alisha Berger (a new mom) and Arianne Chernock; and to the remarkable editors who work on the op-ed columns at the *Times* with amazing care, diligence, and tact: Karen Freeman, Linda Cohn, and Susan Kirby, and the now-retired Steve Pickering.

Finally, this book would never have happened without the energy and expertise of a remarkable pair of creative and sharp-eyed editors who guided me throughout the project: Paul Golob, editorial director of Times Books at Henry Holt and Company, and Alex Ward, who is in charge of book development for the *New York Times*. It would be impossible to thank them enough. Paul was abetted in his efforts by his quiet and efficient assistant, Brianna Smith, and I am grateful to her as well.

INDEX

ABC-Paramount Records, 326
ABC TV, 21
Aber, J. Lawrence, 223
Abraham Lincoln (aircraft carrier), 266, 278, 287
Abramson, Stacy, 93
Abu Ghraib prison, 270–72, 332
Acheson, Dean, 255
"Act Now" (Shultz), 256
Adams, Bob, 111
Addolorato, Robert, 81
Advancement Project, 168
affirmative action, 193
Afghanistan war, 263, 264, 269, 289, 294
AFL-CIO, 110, 136
African Americans
    Bush and, 198–200
    child tax credit and, 115–16
    civil rights heroes and, 315–17
    death penalty and, 103–6
    elderly voters intimidated, 201–8
    false arrests and, 182–84
    gay marriage and, 230
    gospel music, 327
    hate crimes vs., 164–66
    high school diplomas and, 331
    integration of baseball and, 308–10
    King's dream for, 161–62
    male unemployment, 23–25, 200
    Oneonta police sweep of, 180–82
    peer pressure, education and, 174–76
    Republicans and, 193–94
    segregated schools and, 166–68
    self-destructive culture and, 172, 173
    special treatment of, as reporters, 191–92
    Tulia drug arrests of, 5–6, 37–62
    violence in inner cities and, 156–57, 161–62, 172–73
    voter disenfranchisement and, 196, 199–208
after-school programs, 222, 231
AIDS, 172
air marshals, 237–39
Akerlof, George, 133
Alabama, 83–85

Alabama Court of Criminal Appeals, 85, 87
Al Jazeera (satellite TV station), 268
Allen, Fred, 92–94
Allen, Maury, 314
All Things Considered (NPR show), 92
Alphonso X, king of Spain, 255
Al Qaeda, 240, 247, 248, 268–70, 289, 294, 329
Alsup, Traci, 211
Alternative Schools Network, 127
America
    danger of ignorance in, 328–34
    optimism of postwar, 4, 5
    promises betrayed in, 5, 7–10
American Civil Liberties Union, 62, 238–39
American heroes
    astronauts as, 305–7
    baseball players as, 308–15
    civil rights movement and, 315–17
    musicians as, 321–27
    Sargent Shriver as, 318–20
"America the Beautiful" (song), 327
Amnesty International, 105
Andrews, Tom, 251
anti-sodomy laws, 229
Arlington National Cemetery, 299, 300
Ashcroft, John, 48, 50, 51, 53
Asian immigrants, 143
assault weapons ban, 231, 232
Associated Press, 28
astronauts, 305–7
Austin, Texas, police, 72, 76

Baathist army, 273
Babbio, Larry, 121, 122
Baghdad
    bombing of, 16
    security problems in, 267–68
bankruptcy, 9, 118–19, 220
Banks, Delma, Jr., 102–6
Banks, Medell, Jr., 83–88
Banks, Victoria, 83–88
Barbour, Haley, 212–13
Barnicle, Mike, 191

Barrett, Craig, 138–39
baseball, 308–15
Bayardo, Roberto, 74–75
Beatles, 321–22, 325
Bechtel Group, 255, 256
Belton, Jayla, 71–76, 78
Belton, Judy, 72, 75
Benjamin, Medea, 149
Bergmann, Joe, 123, 124
Berlinger, Tom, 205
Bernstein, Jared, 111, 117–18, 131
Beyond Shelter, 133–34
Bill of Rights, 332
bin Laden, Osama, 247, 268–70, 289, 294
Blackburn, Jeff, 49, 53
Blackmun, Harry A., 99–101
blackout of August 2003, 18, 242–45
black separatism, 162, 163
Blair, Jayson, 190–92
Blair, Tony, 252
Blocker, David, 175
blues music, 323–25
Bob Jones University, 194, 196, 197
Bolles, Gene, 290
Boorstin, Bob, 247
"Borrowing to Make Ends Meet" (report), 112–13
Boston Globe, 31, 172, 191
Bowie County, (Texas), 103
Brackins, Angjell, 126
Bradley, Omar, 306
Branca, Ralph, 310
Brando, Marlon, 294
Brazzil, Jim, 93
Brinkley, David, 15, 301
Brookins, Freddie, Jr., 6, 45–47, 60
Brookins, Freddie, Sr., 6, 46–47, 59–61
Brooklyn district attorney's office, 79–80
Brooklyn Dodgers, 308–10
Brown, David M., 305
Brown & Root, 261
Bryant, Yul, 39
Buckley, James, 90
Bureau of Labor Statistics, 117
    household vs. payroll survey, 143
Burke, Ken, 40

Burnout 2 (video game), 153
Bush, Barbara, 273
Bush, Columba, 198
Bush, George Herbert Walker, 194, 289, 328
Bush, George W.
  announces combat in Iraq over, 266, 278
  Azores meeting and, 250–51
  blacks and, 173, 194, 195, 198–200
  black voter suppression and, 202
  Columbia disaster and, 307
  "compassionate" conservatism and, 221–22
  cuts in services and, 215–16, 222–23
  death penalty and, 102
  economic troubles and, 117–18, 128–34
  election of 2004 and, 332
  fiscal policy of, 133
  gay marriage ban and, 226–28
  health programs for children and, 219–21
  Iraq and, 5, 241, 248, 250–52, 254, 268–70, 272–75, 287–88
  Iraq and, costs, 16–18, 267
  Iraq and, deaths of troops, 278, 286, 297, 298
  Iraq and, reconstruction contracts, 256
  Iraq and, troops let down by, 265–67, 294–96
  Iraq as Vietnam of, 299–301
  job losses and, 123–25, 198
  malpractice suits and, 224–26
  media and, 21
  NAACP and, 198–99
  overtime pay and, 109–11
  poor, cuts for services for, 222–23
  reality and, 289, 291
  school funding cuts and, 16–18, 216–18
  September 11 commission and, 286
  state budget crises and, 214–16
  tax credits for poor and, 114–16
  tax cuts and, 10, 130–32, 134, 215–16
  Tulia false arrest scandal and, 48
  white collar unemployment and, 135
  working families and unemployed and, 130–32
  youth joblessness and, 127
Bush, Jeb, 198, 201, 205, 206
Bush, Jenna, 273
Bush, Laura, 16
Bushey, Morgan, 131
Butler, Samuel, 331
Butterfield, Fox, 232
Butts, Antowine, 79–80
Butts, Mark Dale, 165
Byers, Joshua T., 297
Byrd, James, Jr., 164, 166

California
  budget crisis, 18, 129, 214, 215
  new immigrants in, 143
Campaign for Tobacco-Free Kids, 147
Candid Camera (TV program), 321
Cantor Fitzgerald, 235
capital murder. *See also* death penalty
  children convicted of, 3–4, 71–78
  empathy for white vs. black defendants, 177–79
  mentally retarded and, 84–88
  wrongful convictions and, 89–93
Casanova, Jose, 296
Catholics, 197
Center for American Progress, 247
Center for Labor Market Studies, 23, 26, 127, 142
Center for Strategic and International Studies, 274
Center on Budget and Policy Priorities, 115, 116, 219, 220
Centers for Disease Control and Prevention, 146, 245
Central American immigrants, 143
Central Intelligence Agency (CIA), 247
Centurion Ministries, 91
Century Foundation, 118
CEO compensation, 27, 124
Chalabi, Ahmad, 274–75
Chaney, James, 197
Chang, David, 156
Chapman, Ron, 54, 57, 58

Charles, Ray, 325–27
Chavez, Kenneth, 263–64
Cheney, Dick, 130, 194, 250, 254, 286, 295
    Halliburton and, 258, 259, 261–262
Chicago, jobless youth in, 8–9, 125–27
Chicago Tribune, 332
child abuse, 22, 71, 73–75
child labor, 110, 148–50
children
    guns and, 150–52
    health coverage for, 200, 219–21
    homeless, 22
    murder of, by mother, 177–79
    nutrition program cuts, 17
    programs for, cut, 194, 222, 231–32
    racist games for, 155–57
    tax cuts and, 115–16
    tobacco industry and, 145–47
    tsunami and, 32
    violence and, 170–73
    violent toys for, 153–55
Children's Defense Fund, 116, 195, 199
Children's Health Fund, 244
Children's Research and Education
    Institute, 116
child tax credits, 114–16
China
    jobs offshored to, 138
    Nike workers in, 149
CHIP (children's health insurance
    program), 219–22
Cinema Paradiso (film), 229
Cisco Systems, 137
cities, plight of, 231–33
civil liberties, 10
civil rights movement, 10, 315–17
    betrayed by violence in black
        community, 162, 171–73
Clapton, Eric, 324
Clark, Frank, 68
Clark, Laurel, 305, 306
Clarke, Richard, 267
class warfare, 28
Cleveland budget cuts, 232
Cline, Donald J., Jr., 296
Clinton, Bill, 48, 51, 231–32, 328

Clinton, Hillary Rodham, 50–51
Clizbe, John, 32
Coalition for the Homeless, 22
Cobb, Gary, 76–78
Cochran County, Texas, 40–41
Cohen, Steven, 81
Colbert, Carlos, 165
Coleman, Tom, 38–46, 48–56, 58, 60–62
college education
    aid for lower-income youth, 330
    black male employment and, 25
    black peer pressure and, 174–76
college graduates, job losses and, 131,
    143
Colorado, new immigrants in, 143
Colorado Army National Guard, 263
Columbia space shuttle disaster, 305–7
Committee for the Liberation of Iraq,
    255–56
Communication Workers of America,
    122, 136
Community Service Society, 200
compassionate conservatism, 211–13,
    221–22
Comstock, Barbara, 51
Concerned Citizens for a Better Tunica
    County, 167
confessions
    children and, 71–73, 76, 78
    mentally retarded and, 94–96
Congress of Racial Equality, 316
Conley, Chandra, 97, 98
Conover, Paul, 13–15
conservative values, 7
Consumer Reports, 147
consumers' rights, 10
contract workers, 143
Corallo, Mark, 51
Cordesman, Anthony, 274
Cornyn, John, 47–49, 53–56
corporations
    Iraqi reconstruction and, 256–57
    labor compensation vs. profits of,
        26–28
    layoffs and, 124
    offshoring of jobs and, 135–41

power of, 333
  tax cut on dividends and, 134
  tax shelters and, 116, 260–62
Coughlin, John, 64, 65
Council on Foreign Relations, 242
Courtney, Marcus, 136
Cowherd, Leonard, III, 277–78
Cowherd, Sarah, 277–78
credit card debt, 112–14
criminal justice system
  abuses and black community, 173
  children and, 3–4, 71–78
  cuts in funds and, 231–33
  mentally retarded and, 84–88
  rights of accused and, 10
  Tulia scandal, 5–7, 37–62
  white vs. black defendants and,
      177–79
  wrongful convictions and, 89–93
Curnow, Shelly, 226–27
Curry, Jack, 145

Daily News, 190
Dana, Mazen, 279
Daniel, Candace, 79
David Copperfield (Dickens), 141
Davis, Tom, 263
Dawley, Joyce, 205
Day, Lori Sharpe, 48, 50, 51
Dean, Kenneth, 93
death penalty. *See also* capital murder
  Blackmun and, 99–101
  false confessions and, 95, 96
  innocent and, 89–91, 97–106
  race and, 103–6
  witnesses to executions, 92–94
debt
  bankruptcy rate and, 118–19
  middle class and, 4–5, 9, 329
Deep Blues (Palmer), 325
Dees, Morris, 165
defense contracts, 261–62
Defense Finance and Accounting Service,
    265
Delfay, Bob, 152
Delgado, Hector, 281–83

Delta Airlines, 237
democracy, Middle East and, 251, 257,
    274, 280, 287
Democratic National Convention of
    2004, 231–33
Democratic Party
  demonized by Republicans, 194
  Dixiecrats and, 196, 198
  Mississippi state Medicaid cuts and,
    213
Demos (policy group), 113
Depression, 5, 22
Detroit riots of 1967, 162
DiMaggio, Joe, 310–12, 313–15
"Dirty Dozen" list, 153
disabled
  Medicaid and, 211–13
  veterans, 281–86
Disabled American Veterans, 284
discrimination, in newsrooms, 191–92
Dixie Chicks, 258, 260
DNA testing, 67–70, 95, 97–98
Dockery, Joe Rice, 325
Douglass, Frederick, 333
Draut, Tamara, 114
Dropouts in America (Orfield), 331
drugs
  black community and, 172
  joblessness and, 9
  Tulia false arrests and, 37–62
Dyer, Buddy, 204–6

Earle, Ronnie, 76–78
East Los Angeles, 170
Eastwood, Clint, 324
eBay, 155
economic inequality, growth in, 330
Economic Policy Institute, 110–11, 117,
    131–33
economy. *See also* federal budget
    deficits; income inequality;
    unemployment
  Bush and, 117–19, 128–34
  young people and, 8–10
Ed Sullivan Show (TV program),
    321

education, 4, 5. *See also* college; high
  school; public schools
  black community and, 172, 174–76, 331
  black male employment and, 25
  cuts in funding, 5, 215
  offshoring of white collar jobs and,
    137–39
Edwards, John, 141
Egan, Joseph, 202–3
Einstein, Albert, 31, 32
Eisenhower, Dwight, 320, 326
elderly, programs for, 194
electrical grid, 19, 243–44
Elfvin, John, 67
Ellis County, Texas, 41–42
emergency preparedness, 242–46
"Emergency Responders" (report), 243
employment. *See also* job losses;
  unemployment
  crisis in, for blacks, 200
  globalization and, 329
  immigration and, 142–144
  lag in, despite recovery, 27
  population ratio, 24
Enron Corp., 116
environment, 10
Erie County, N.Y., district attorney's
  office, 68–69
Escobar, Karelia, 123, 125
Essence magazine, 175
Evans, Jim, 85
Everett, David, 184, 185, 187
Ever Sparkle Industrial Toys, 153
evolution, 328, 331
executive compensation, 27, 116, 121

Fahrenheit 9/11 (film), 199
Fair Labor Standards Act, 110
Falgout, Sheree, 98
Falluja, 265–67, 273
Farmer, James, 171, 315–17
Farmer, Michael, 13–15
farm labor, 143
Faulkner, William, 33
FBI, 48, 69
federal budget cuts, 214–18, 223

federal budget deficit, 19, 130, 133, 223,
  289, 329
Feliciano, Richard, 82
Feller, Sid, 326
Feuer, Steven, 237, 238
50 Cent, 157
Figgis, Mike, 324
Figueroa, Jose, 81, 82
fire departments, 233, 235, 245
First African Methodist Episcopal
  Church of Los Angeles, 170
First Judicial Circuit of Alabama, 86
first responders, 244–46
Fiscal Survey of States, 215
Florida
  black voter suppression in, 200–8
  presidential election of 2000, 199
Florida Department of Law Enforcement,
  201–5, 207–8
Florida National Guard, 270
Florida Sunshine Law, 207
Florida Voters League, 205
Fontecchio, Elia P., 298
food pantries and soup kitchens, 128, 129,
  135
food stamps, 17, 22, 23
Ford, Gerald, 328
Fortuna, Andy, 20
Forward Command Post (toy), 153
Fourteenth Amendment, 181
Fourth Amendment, 181
Fox TV, 21
Franks, Tommy, 269
freedom of speech, 29, 332
freedom of the press, 332
freedom riders, 316–17
free trade, 139–41
Fritsch, Jane, 82
From Mali to Mississippi (film), 324

gangs, 9, 231
Garrett, Gerald, 59
Gateway, 137
gays and lesbians, 5
  hate crimes vs., 164, 165
  marriage and, 226–29

General Accounting Office (GAO), 263, 264, 265
Geneva Conventions, 7
Gettleman, Jeffrey, 267
Ghettopoly (game), 155–57
Gibbons, John J., 102
Gibson, Don, 326
Gideon, Leighanne, 92
Gilded Age, 8
Gilmore, James S., III, 95
Girdharry, Compton, 224–26
Givens, Jesse, 278
Givens, Melissa, 278
Global Exchange, 149
globalization, 135–36, 140–41, 329
Gomez, Vernon (Lefty), 314
Gonzalez, Armando, 282–83
Gonzalez, Lori, 170
Goodman, Andrew, 197
Goodman, Carolyn, 197
Gore, Al, 206
Goring-Johnson, Celeste, 182–87
Grand Rapids Police Department, 188
Grand Theft Auto III (video game), 154
Green, Steven, 79
Greenstein, Robert, 220
Grones, Denise, 28, 29
gross domestic product, 26
Group, The (McCarthy), 321
Grubbs, Joe, 41–42
Guadalcanal, battle of, 318–19
Guinan, Michael, 186
gun industry, 150–52
Guns and Ammo magazine, 151–52
Gun World magazine, 151
Gupta, Vanita, 56

Hair, Penda, 168
"hajis," 271, 272
Hall, Kim, 285, 286
Hall, Tyler, 284–86
Hall, Wendy, 261
Halliburton Co., 254, 258–62
Hamilton, Jean, 91
Haney, Craig, 178
Harper, Tim, 228

Harris, Katherine, 207
Harrison, George, 321–22
Hart, Gary, 241, 243
hate crimes, 164–66
Hattiesburg American, 28
Hawk Eagle, Sheldon R., 296
Hawkins, Dennis, 185, 186
HBO (cable TV network), 277
Head Start, 318, 319
health care
    costs, 22–23, 113
    cuts in programs for poor, 17
    debt and, 113, 118–19
    emergency preparedness and, 245
    low-income children and, 219–21
    malpractice suits, 224–26
health insurance, 22, 329
health programs, 19
Heighter, Raheen Tyson, 298
Hidalgo, Olmado, 81–83
high school, jobs and, 25, 143
highways, 10
Hilburg, Alan, 146, 147
Hilton, Paris, 21
hip-hop culture, 156–57, 174
Hiroshima, 328
Hirshorn, Robert, 51
Hispanics
    child tax credit and, 115–16
    Florida voter roll purge and, 200, 207
    high school diplomas and, 331
    jobs and, 143
Hoffmann, John, 129
Holland, Steve, 213
home health care, 17
homeland security, 20, 233, 249
Homeland Security Department, 243
homelessness, 5, 8, 21–23, 133–34
homicide rates, 170. *See also* capital murder
homophobia, 165
Hood, Glenda, 206, 207
Hoover, Herbert, 198, 321
Horton, Willie, 194, 196
hospitals, 245, 246

housing, 19, 22, 23, 118–19, 222
Houston, Texas, police cuts, 232
Human Rights Watch, 95
hunger, 5, 9, 22, 23, 214
Hunt, Tom, 189
Hunter, Tab, 325, 326
Huntsville, Texas, executions, 92–94
Huntsville Item, 92
Hussein, Saddam, 21, 240, 251, 252,
    254–56, 266, 289, 297, 298
Hutchinson, Rick, 83–84, 85
Hyde Leadership Public Charter School,
    175
Hynes, Charles, 79, 80, 185

IBM, 135, 136
"I Can't Stop Loving You" (song), 325–27
ignorance, danger of, 328–33
Illinois, death penalty and, 100–101
immigrants, jobs and, 142–44
Impact Aid program, 216–18
Imperial Hubris (anonymous), 247
income inequality, 8–9, 22–23, 216. *See
    also* wages
Index of Social Health, 22
India, 31, 135–36, 138
Indian Americans, 238
Indonesia, 149
inflation, 117
information technology jobs, 137, 140
infrastructure, 19, 125, 245
inner cities
    college aid and, 329–30
    violence in, 156–57
Innocence Project, 69–70
Institute for Innovation in Social Policy,
    22
integration, 161, 163, 308–10
Intel, 138, 139
interest rates, 112
Interracial Intimacies (Kennedy), 230
interracial marriage
    Bob Jones University and, 197, 198
    laws forbidding, 230–31
Interstate Commerce Commission, 317
Iran, 258

Iraqi civilians, 271–72, 280, 288
Iraqi National Guard, 295
Iraqi police, 280, 295
Iraq war, 7, 10, 247–75
    antiwar protests and, 240–41, 250–51
    Bush's failures in, 265–70, 273–75,
        286–89, 299–301
    costs of, 249, 267, 274, 280–81
    deaths of journalists in, 279–81
    deaths of troops in, 267, 268, 276–78,
        283, 286, 296–98
    erosion of support for, 288
    failure of occupation of, 280–81
    funding of, and cuts in domestic
        programs, 16–18, 19, 20, 214, 231
    Halliburton and, 258–62
    invasion and, 250–52, 306
    media and funding of, 21
    military enlistment extensions and,
        281–83
    mission not defined, 280–81, 294–95
    oil and, 259–60
    planning for, 269
    reconstruction contracts and, 253–58,
        274
    September 11 attacks and, 254, 329
    Shultz and, 255–56
    troop estimates and, 266
    UN and, 279
    Vietnam and, 296–98
    war on terror and, 247–49, 251, 267,
        279
    wounded and disabled troops and, 4, 5,
        9, 281–88, 290–93
Isay, Dave, 93
Islamic terrorist groups, 251, 279

Jackson, Leonard, 156, 170–71
Jaffee Center for Strategic Studies, 289
JCPenney, 153
Jefferson County, Louisiana, district
    attorney's office, 98
Jenkins, Vincent, 66–69, 70
Jenney, Timothy, 217–18
Jhingory, Caroline, 174
Job Corps, 318

jobs, 4. *See also* unemployment
  blacks and, 317
  Bush and losses of, 117–19, 123–25,
    128–34
  new immigrants and, 142–44
  rebuilding infrastructure and, 19
  shifted offshore, 135–41
  Verizon layoffs and, 120–22
Johnson, Elizabeth, 182
Johnson, Josiah, 182
Johnson, Lyndon B., 15, 280, 297, 301,
  319
Johnson, Richard, 182
Johnson, Robert, 323
Johnson, Tommy, 323
Jolliff, Rose, 90
Jones, Bob, Jr., 197
Jones, Elaine, 49, 59
Jordan, Barbara, 332
journalists
  bogus reporting by, 190–92
  discrimination and, 191
  killed by U.S. troops, 279
  seizure of recordings of, 28–30
juries, 103
Justice Department
  Tulia false arrest scandal and, 47, 48,
    50–52, 56
  Tunica school board and, 167–68
juvenile deliquency programs, 222

Kahn, Roger, 308, 309–10
Kamstra, Sue, 134
Kamstra, William, 134
Kasich, John, 195
Katzenbach, Nicholas deB., 240–41
Keahey, Robert, 84–85, 86–88
Kellogg Brown & Root, 259, 262
Kelly, Tom, 47–48
Keltner, Ken, 313
Kendall, George, 104
Kennedy, Edward M., 218, 223
Kennedy, John F., 280, 306, 319–21, 325
Kennedy, Randall, 230
Kennedy, Robert F., 317
Kerry, John, 141, 205, 300, 332

Kindler, James, 83
King, John William, 164
King, Martin Luther, Jr., 161–63, 171, 316
Kinhill Kramer corporation, 261
Kirkpatrick, Clifton, 252
Kirkuk, 278
Kirtley, Jane, 30
Knight, Philip, 148–50
Konz, Antoinette, 28, 29, 30
Ku, Leighton, 220
Ku Klux Klan, 317
Kulongoski, Ted, 214
Kutz, Gregory, 264
Kuwait, 262
Kyser, Jack, 215

labor compensation, 26–28
Labor Department, 110, 111
labor unions, 149, 330
Lamar, Lawson, 204
Landstuhl Regional Medical Center, 290,
  293
Last Letters Home (HBO documentary),
  277
"Leave No Child Behind" slogan, 195.
  See also No Child Left Behind Act
Lee, Thea, 136
LeFrem, Maude, 239–40
"Left Behind in the Labor Market"
  (report), 126–27
Legal Services, for the poor, 318
Lemus, David, 81–83
Lennon, John, 322
Leno, Jay, 21
Letterman, David, 21
Lewinsky, Monica, 248
Lewis, Timothy K., 102
Libya, 258, 259
Lincoln, Blanche, 115, 116
Lindbergh, Charles, 313, 314
Lineberger, James A., 237
Lion & Lamb Project, 153
Little Creek Naval Amphibious Base,
  217
Littleton, Colorado, massacre, 151, 152
Look, 163

Los Angeles
  job market in, 133–34
  riots of 1992, 155
  violence in, 169–71
Los Angeles Council of Churches, 156, 170
Los Angeles County Sheriff's
    Department, 232
Los Angeles Times, 251
Lott, Trent, 196–98
Louisiana Crisis Assistance Center, 98
Louisiana death row, 97
Louisiana State Supreme Court, 98
Love, Cash, 44
Love, Rondell, 97–99
Loving v. Virginia, 230
low-income families
  credit card debt, 113
  cuts in health coverage and, 219–21
  cuts in programs to aid, 17
  tax cuts and, 115
  workers displaced by immigrants, 143
Lydon, Michael, 326
Lynch, Jessica, 290
Lyner, Mary Ellen, 90

MacArthur, Douglas, 321
McCain, John, 280, 297
McCarthy, Mary, 321
McCartney, Paul, 322
McCoy, Billy, 213
McCullers, Shawn B., 238
McCutchen, Tammy, 110
McEachern, Terry, 39, 49, 54
McGeogh, Holly, 278
McVeigh, Timothy, 96
Maines, Natalie, 258
malpractice suits, 224–26
Manhattan district attorney's office, 82
Mantle, Mickey, 312
manufacturing jobs, 143–44
Markee, Patrick, 22
Marquez, Mario, 179
Marshall Plan, 10
Martinez, Jesus "Poppy," 78–80
Matthews, Pauline, 98, 99
Matthews, Ryan, 97–99

Maupin, Keith, 268
Mayaguez (ship), 299–300
Mays, Judy, 225–26
Mays, Willie, 310–12
media, 21–23, 331, 332
Medicaid, 211–13, 215, 219–20
Medicare, 17, 212, 222
Mejia, Camilo, 270–72
Melia, John, 283
Memphis sanitation workers strike, 162
mentally retarded, 95–99, 179
"Mentally Retarded and the Death
    Penalty, The" (report), 95–96
Metallic Lathers Union, 128–29
Mexican immigrants, 143
Mfume, Kweisi, 155, 198
Michigan State Police, 187–89
Microsoft, 135, 136
middle aged
  bankruptcy and, 118
  job losses and, 123–24
middle class
  bankruptcy and, 118–19
  Bush tax cuts and, 10, 132
  credit card debt and, 113
  income declines of, 17, 23, 329
  offshoring of jobs and, 136, 139–41
  white swing voters, 194
Milczark, Matthew G., 297
military
  Bush and, 265–67, 294–96
  deaths of, in Iraq, 248, 268, 269, 273,
      276–78, 283, 296–98
  journalists and, 279
  lack of attention to, at home, 283
  lack of economic opportunity and, 9
  occupation of Iraq and, 249, 254
  pay problems and, 263–65
  refusal of, to return to Iraq, 270–72
  schools cuts and, 216–18
  support for, 254
  wounded in Iraq, 281–87, 291–93, 329
military reservists, 233, 263–65
Mills-Harris, Sheila, 16
minimum wage, 110
Miringoff, Marc, 22, 23

miscegenation laws, 230–31
Mishel, Lawrence, 131
Mississippi
    cuts in Medicaid in, 211–13
    Delta blues, 324–25
    desegregation in, 316–17
    school segregation and, 166–68
Mississippi Health Advocacy Program, 212
Mississippi House Public Health and Human Services Committee, 213
Mitchell, Martin, 80
Mittleberg, Scott, 183–86
Mode, Marilyn, 186
Modern Sounds in Country and Western Music (album), 326
Monroe, Marilyn, 315
Moore, Joe, 38, 42–43, 49, 59, 61
Moore, Michael, 199
Morales, Geo, 201–2
Morales, Thomas, 81–83
Morial, Marc, 157, 172, 173
Motorola, 137
Moyers, Bill, 319
multinational corporations, 141, 262
Mumma, Samuel, 238
Murdock, Londell, 169
Murray, Jim, 312
Murray, LaCresha, 71–78
Murray, R. L., 71, 75, 77
Murray, Shirley, 71–72, 75
Muslim world, 281

NAACP Legal Defense and Educational Fund, 6, 39, 46, 49, 53, 56, 59, 62, 104
National Association for the Advancement of Colored People (NAACP), 48, 155, 157, 198
National Association of State Budget Officers, 215
National Center for Children in Poverty, 223
National Center for Disaster Preparedness, 245, 246
National Employment Law Project, 132

National Governors Association, 214
National Religious Broadcasters Convention, 221
National Shooting Sports Foundation, 150, 152
National Urban League, 157, 171, 172, 173, 200
Native Americans, 331
NATO, 10
NBC News, 190
Nelly, 157
NeoIT, 137
Neufeld, Peter, 69
Newark riots of 1967, 162
Newark Star-Ledger, 109
New Deal, 110
New Jersey Turnpike police, 189
Newman, Harry, 135
Newsweek, 178, 298
New York
    crime reduction in, 232
    economic problems of, 128
    September 11 attacks and, 234–36, 239–41
    young people without jobs in, 9, 125
New York Giants, 310–12
New York magazine, 311, 312
New York Police Department, 64, 182–187
New York Times, 31, 51, 82, 114, 115, 131, 145, 161, 162–63, 180, 190, 216, 222, 232, 240, 247, 248, 267, 270, 277, 296, 313, 327, 330
    Magazine, 290
New York Yankees, 310–12, 315
Nguyen, Lap, 150
Nguyen, Thuyen, 150
Nike, 148–50
Nixon, Richard, 100
No Child Left Behind Act, 199, 222–23
nonviolence, 161–62, 316
North American Electric Reliability Council, 243
Northeastern University, 125–27
Norton, Linda, 73–74

Oceana Naval Air Station, 217
O'Connor, Sandra Day, 101

Office of Economic Opportunity, 319
"Offshore Outsourcing" (conference of
    2004), 137–39
offshore tax havens, 116, 260–62
oil
    foreign, 19, 329
    Iraq and, 254, 257, 258, 287
O'Malley, Martin, 232–33
Ondersma, Rachel Ellen, 187–89
O'Neill, Paul, 266–67
O'Neill, Tip, 223
Oneonta, N.Y., police, 180–82
On the Waterfront (movie), 294
Orange County, Florida, 206–8
Orange County League of Voters, 202
Oregon, budget crisis in, 5, 214–16
Orfield, Gary, 331
Orlando, Florida, black voters in,
    201–8
overseas factories, 148–50
overtime pay regulations, 109–11
Owen, C. Penn, Jr., 166, 168
"ownership society," 333

Padilla, John, 63–65
Pagein, Robert, 120–22
Palladium nightclub murders, 81–83
Palmer, Robert, 325
Panhandle Regional Narcotics Trafficking
    Task Force, 56
Pardon, John, 140, 141
Pareles, Jon, 327
Parkerson, Harvey E., III, 297
Parks, Bernard C., 170
Patriots (Zorthian), 287
Pattison, Scott, 215
Peace Corps, 318, 319
Pear, Robert, 17, 222
Pennsylvania, 143
Perry, Rick, 57, 58, 62, 96
Peterson, Alyssa R., 296
Philadelphia, Mississippi, 197
Philadelphia Inquirer, 238
Phipps, Ivory L., 297
Pickett, Carroll, 93

Pickett, Jerry, 112, 114
Pickett, Julie, 112, 114

Piel, Eleanor Jackson, 66–70
Pilate, Cheryl, 90
Pillot, Joey, 81–82
Pimp Juice, 157
"P.I.M.P" (song), 157
Plan of Attack (Woodward), 269
PlayStation 2, 154
Plumb, Ralph, 134
police
    brutality, New York, 63–65
    cuts in funds for, 231–33
    emergency preparedness and, 245
    Tulia arrests and, 38–62
Poole, Eugene, 205
poor, 130
    Bush cuts and, 17, 194, 214, 222–23
    child tax credits and, 114–16
    health coverage for, 219–20
    King and, 161, 163
Pop, Iggy, 146
Porter, Anthony, 100–101
Porter, Cole, 321
*"Post-Conflict" Lessons of Iraq and
    Afghanistan, The* (report), 274
Postman, Neil, 21
poverty rates, 9, 10, 17
Powell, Colin, 193–94, 269
Powell, Jane, 212
Powers, Francis Gary, 320
Presbyterian Christian High School, 28
prescription drug prices, 5, 10
Present at the Creation (Acheson), 255
presidential election of 2000, 206
    of 2004, 201–3, 206–8, 332
prison
    blacks and, 172
    innocents sent to, 5, 6, 69
Privacy Protection Act (1980), 30
Procter & Gamble, 137
productivity, 26–28, 135, 140
prostitution, 9
public housing, 10, 222

public schools
   black children and, 173
   cuts in funding for, 10, 16–19, 199,
      200, 214–18, 222, 245, 246, 331
   segregation and, 167–68
Purdum, Todd, 240
Pye, J. C., 169

race
   Blair and, 190–92
   death penalty and, 102–4, 105
   empathy for defendant, 178–179
   Ghettopoly game and, 155–57
racism, 173
   blues and, 323
   hate crimes and, 164, 165
   Republicans and, 196–98
   segregation vs., 317
Rajcoomar, Bob, 236–39
Rajcoomar, Dorothy, 238
Ramadi, 271, 295
RAND Corporation, 245
rape convictions, 66–69
Ray Charles: Man and Music (Lydon), 326
Reagan, Ronald, 197, 223, 255
reality-based community, 291
Reasonover, Ellen, 89–91
recession of 2000–2001, 24, 26–28, 126, 142
Redlener, Irwin, 244–46
Reese, Pee Wee, 308–10
Reich, Robert, 10
Reichman, Deborah Gar, 226–27
religious community, 251–52
Republican National Convention of
   2000, 193–95, 199
Republicans
   child tax credits and, 116
   Medicaid and, 211–13
   racism and, 196–99
   southern strategy, 194, 196
   voter suppression and, 206–8
Rice, Condoleezza, 269
riots of 1968, 163
RJ Reynolds Tobacco Company, 147
ROAR tour, 146–47

Roberts, Audrey, 9, 126
Robinson, Amy, 165
Robinson, Jackie, 308–10
Robinsonville, Mississippi, 166–68
Rockstar Games, 154
Rodriguez, Frankie, 79, 80
Rohde, David, 82
Rojas, Juan, 78
Romero, Daniel, 263
Rooks, Andy, 169
Roosevelt, Franklin D., 8, 111, 313
Rostow, Walt, 240–41
Rube, Melanie, 29
Rudman, Warren, 243
Rumsfeld, Donald, 258–59, 269, 272
Russia, 138
Ruth, Babe, 314
Rutkowski, Mike, 228
Ryan, George H., 100–101

Sack, Robert, 63–65
Saginaw, Mississippi, police, 232
Salenger, Marvin, 63–65
Salpeter, Jay, 79
Sandburg, Carl, 8
San Jose Mercury News, 138, 139
Santorum, Rick, 229
Sarge (Stossel), 318
Scalia, Antonin, 28–30
Scheck, Barry, 67, 69–70
Schilling, Curt, 145–46
Schlumberger Ltd., 254
School Without Walls, 16
Schumer, Charles, 50, 235
Schwarzenegger, Arnold, 318
Schwerner, Michael, 197
Scorsese, Martin, 324
Securities and Exchange Commission,
   260–61
segregation
   freedom riders and, 316–17
   schools and, 166–68
   Thurmond and, 196–97
Seidenberg, Ivan, 121, 122
Self, Ed, 53

Sellas, Nicoletta, 228
senior citizens, 113, 211–13
September 11 attacks
    aftermath of, 7, 239
    commission on, 286
    Iraq war and, 248, 254, 269, 273, 289,
        298, 329
    job losses after, 123
    racial profiling after, 236–39
    shock of, in New York, 234–236
    unpreparedness for, 243
Sessions, William, 102, 106
Shakespeare, William, 32
Sharpton, Al, 316
Shaw, Derrick, 72, 75
Shays, Christopher, 264
Shepard, Matthew, 164
Shine, Patrick, 265
Shinseki, Eric, 266
Shriver, Eunice Kennedy, 319
Shriven, Maria, 318
Shriver, Sargent, 318–20
Shultz, George, 255–56
Shynvwelski, Alfonso, 128
Silicon Valley, 139
Simon, Paul, 244
Simpson, Eugene, Jr., 291–93, 294
Simpson, O. J., 248
Sivits, Jeremy, 270, 271
60 Ft. Dolls, 146
Sixty Minutes (TV program), 273
Skoal, 146, 147
smokeless tobacco, 145–47
Smokeless Tobacco Council, 146
Social Security, 10, 19, 329, 330
Sojourners (journal), 252
Solow, Robert, 133
Sothern, Billy, 98
Southern Asia, tsunami and, 31–33
Southern Baptist Convention, 251
Southern Echo, 167
Southern Poverty Law Center, 164–65
South Los Angeles, 169–71
Special Olympics, 318
Spitzer, Eliot, 182
Sri Lanka, 31, 32

standard of living, 10, 136, 141
Starr, Edwin, 255
Starr, Ringo, 322
"Start 'Em Young" (study), 151
state budget crises, 17, 125, 214–16, 219–21
State Department, 251
State of Emergency (video game), 154–55
States' Rights Democratic Party
        (Dixiecrats), 196
State University of New York at
        Oneonta, 180
Steinkampf, Michael, 85, 87–88
Stewart, Larry, 37, 41, 46
stock dividends, taxes on, 125, 134
Stossel, Scott, 318
Sugarmann, Josh, 151
Sullivan, Ed, 325
Sum, Andrew, 23–27, 127, 142, 143
Sundance Film Festival, 324
Suskind, Ron, 290–91
Swanson, Linda, 46
Swartworth, Sharon T., 298
Swisher County, Texas, 41

Task Force on Homeland Security, 232
taxes
    cuts for wealthy, 19, 116, 117, 129–34,
        195, 200, 215, 223, 233, 330
    low-income families and, 17, 114–16
    in NYC, 129
    offshoring of jobs and, 136–37
    permanently unemployed and, 25
tax shelters, 260–62
technological advances, 10
Tennessee Supreme Court, 230
terrorism
    preparedness for, 242–247
    war on Iraq and, 247–49, 269–70,
        274–75
Tessler, Joanna, 228
Texas
    anti-sodomy laws, 229–30
    cuts in social services, 129
    death penalty and, 92–94, 96, 102–4,
        106
    health care for children and, 219–20

"Lawman of the Year" award, 40, 49, 53–55
narcotics trafficking task forces, 56
new immigrants in, 143
Texas Board of Pardons and Paroles, 58–59
Texas Commission on Law Enforcement, 40
Texas Court of Criminal Appeals, 46, 53, 56–58
Texas state attorney general's office, 47–48
Texas State Children's Health Insurance Program (SCHIP), 219
Texas State Legislature, 58
Thomas, Clarence, 173, 194
Thomas, Ezzie, 202, 208
Thomson, Bobby, 310
Thurmond, Strom, 196–97
Tikrit, 292
Tinch, Nomoya, 175
tobacco industry, 145–47
Tonic (rock group), 146
toys, 153–57
Transportation Security Administration, 238
Travis County, Texas, 74, 76
Truman, Harry, 9–10, 217
Trzaska, Gary, 165
tsunami of 2004, 31–33
Tucker, Dianne, 84, 85, 87
Tulia, Texas, drug sting on black citizens of, 5–6, 37–62
Tulia Legal Defense Project, 39
Tull, Tanya, 133, 134
Tunica County, Mississippi, school board, 166–68
Tunica Institute of Learning, 167
Tunnell, Guy, 204, 205, 207–8
TWA, 123
Two-Income Trap, The (Warren), 118

underemployment, 9, 19–20, 24, 129, 142, 143
unemployment
    black community and, 173
    black male, 23–25, 200

Bush and, 123–25, 129–31
California and, 133–134
long-term, 132
New York and, 128–29
official statistics, 24
offshoring of jobs and, 135–39
recovery after 2001 and, 142
tax cuts for wealthy and, 117
total, 9, 17, 19
youth and, 9, 125–27
Union Rescue Mission, 134
United Nations, 10, 279, 281
United Spinal Association, 283
United States Central Command, 269, 273
U.S. Army National Guard, 233, 263–65, 268
U.S. Army Reserve, 295
U.S. Conference of Mayors, 22, 232
U.S. Congress, 17, 82, 218, 243–44, 256–57
U.S. Constitution, 29, 30
U.S. House of Representatives, 116
    Budget Committee, 195
    Committee on Government Reform, 263
U.S. Marines, 267, 270, 281–83, 295
U.S. Senate, 48–49, 54, 56, 115, 116
U.S. Supreme Court, 28–30, 194, 229–30, 316, 331
    death penalty and, 99–104, 106
U.S. Tobacco Company, 146
"Unprecedented Rising Tide of Corporate Profits and the Simultaneous Ebbing of Labor Compensation, The" (study), 26–27
Urban Outfitters, 155
USA Today, 134, 288
usury, 112

Valdez, Ruben, Jr., 298
VandeGeer, Diana, 299, 300
VandeGeer, Richard, 299–300
VandeGeer, Michelle, 300
Vanuatu, 261

Vashistha, Atul, 137, 138z
Verizon Communications, 120–22
veterans programs, 17
video games, 153–154
Vietnam, Nike and, 149, 150
Vietnam Labor Watch, 150
Vietnam Memorial, 15, 299
Vietnam Veterans of America
     Foundation, 300
Vietnam War, 4, 7, 13–15, 163, 280, 287,
     296–300
violence
   black community and, 161–63, 172–73
   cuts in funds for police and, 231–33
   inner cities and, 156–57
   Los Angeles and, 169–71
Violence Policy Center, 151
Virginia Beach public schools, 217–18
Virginia Racial Integrity Act, 230
Vitale, Lisa, 224–25
Volunteers in Service to America
     (VISTA), 318
voter suppression, in Florida, 201–8
voting, ignorance and, 330

Wachtler, Sol, 87
Wafer, Billy Don, 39
wages, 10, 20, 113, 117–18, 121, 131, 140
   offshoring of white-collar jobs and,
     136, 139
   overseas factories and, 149
   productivity and, 26–28
   unemployment and, 131
Wallis, Jim, 252
Wall Street Journal, 18, 118, 134, 253–54,
     247, 248
war on terror, 258, 267, 289
Warren, Elizabeth, 118
Washington, Earl, Jr., 94–97
Washington Alliance of Technology
     Workers, 136
Washington Heights Ecumenical Food
     Pantry, 128
Washington Post, 256
Watts, J. C., 194
Waxman, Henry, 258–60

wealthy
   tax cuts and, 10, 115, 116, 117, 125, 129,
     215–16, 223, 233, 330
   total wealth of top 1 percent, 8
weapons of mass destruction, 266, 328
Weber, Shirley, 293
Weindler, Rudy, 234
Weinraub, Bernard, 327
welfare reform, 134
Wenders, Wim, 324
When Your Youngster Wants a Gun
     (pamphlet), 150–51
White, Donald, 43
White, Kareem, 38, 44
White, Kizzie, 43–45
White, Mattie, 42–44
White, Tonya, 6, 39, 43, 45
white collar job losses, 135–39, 141
Whitehead, Richard, 102–3
whites
   arrest of, in Tulia, 37, 38, 43
   hate crimes vs., 165
   police treatment of, vs. blacks, 189
   private schools in South for, 167
white supremacists, 164, 165, 196–97
Whitmire, John, 58
Wilkins, Roy, 171, 316
Willard, Erick, 41
Willett, Jim, 92
William Moses Kunstler Fund for Racial
     Justice, 39, 62
Williams, Rebecca, 95
Williams, Ted, 311
Win Without War, 251
Witmer, Charity, 268
Witmer, John, 276
Witmer, Michelle, 268, 276–77
Witmer, Rachel, 268
Witness to an Execution (documentary),
     92–94
Wolfowitz, Paul, 272
Wong, Edward, 295
Woodward, Bob, 269, 289
workers' rights, 10, 109–11
working families
   Bush and, 130–32, 214–16

child tax credit and, 114–116
food pantries and, 129, 135
working poor, 23, 220, 223
World's Wackiest Police Videos, 187
World Trade Center collapse, 234–36,
244–45. *See also* September 11, 2001
attacks
World War II, 5, 313, 318
Wounded Warrior Project, 283
Wuest, Jack, 127
Wyden, Ron, 256–57

Yahoo, 155
Yates, Andrea, 177–79
"Year of the Blues," 323
Young, Whitney, Jr., 171–73, 316
youth
joblessness and, 8–9, 125–27, 143
violence in inner cities and, 156–157

Zasadny, Paula, 278
Zinni, Anthony, 273
Zorthian, Barry, 287

ABOUT THE AUTHOR

BOB HERBERT has been an op-ed columnist for the *New York Times* since 1993. He was previously a correspondent for NBC News and a reporter, columnist, and member of the editorial board for the *New York Daily News*. He has taught journalism at Brooklyn College and at Columbia University, and he has won numerous awards for his reporting and commentary. He lives in New York City.